A Rainy
Day in
New York

A Rainy Day in New York

레이니 데이 인 뉴욕

초판 1쇄 인쇄 2020년 12월 3일
초판 1쇄 발행 2020년 12월 3일

지은이 | 고성란
펴낸이 | 조치영
펴낸곳 | 스크린영어사
편집주간 | 스크린영어사 편집부
디자인 | 류형태 (주)코치커뮤니케이션
경영지원 | 정연희
인 쇄 | 삼성인쇄

주소 서울 특별신 관악구 신림로 137
전화 (02) 887-8416
팩스 (02) 887-8591
홈페이지 www.screenplay.co.kr

등록일자 1997년 7월 9일
등록번호 제 16-1495

ISBN 978-89-6415-078-8 13740
ISBN 978-89-87915-11-1 (세트)

A Rainy
Day in
New York

레이니 데이 인 뉴욕

스크린영어사
Screen English Publishing co.

〈A Rainy Day in New York〉를 시작하며

영화 "A Rainy Day in New York"은 2020년에 개봉된 영화로, 두 주인공, 개츠비와 챈의 전지적 관점으로 번갈아 가며 전개된다는 점이 흥미로우며, 우디 앨런 감독 특유의 작품 색이 돋보인다. 영화 제목에서 나타나듯이, 이 영화는 비와 깊은 연관성을 보인다. 비가 오기 시작하면서 영화 속 주인공들의 하루의 계획이 무너지고, 비를 맞으며 본인들이 갖고 있던 편견과 가면을 벗고 마음 속에 감춰진 거짓에서 벗어나는 모습을 보여준다. 이 영화는 앞서 말한 주인공들이 솔직하게 변화하는 모습과 매력적인 재즈 음악, 그리고 그와 어우러지는 비오는 뉴욕의 운치있는 풍경을 통해 바쁜 현대 사회를 살아가는 우리들에게 촉촉한 마음을 느끼게 해준다.

영어를 학습하는 사람과 가르치는 사람이 공통적으로 가지는 관심 중에 하나는 "어떻게 하면 영어를 흥미롭고 재미있게 배우고 가르칠 수 있을까?"라는 것이다. 빠르게 발전하고 움직이는 현대 시대에 영화라는 것은 언어학습에 있어서 상당한 도움을 줄 수 있는 도구가 된다. 학습자가 좋아하는 영화를 자발적으로 선택하는 것은 영어 학습에 충분한 동기부여가 되며, 흥미를 가지고 반복적으로 본다면 실력 향상에 큰 도움이 된다.

"A Rainy Day in New York" 영화를 보면 다양한 표현의 말뭉치와 속어가 쓰인다. 말뭉치는 습관적으로 함께 나타나는 단어들의 집합체로 두 개 이상의 단어가 모여 하나의 표현을 이룬 것이다. 영화를 통해 반복적으로 쓰이는 말뭉치를 기억한다면, 다양한 문장을 표현하는데 사용되어, 유창성과 정확성을 높이고 영어에 대한 자신감도 증가할 수 있다. 영어를 하나의 단어로만 표현하는 것이 아니라 구 동사와 말뭉치를 사용하여 표현할 수 있게 된다면 훨씬 세련되고 수준 높은 영어를 사용하게 되는 것이다. 또한 이 영화에는 많은 속어(slang)들이 쓰인다. 학생들이 해외 경험을 해보지 않는다면 학교에서 배운 영어로는 이해 못할 표현들이 많이 있다. 그러므로 영화를 통해 다양한 환경에서 사용되는 속어들을 배운다면 실생활 표현을 이해하는데 도움이 될 것이다.

외국영화를 본다는 것은 단순히 외국어만 배우는 것이 아니라 그 나라의 문화적인 측면도 같이 학습하는 것으로 단순한 언어습득 그 이상의 것이다. 영화에는 그 사회의 경제적, 문화적, 역사적인 측면을 담고 있기 때문에 영화를 통해 그 국가의 사람들이 가지고 있는 다양한 생각이나 행동을 이해할 수 있게 된다. 따라서 한 편의 영화는 어쩌면 영어교재보다 더 좋은 배움의 수단이 될 수 있다.

뉴욕 맨해튼은 낭만의 도시로 누구든 한 번쯤 가보고 싶은 꿈의 도시이다. 이 영화는 맨해튼의 유명한 관광지와 문화명소, 그리고 유명한 레스토랑, 호텔, 그리고 술집들을 언급하면서 실제로 낭만적인 뉴욕을 관광하는 느낌을 갖게 해 준다. 만약 뉴욕을 여행할 계획이 있다면, 무비토크에서 설명한 곳을 따라 "A Rainy Day in New York"을 따라 걷는 뉴욕 관광코스를 만드는 것을 추천한다.

영화 "A Rainy Day in New York"은 우연이라고 하기에는 너무나 필연적인 세 주인공의 사랑을 보여주며, 만날 운명은 결국 만나게 되어 있다는 운명적 만남을 보여 준다. 만일 현재 우연으로 수 없이 반복적인 만남을 가지는 사람이 있다면, 나의 운명적인 사랑이 아닐까 한번 생각해보며 새로운 사랑으로 셀레이는 낭만적인 계절이 되었으면 한다.

고성란

Contents

콜론(:)의 용법

한국어에는 거의 없는 용법이지만 영어에서는 많이 사용되는 중요한 용법이니 잘 알아두자.

1. 콜론 앞은 붙이고 (한 칸 띄우면 안 됨) 콜론 뒤는 반드시 한 칸 띄워야 한다.

2. 보통 3개 이상을 나열할(list) 때 콜론을 사용한다.

3. 콜론 앞의 문장이 완벽한 문장(complete sentence)이어야 한다.

   · 콜론 앞이 명사로 끝나거나

   · 콜론 앞이 the following 또는 as follows로 끝나야 한다.

4. 나열되는 명사들은 콤마(,) 또는 세미콜론(;)으로 구분해준다.

   예: I have three favorite actors: Paul Newman, Woody Allen, and Harrison Ford.

   　　We took the following: a tent; two sleeping bags; and a lantern.

A Rainy
Day in
New York

레이니 데이 인 뉴욕

Chapter 1

뉴욕에서 애슐리와 개츠비 시작

Ashleigh and Gatsby'
Start in New York

시간 00:00:00 ~ 00:07:50

Students walk past stately buildings on the bucolic campus of Yardley College in upstate New York. A small lamppost banner reads: Yardley College.

Camera dollies back to reveal more students in the classroom.

GATSBY: (voice over) This is Yardley...which is supposed to be a very good liberal arts school, and definitely tony enough for my mother with its beautiful rural campus...

Camera holds on the campus.

GATSBY: (voice over) ...which is total bullshit because you get ticks walking in the grass.

Welles, a handsome undergraduate student, sits at a desk in a classroom with a bored expression on his face. Other students are sitting around him.

GATSBY: (voice over) Yardley has more structure than the first college I went to.

학생들이 뉴욕 주 북부에 야들리 대학의 전원 캠퍼스에 있는 위엄있는 건물들 사이를 지나간다. 작은 가로등 기둥에 '야들리 대학교'라고 쓰여져 있다.

카메라가 교실에 더 많은 학생들을 보여준다.

개츠비: (해설) 이곳은 '야들리' 대... 문과 대학으로 아주 유명하고 전원풍의 아름다운 교정이 엄마의 고급 취향에도 딱 맞았지만.

카메라가 캠퍼스를 비춘다.

개츠비: (해설) 빛 좋은 개살구지, 풀밭엔 진드기가 가득하다.

캐츠비 웰스, 잘생긴 대학생이 지루한 표정으로 책상 앞에 앉아있다. 다른 학생들이 그 주변에 앉아있다.

개츠비: (해설) 여긴 몇 달 다닌, 저번 학교보다 빡세다.

- **stately**
  위엄있는

- **bucolic**
  전원의

- **liberal arts school**
  문과대학, 교양학부

- **tony**
  멋진
  fashionable among wealthy or stylish people

- **bullshit**
  헛소리

- **tick**
  진드기

- **structure**
  구조

Camera dollies back to reveal more students in the classroom.

GATSBY: (voice over) I lasted a few months at one of those serious Ivy League pseudo-intellectual joints, which my mother thought would give me an "appropriate" education.

Gatsby enters his room, then stops at his desk and starts to take books out of his backpack. Among the posters on the wall in the room are a John Dillinger wanted poster, An H.L. Mencken quote, and a poster for a Veronica lake movie.

GATSBY: (voice over) She says I have a high I.Q. and I'm not living up to my potential, even though last weekend I made twenty grand playing poker.

Gatsby opens a drawer in his desk, then takes out a candy bar and flips it into his hand.

GATSBY: (voice over) But I'll get to that. Yardley's where I met Ashleigh on the school paper.

Gatsby opens the door and walks out of the dormitory. He looks at his cell phone, then puts it in his pocket.

GATSBY: (voice over) That's my girlfriend, Ashleigh Enright. My dad knew one of her father's banks in Arizona, and naturally, with those family credentials, my mother wants us to get married, sight unseen.

Camera pans, off Gatsby, to reveal Ashleigh Enright, Gatsby's attractive blonde girlfriend, who is walking down a path toward the dormitory. Camera dollies in as Ashleigh hops up giddily and waves her hand at Gatsby. She walks hurriedly toward him.

카메라가 교실에 더 많은 학생들을 보여주며 뒤로 이동한다.

개츠비: (해설) 제대로 된 교육을 받으라며 엄마가 보
냈던 말만 아이비리그인 사이비 지성의 전
당.

개츠비가 기숙사 방으로 들어가고 책상에 멈춰서 가방에서 책들
을 꺼내기 시작한다. 방의 벽에는 수배중인 죤 딜링거 포스터,
Mencken 인용구와 베로니카 호수 영화에 포스터가 있다.

개츠비: (해설) 엄만 내가 머린 좋은데 제대로 쓰질 않
는다나 지난 주말에도 포커로 이만불이나
땄는데.

개츠비는 책상 서랍을 열고 캔디바를 꺼내 손안으로 톡 던진다.

개츠비: (해설) 그 얘긴 나중에 다시 하고. 애슐리는
학교신문을 만들다 만났다.

개츠비는 문을 열고 기숙사 밖으로 나온다. 그는 휴대폰을 보고 주
머니에 넣는다.

개츠비: (해설) 내 여자친구, 애슐리 엔라잇. 아빠가
거래하던 애리조나의 은행이 걔네 아버지
건데 엄만 배경만 보고 무조건 개랑 결혼하
란다.

카메라가 개츠비에게 꺼지고, 개츠비의 매력적인 금발의 여자친구
애슐리 앤라잇이 기숙사 쪽으로 길을 걸어가고 있다. 애슐리가 들
떠서 뛰며 내려오고, 개츠비에게 손을 흔들며 서둘러 걸어간다.

- **pseudo-intellectual**
  사이비 지성의

- **I.Q. (Intelligence Quotient)**
  지능지수

- **live up to**
  (기대 등)에 부응하다

- **potential**
  가능성

- **grand**
  (비격식) 천 달러(파운드)

- **flip**
  (손가락으로) 튀기다, 가볍게 치다 (던지다)

- **I'll get to that.**
  다음에 다시 할게

- **sight unseen**
  실물을 보지 않고

- **giddily**
  (너무 좋아) 들떠서

I'm not living up to my potential.
live up to ~는 '(기대 등)에 부응하다' 하
는 의미로 '내가 가진 가능성에 부응하지
못하고 있다' 라는 뜻으로 사용된다.

I'm not living up to my potential.
나는 내가 가진 가능성에 부응하지 못하고 있다.

GATSBY: (voice over) It's the one area I agree on with my mother, because even though we've only been goin' out for a few months, I'm hopelessly in love with Ashleigh.

Ashleigh hurries.

ASHLEIGH: (excited breath) Gatsby! I got an interview with Roland Pollard.

GATSBY: Ohhh, my gosh, that is amazing!

Gatsby and Ashleigh embrace.

ASHLEIGH: (giggles excitedly)

GATSBY: How did you land that?

Ashleigh steps back and gestures excitedly at Gatsby.

ASHLEIGH: Um, well, he has a new movie coming out this fall...

GATSBY: Mm-hm.

ASHLEIGH: (inhales) ...and the assignment originally went to Priscilla McCain, but she's totally got mono, so I'm doing it.

GATSBY: Gee, mono's like a two-credit course at this school.

ASHLEIGH: (sighing) Oh...

GATSBY: Well, listen, Ashleigh, I think this is great for you.

ASHLEIGH: Yeah.

GATSBY: When, w-when, when is it?

개츠비: (해설) 그래도 그건 웬일로 나랑 통하신 셈. 왜냐하면 만난 지는 몇 달 안 됐지만 난 미치도록 사랑에 빠졌으니까.

애슐리는 서둘러 온다.

애슐리: (기쁘게 숨쉬며) 개츠비! 나 롤란 폴라드 감독 인터뷰 맡게 됐어.

개츠비: 완전 대박!

개츠비와 애슐리가 껴 안는다.

애슐리: (기쁘게 웃으며)

개츠비: 어떻게 맡았어?

애슐리는 뒤 걸음질을 하고 게츠비에게 기쁘게 제스처를 한다.

애슐리: 이번 가을에 신작이 나오는데.

개츠비: 음.

애슐리: (숨을 들이 마쉬며) 원래 인터뷰 맡았던 애가 이번 가을에 신작이 나오는데 전염성 단핵증에 걸려서 나한테 넘어왔어.

개츠비: 무슨 필수과목처럼 다들 걸리네.

애슐리: (한숨쉬며) 오…

개츠비: 정말 잘됐다.

애슐리: 응

개츠비: 언제야?

- **area**
  분야

- **mono**
  mono (美 비격식) 선열(림프선이 붓는 감염 질환) mono · nucle · osis (美 또는 의학)

- **Gee**
  (놀람감탄을 나타내어) 야

How did you land that?
land는 '차지[획득]하다' 라는 의미로 How did you land that?는 어떻게 맡았어?라는 뜻이다.

How did you land that?
어떻게 맡았어?

ASHLEIGH: Uh, it's the twenty–eighth of this month.
GATSBY: Mm–hm.

Ashleigh and Gatsby walk.

ASHLEIGH: A Saturday.
GATSBY: Okay. And it's on campus?

Ashleigh shakes her head and smiles.

ASHLEIGH: It's in Manhattan.

Gatsby crosses and stops in front of her. Ashleigh stops and smiles at him.

GATSBY: It's in Manhattan?
ASHLEIGH: Uh–huh!
GATSBY: Are you serious?
ASHLEIGH: (inhales, nodding)

Gatsby sits down on a bench. Ashleigh takes off her backpack and puts it down on the bench.

GATSBY: This is fantastic! We're always talkin' about going
                  into Manhattan for a special weekend.
ASHLEIGH: (chuckles)

Gatsby gestures at Ashleigh, who is opening the backpack.

GATSBY: Okay. Look, I'm gonna make a reservation at the
                  Carlyle. That's the place I'm always tellin' you
                  about with the...
ASHLEIGH: (very soft chuckle)

애슐리: 이달 28일,

개츠비: 음.

애슐리와 개츠비는 걸어간다.

애슐리: 토요일이야.

개츠비: 그렇구나, 우리 학교에서?

애슐리는 머리를 흔들고 웃는다.

애슐리: 아니, 맨해튼에서.

개츠비가 걷고 애슐리 앞에서 멈춘다. 애슐리는 멈춰서서 그에게
웃는다.

개츠비: 맨해튼?

애슐리: 응!

개츠비: 진짜?

애슐리: (머리를 끄덕이며 숨을 들이쉰다)

개츠비가 벤치에 앉고 애슐리는 가방을 벗으며 벤치에 내려둔다.

개츠비: 잘됐다! 잘됐다! 우리 뉴욕 주말 여행 꿈꿨
었잖아.

애슐리: (웃는다)

게츠비는 애슐리에게 제스쳐를 하고 애슐리는 가방을 연다.

개츠비: 칼라일 호텔 예약해야겠다. 거기 바 얘기했
었지.

애슐리: (부드럽게 웃으며)

■ take off
(옷, 가방 등을) 벗다

Are you serious?
그 얘기는 믿을 수 없다는 의구심을 표할
때 쓰이는 표현으로 '진심이야?' 정말이
야? '진짜?' 라는 뜻으로 쓰인다.

Are you serious?
진심이야? 정말이야? 진짜?

Ashleigh puts a stack of books into the backpack.

GATSBY: ...the piano player at the bar. He sings those old Broadway tunes. And, uh, I'll take you out for lunch and dinner. How does that sound? Maybe I'll show you around the city.

ASHLEIGH: Yeah.

GATSBY: Yeah?

ASHLEIGH: I mean...it'll cost a fortune.

Gatsby shakes his head at her.

GATSBY: Nah, relax, I'm loaded. I scored twenty big ones last Sunday.

Ashleigh closes her backpack and buckles it.

ASHLEIGH: Not another crap game?

GATSBY: No–no–no, stud poker this time. I'm sittin' there with three tens, and some guy with aces up keeps raising me.

Ashleigh puts on her backpack, then Gatsby stands up.

ASHLEIGH: Oh. How do you get all the money to play in such a big poker game?

GATSBY: Well, my horse came in this weekend. I'm telling ya, this is why I gotta go to Vegas.

ASHLEIGH: (exhaling very softly) Oh...

GATSBY: I–I–I–I'm a gambler, I don't know how else to put it.

애슐리는 가방에 책들을 넣는다.

개츠비: 피아노 연주에 뮤지컬 곡들 불러줘.
밥은 나가서 먹어. 어때? 시내구경도 시켜
줄께

애슐리: 좋아.

개츠비: 응.

애슐리: 근데 돈 너무 많이 들겠다.

게츠비는 그녀에게 고개를 가로 젓는다.

개츠비: 걱정 마, 지갑 두둑해. 주말에 이만불 땄거
든.

애슐리는 가방을 닫고 잠근다.

애슐리: 또 주사위 도박?

개츠비: 아니, 이번엔 스터드 포커. 난 트리플이었
는데 투페어가 계속 쫓아 오더라구.

애슐리는 가방을 메고 게츠비는 일어난다.

애슐리: 그런 큰 판에 낄 돈은 다 어디서 구해?

개츠비: 주말에 경마에서 땄지. 라스베이거스에 가
야 되는데.

애슐리: (부드럽게 숨을 내쉬며) 오…

개츠비: 난 타고난 꾼인가 봐. 뭐라 해야 할지 모르
겠어.

■ tune
곡, 곡조, 선율

■ How does that sound?
어때? 괜찮을까?

■ Nah
아니(No)

■ I'm loaded
돈이 많아

■ ace up
이기다, 비장의 무기가 있다

■ crap game
(일종의) 주사위 도박

■ Vegas
Las Vegas' 의 약자

■ put
설명하다

It'll cost a fortune.
fortune은 '재산, 자산, 큰돈' 이라는 뜻
으로 It'll cost a fortune to + 동사 원형
~하는 데 돈이 많이 들거야' 라는 뜻으로
사용된다.

Zoom In

It'll cost a fortune.
돈이 많이 들거야.

Ashleigh and Gatsby walk, camera dollying in with them.

ASHLEIGH: Gosh…I've always wanted you to have to show me around Manhattan.

Gatsby wraps his arms around Ashleigh

GATSBY: I know, this is gonna be absolutely fantastic.

ASHLEIGH: (soft chuckle, followed by excited breath)

Gatsby and Ashleigh turn and walk.

GATSBY: Hey, I'm gonna maybe get in touch with my dad's ticket broker, he can get us tickets to "Hamilton" how does that sound?

Ashleigh nods hesitantly at him.

GATSBY: Actually, I don't want to let my parents know I'm in town that weekend.

ASHLEIGH: Oh. Why not?

Gatsby gestures at Ashleigh

GATSBY: My mother's having her big annual Fall Gala and she's apoplectic I'm not coming, and…

ASHLEIGH: Mm.

GATSBY: …you know, I told her I had a major paper due. Otherwise, I'd have to put in an appearance, and…

ASHLEIGH: (sighs excitedly).

애슐리와 개츠비는 걸어가고 카메라도 따라간다

애슐리: 네가 맨해튼 구경시켜주길 기다렸었는데.

개츠비는 애슐리를 팔로 안는다.

개츠비: 정말 좋을 거야.

애슐리: (부드럽게 웃으며 흥분된 숨을 쉰다)

게츠비와 애슐리가 방향을 돌려 걸어간다.

개츠비: 아빠 암표상한테 연락해서 '해밀튼' 표도 구
해볼까?

애슐리는 그에게 망설이며 끄덕인다.

개츠비: 아니다, 부모님한텐 간다고 안 할래.

애슐리: 왜?

개츠비는 애슐리에게 제스처를 한다.

개츠비: 엄마는 연례 가을 파티를 여는데 내가 가기
싫어서 엄마는 졸도할 지경이고…

애슐리: 음.

개츠비: 급한 리포트 있다고 해놨거든 그렇지 않으
면 내가 잠깐이라도 얼굴을 내밀어야 되거
든.

애슐리: (한숨을 쉰다)

- **get in touch with**
  연락하다

- **apoplectic**
  (화가 나서) 졸도할 지경인

- **due**
  ~하기로 되어 있는(예정된)

- **otherwise**
  그렇지 않으면

- **put in an appearance**
  (모임 따위에) (잠깐) 얼굴을 내밀다

How does that sound?
How would you like that?과 같은 의
미로 '어때?, 괜찮을까?라는 뜻이다.

How does that sound?
어때? 괜찮을까?

GATSBY: ...it's like death, it's like having...drinks with a hundred bullshit people, not one of which has ever been turned down by a co—op.

Ashleigh looks up and smiles dreamily.

ASHLEIGH: God, I can't believe it. An interview with the director of "Winter Memories".

GATSBY: (chuckling) Yeah. Hey...

Camera holds as Gatsby stops, then Ashleigh stops and turns toward him.

GATSBY: ...didn't we see "Winter Memories" together on our first date?

Ashleigh nods at him.

ASHLEIGH: (inhales deeply, nodding)

GATSBY: I think so.

ASHLEIGH: I'm just so excited. I mean, you have to help me come up with a list of profound questions to ask him.

Gatsby and Ashleigh walk.

ASHLEIGH: I don't want to come off like a twit.

GATSBY: You're not gonna come off like a twit.

GATSBY: And actually, now that I'm thinking about it, we can't stay at the Carlyle, it's too close to my parents' house...

ASHLEIGH: (very softly, nodding) Oh.

GATSBY: ...but I want you to have a park view?

개츠비:	그 파티는 죽음이야. 손님들이라곤 전부 돈 많고 연줄 좋은 허세들이지.

애슐리는 위를 올려보고 꿈을 꾸는 듯이 웃는다.

애슐리:	믿어지질 않아. '윈터 메모리즈' 감독과 인터뷰라니.
개츠비:	(웃으며) 응.

카메라는 게츠비가 멈추는 것을 비추고, 애슐리는 그에게로 향해 멈춰서 돌아선다.

개츠비:	우리 첫 데이트 때 그 영화 보지 않았나?

애슐리는 그에게 끄덕인다.

애슐리:	(고개를 끄덕이며 깊이 숨쉰다)
개츠비:	맞아.
애슐리:	너무 신나. 질문 리스트 짜는 거 도와줘야 해.

개츠비와 애슐리는 걸어간다.

애슐리:	멍청해 보이기 싫어.
개츠비:	그래 보일 리가 있나.
개츠비:	근데 칼라일은 안 되겠다. 집이랑 너무 가까워.
애슐리:	(부드럽게 머리를 끄덕이며) 응.
개츠비:	그래도 공원이 보이려면…

- **turn down**
  거절하다

- **co-op**
  condominium

- **come up with**
  생각해 내다

- **profound**
  심오한

- **come off = seem**
  보이다

- **twit**
  멍청이

You're not gonna come off like a twit.
twit은 '멍청이' 라는 뜻이고 come off 은 seem(보이다)과 같은 뜻으로 이 문장은 '너는 멍청이처럼 보이지 않을 거야' 라는 뜻으로 쓰인다.

You're not gonna come off like a twit.
너는 멍청이처럼 보이지 않을 거야.

Gatsby snaps his fingers.

GATSBY: (snapping fingers) You know what?
We're gonna stay at the Pierre.
That way you can have a park view, it's a safe
distance from my parents' house...

ASHLEIGH: (very softly) Oh.

GATSBY: ...and then after dinner we're gonna go to the
Carlyle, we'll go to the bar, and, a–a–a–and
spend some time there. It's, it's very old New
York. Uh, uh, I, I really love it.

ASHLEIGH: (very softly, nodding) Uh–huh.

GATSBY: The murals are by Ludwig Bemelmans.

ASHLEIGH: Oh, wow.

Gatsby and Ashleigh turn and walk on another path. Ashleigh gestures at
Gatsby, holding up two fingers.

ASHLEIGH: Yeah, I've... I've only been to Manhattan twice,
you know. Once when I was two and then once
when I was twelve.
All I remember is, we got incredible bargains.
I mean, my parents could not believe that you
could buy a Birkin bag and a Rolex on a blanket
off the street...

GATSBY: (chuckles)

ASHLEIGH: ...for only two hundred dollars! (soft breath and light
chuckle)

Ashleigh walks, then Gatsby follows her.
A greyhound bus moves down a rural highway. The bus destination sign reads:
Go Greyhound

개츠비는 손가락으로 딱소리를 낸다.

개츠비: (손가락으로 소리를 내며) 있잖아.

피에르에 묵으면 되겠다.

공원도 보이고, 부모님 집과도 거리가 있
고.

애슐리: (부드럽게) 오.

개츠비: 칼라일 호텔 바는 저녁 먹고 가면 되니까.

올드타운이라 좋아.

애슐리: (부드럽게 고개를 끄덕이며) 응.

개츠비: 베멀먼즈의 벽화도 있고.

애슐리: 우와.

개츠비와 애슐리는 돌아서 다른 길로 걸어간다. 애슐리는 두 손가
락으로 개츠비에게 제스쳐를 한다.

애슐리: 난 맨해튼 딱 두 번 가봤어. 두 살 때랑 열두
살 때.

기억나는 거라곤 폭탄 세일뿐인데. 버킨 백
이랑 롤렉스 시계를 길에서 팔아 깜짝 놀랐
잖아.

개츠비: (웃는다)

애슐리: 그것도 겨우 200불에. (부드러운 숨을 쉬며 가벼운
웃음을 지으며)

애슐리는 걸어가고 개츠비는 따라간다.
그레이하운드 버스가 시골길 아래로 이동한다. 버스에 목적지 표시
에는 "그레이하운드를 간다"라고 적혀있다.

- mural:
  벽화

- Ludwig Bemelmans
  [1898-1962] 루드비히 베멀먼즈, 오스트
  리안 미국인 어린이책 작가

- blanket
  담요

You know what?
대화 도중에 다음에 하는 말을 강조하거
나, 상대방의 주의를 끌 때 "You know
what?"(있잖아, 정말이지)으로 시작한
다.

You know what?

있잖아, 정말이지.

Gatsby and Ashleigh sit on their seats in the bus as it moves down the highway. Other passengers are sitting around them in the crowded bus. Ashleigh, who has been reviewing her notes for the interview, looks up at Gatsby.

ASHLEIGH: Are there any other questions you can think of that I can ask him?

GATSBY: (exhales through closed lips, thinking) Find out who influenced him more on love, Denis de Rougemont or Ortega y Gasset.

ASHLEIGH: (chuckles softly) How do you always know all that stuff?

Gatsby shrugs at her.

GATSBY: I read, I just don't read what they give us in school. I mean, do I really care who wins between Beowulf and Grendel? No, I don't. Maybe if I had a little money on it, but...

Ashleigh shakes her head and grimaces at him.

ASHLEIGH: (inhales deeply, then sighing tensely) Mm...I don't know why I'm so nervous. I just...No college reporter's won a Pulitzer, right? I don't think so.

GATSBY: You're gonna be fine. Don't put so much pressure on yourself. I think it'll be great.

ASHLEIGH: (softly, nodding) Uh–huh.

GATSBY: Listen, I want to see the Weegee photos at MOMA, and I booked us a dinner at Daniel, which is kind of a nice place, we can dress up for it, it'll be really nice.

버스가 고속도로로 달릴 때 개츠비와 애슐리가 버스에 앉아 있다.
붐비는 버스안에 그들 주변에 다른 승객들이 앉아 있다. 애슐리는
인터뷰할 노트를 다시 보면서 개츠비를 쳐다본다.

애슐리: 다른 질문 또 뭐 없을까?

개츠비: (닫힌 입술로 숨을 내쉬고 생각하며) 사랑에 관해 누
구한테 더 영향 받았나 '드니 드 루주몽',
'오르테가 이 가세트' 중에.

애슐리: (부드럽게 웃으며) 그런 건 어떻게 다 알아?

개츠비가 어깨를 으쓱한다.

개츠비: 내가 좀 읽잖아 학교 과제만 빼고. 베어울프
와 그렌델 중 누가 이기는지는 관심 없어.
내기를 한다면 모를까.

애슐리는 머리는 저으며 그에게 얼굴을 찡그린다.

애슐리: (깊이 숨을 들이쉬며 긴장의 한숨을 내쉬며) 왜 이렇게
떨리지. 퓰리처상 받은 학생기자는 아직 없
었지?

개츠비: 잘할 거니까 너무 스트레스 받지 마.

애슐리: (부드럽게 끄덕이며) 응

개츠비: 현대미술관에서 위지 사진전도 보고. 저녁
은 차려 입고 '다니엘'에서 먹는 거야.

- **grimace**
  (at) 얼굴을 찡그리다

- **MOMA(Museum of Modern Art)**
  현대미술관

- **Daniel**
  뉴욕 북동주지역에 있는 새로운 프랑스 상
  류층 레스토랑

> **Don't put so much pressure on
> yourself.**
> put pressure on+ sb '압력을 가하다'
> 라는 뜻으로, 이 표현은 '자신을 너무 압
> 박하지마, 스트레스 받지마(Don't get
> stressed)' 라는 뜻으로 사용된다.

Z**oom** In

Don't put so much pressure on yourself.

자신을 너무 압박하지마, 스트레스 받지마.

GATSBY: And I splurged on the suite at the Pierre. What the hell, right? It's poker winnings, it's not even real money.

PIERRE – MANHATTAN

Pedestrians walk on the sidewalk and cars cross on the street across from the park. A taxi enters, then stops at the curb. As the Pierre doorman enters, then opens the taxi door.

PEDESTRIANS & PIERRE DOORMAN: (low and indistinct chatter)

Gatsby and Ashleigh get out of the taxi.

PIERRE/ HALLWAY

A bellman enters, carrying Ashleigh and Gatsby's bags, and opens the door to a lavish suite. The bellman walks into the suite as Ashleigh and Gatsby enter and follow him.

ASHLEIGH: (soft gasp)

GATSBY: (whispering very softly) Oh...

Ashleigh glances over her shoulder at Gatsby and smiles at him.

ASHLEIGH: Gatsby, (giggling) it's beautiful!

GATSBY: Well, I wanted to do something special.

As they enter the living room, Ashleigh gestures at a vase flowers on a coffee table.

ASHLEIGH: Wow. (soft breath) Oh, and the flowers.

GATSBY: That's not me, I don't know what that is.

Off the bellman, Ashleigh gestures at a bottle of champagne on the coffee table.

ASHLEIGH: Champagne. Wow. (inhales softly)

개츠비: 그리고 나는 피에르 호텔 스위트룸에서 돈
            을 펑펑 쓸거야. 뭐 어때, 어차피 포커로 딴
            돈인데.

멘하탄 피에르 호텔
보행자들이 보도 위를 걸어가고 차들이 공원에서 다닌다. 택시가
들어와서 연석에서 멈춘다. 피에르 호텔 안내원이 와서 택시문을
연다.

보행자와 피에르 호텔 안내원:　　　　(낮은 명확하지 않은 목소리)

게츠비와 애슐리가 택시에서 내린다.

피에르 호텔 복도
직원이 와서 애슐리와 개츠비의 가방을 들고 호화로운 스위트룸으
로 문을 열어준다. 애슐리와 개츠비가 직원을 따라 방으로 들어온
다.

애슐리: (부드러운 숨을 쉰다)
개츠비: (낮은 목소리로 속삭이며) 오.

애슐리는 개츠비의 어. 위로 보며, 그를 보며 미소를 짓는다.

애슐리: 개츠비, 완전 예쁘다!
개츠비: 특별한 추억이 됐으면 했어.

그들이 방으로 들어왔을 때 애슐리는 커피 테이블에 꽃병을 가리킨
다.

애슐리: (부드러운 목소리로) 꽃까지.
개츠비: 그건 내가 한 건 아냐. 그게 뭔지 난 몰라.

직원은 나가고 애슐리는 커피 테이블 위에 샴페인 병을 가리킨다.

애슐리: 샴페인도 있고. (부드럽게 숨을 쉬며)

- **splurge**
  돈을 물 쓰듯 쓰다

- **lavish suite**
  호화로운 스위트 룸

- **That's not me**
  '내가 주문한 것이 아니야' 라는 뜻.
  i.e., 'I did not order the flowers'

- **I wanted to do something
  special.**
  특별한 것을 하고 싶었어

I don't know what that is.
'나는 그 꽃들이 어떻게 여기 있는지 모
른다는 뜻.
i.e., 'I don't know how those
flowers got here.

I don't know what that is.
그게 뭔지 난 몰라.

Ashleigh looks up through a window at a view of central park.

ASHLEIGH: Oh, look at that view!

Gatsby looks at Ashleigh and smiles at her

GATSBY: Wanted it to be high enough so you could see Central Park.

ASHLEIGH: (sighs) Central Park. Exciting. (excited chuckle)

GATSBY: (to bellman) Thank you so much, sir. I really appreciate that.

ASHLEIGH: Oh.

Ashleigh walks, camera panning with her to again reveal. The bellman, and Gatsby, sitting on the edge of the bed. Gatsby tips the bellman, who hands him the passkey.

GATSBY: Thank you.

The bellman walks.

ASHLEIGH: Do you think that, uh...later maybe we could take a carriage ride?

GATSBY: Yeah.

ASHLEIGH: If it doesn't rain.

The sound of the bellman leaving the room is heard.

GATSBY: We could ride in the rain. It's very moody. It's very romantic. I prefer it.

ASHLEIGH: What time is it?

Gatsby looks at his wristwatch.

애슐리는 셀트럴 파크의 경치를 창문을 통해 본다.

애슐리: 경치 좀 봐.

개츠비는 애슐리를 보며 웃는다.

개츠비: 센트럴 파크가 보이는 방으로 했지.

애슐리: 센트럴 파크. 설렌다. (흥분되어 웃는다)

개츠비: 감사합니다.

애슐리: 오.

애슐리는 걷고 그녀를 비추는 카메라는 직원과 침대 가장자리에 앉아있는 개츠비를 비춘다. 개츠비는 직원에게 팁을 주고 직원은 개츠비에게 패스키를 건넨다.

개츠비: 감사합니다.

직원은 걸어나간다.

애슐리: 이따 마차도 탈 수 있을까?

개츠비: 그럼.

애슐리: 비만 안 오면.

방을 떠나는 직원의 소리가 들린다.

개츠비: 오면 어때. 분위기 있고 로맨틱하잖아. 난 더 좋아.

애슐리: 몇 시야?

개츠비가 그의 시계를 본다.

■ take a carriage ride
마차를 타다

■ moody
분위기 있는

■ wristwatch
손목시계

I really appreciate that.
really의 위치에 따른 의미차이.
I don't really know about that.
= 나는 그거 별로 안좋아해.
I really don't know about that.
=나는 그거 완전 안좋아해.

I really appreciate that.
정말 고마워.

GATSBY: Yeah, we should go, 'cause his hotel's downtown. There might be a little bit of traffic.

Ashleigh walks around the bed.

ASHLEIGH: Oh, it's far?

GATSBY: It's in Soho. You're gonna like Soho.

Ashleigh opens her suitcase, which is at the end of the bed.

GATSBY: It was filled with creative people. Then it got commercial and expensive, so all the creative people moved to Tribeca. But then that got expensive, so they all moved to Brooklyn.

Ashleigh takes a notebook out of her suitcase.

GATSBY: Next move is back in with their parents.

Ashleigh puts the notebook into her handbag.

THE WOOSTER
Some pedestrians cross on the sidewalk in front of the Wooster hotel. A hotel windows read: The Wooster.

GUESTS & WOOSTER BELLMAN: (low and indistinct chatter)

A taxi stops on the street, then Ashleigh and Gatsby get out of the taxi and walk toward the entrance to the hotel.

Ashleigh and Gatsby enter and walk across the stately lobby of the hotel.

ASHLEIGH: He's only giving me an hour.

GATSBY: That's good, we have a one-thirty lunch reservation.

개츠비: 가야겠다. 시내라 막힐지도 몰라.

애슐리는 침대 주변으로 걸어간다.

애슐리: 멀어?

개츠비: 소호에 있어. 너도 좋아할 거야.

애슐리는 침대 끝 쪽에 있는 가방을 연다.

애슐리: 예술가들의 거리. 그러다 임대료가 올라 다들 트라이베카로 갔어. 근데 거기도 비싸져서 브루클린으로 갔지.

에슐리는 가방에서 노트북을 꺼낸다.

개츠비: 담엔 부모 집으로 돌아가야 할지도.

애슐리는 가방에 노트북을 넣는다.

우스터
몇몇 보행자는 우스터 호텔 앞에 보도를 걸어간다. 호텔 창문엔 "더 우스터"라고 쓰여있다.

손님들과 우스터 호텔 직원들: (낮고 명확하지 않은 목소리)

택시가 거리에 멈추고 애슐리와 개츠비가 택시에서 내려 호텔 입구 쪽으로 걸어간다.

에슐리와 개츠비가 빌딩안으로 들어가서 우아한 호텔 로비로 걸어간다.

애슐리: 한 시간밖에 안 준대.

개츠비: 잘됐네. 1시 반에 점심 예약이니까.

- **indistinct**
  또렷하지 않은, 흐릿한

- **get out of**
  (차)에서 내리다

- **stately**
  당당하게, 우아하게

- **reservation**
  예약

There might be a little bit of traffic.
traffic은 '차량들, 교통(량)'이고 might be는 추측을 나타내는 '~일지도 모른다'라는 뜻으로, '차가 막힐지도 모른다'라는 뜻으로 사용된다.

There might be a little bit of traffic.
차가 막힐지도 몰라.

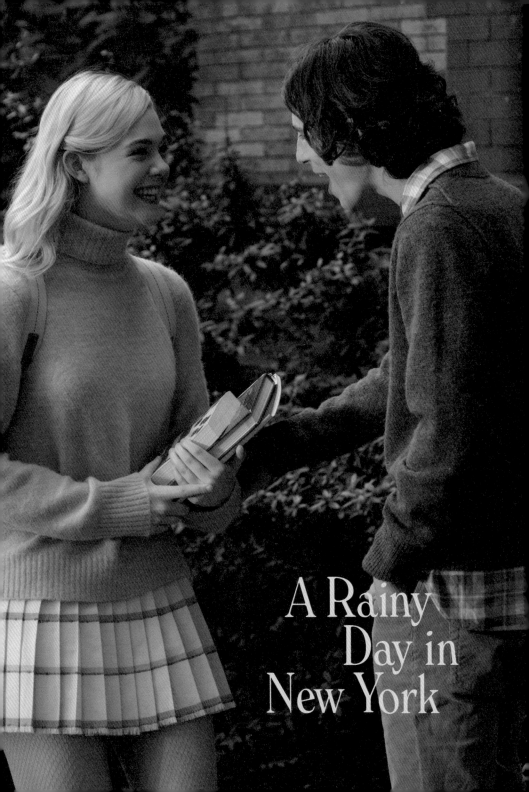

A Rainy
Day in
New York

A Rainy
Day in
New York

ASHLEIGH: Oh. Well, what are you gonna do while I'm upstairs?

Ashleigh turns and leads Gatsby, camera dollying with them to reveal the front desk.

GATSBY: I don't know. I'll...stroll around Soho, maybe visit my brother. I can't tell you how nice it is to be back in the city. Tell you the truth, if it weren't for you, I don't know if I'd ever find my way back to Yardley.

ASHLEIGH: Well, what would you do?

Ashleigh and Gatsby, step to the front desk, camera panning with them to reveal a desk clerk, standing behind the front desk.

GATSBY: Find some brilliant way to ruin my life.

ASHLEIGH: (chuckles softly, then inhales)

Ashleigh looks at the desk clerk.

ASHLEIGH: (to desk clerk) Hi, um, I'm here for Mister Roland Pollard.

애슐리:　나 일할 동안 뭐 할 거야?

애슐리가 돌아서 개츠비로 가고 카메라는 프론트 데스크를 비춘다.

개츠비:　글쎄, 소호를 거닐든지 형네 집에 들르든
지. 오랜만에 시내에 오니까 정말 좋다. 너
만 아니면 학교로 안 돌아갔을걸.

애슐리:　안 가면 뭐 하려고?

애슐리와 개츠비는 프론트 데스크로 가고 카메라는 프론트 데스크
뒤에 서있는 데스크 직원을 그들과 함께 비춘다.

개츠비:　인생 망칠 멋진 방법을 찾아봐야지.

애슐리:　(부드럽게 웃고, 숨을 들이쉰다)

애슐리는 데스크 직원을 쳐다본다.

애슐리:　롤란 폴라드 감독님 뵈러 왔는데요.

■ stroll around
거닐다

■ if it weren't for you
without 또는 but for (~이 없다면)과 같은
뜻으로 '만일 너가 없다면' 이라는 의미

What are you gonna do?
gonna do는 going to do의 대화체 표
현으로 흔히 사용되며 '뭐할 예정이니?
뭐할 거니?' 라는 뜻이다.

What are you gonna do?
뭐할 예정이니? 뭐할 거니?

41

Chapter 2

애슐리의 인터뷰

Ashleigh's Interview

시간 00:07:50 ~ 00:17:09

THE WOOSTER/ ROLAND'S SUITE
An assistant and Ashleigh stop and look at Roland.

ASSISTANT :   Roland, this is Ashleigh Enright...

Ashleigh smiles nervously at Roland.

ASHLEIGH :   (to Roland) Hi.
ASSISTANT :   ...from Yardley.

Roland Pollard, a middle-aged film director, enters and walks toward Ashleigh.

ROLAND   How do you do?
ASHLEIGH :   Ashleigh, this is Roland.

Ashleigh stops beside the assistant and shakes hands with Ashleigh. The assistant looks at Roland.

ASHLEIGH :   The screening's all set up. We're running on a really tight schedule.

우스터 호텔에 로랜드의 스위트룸
조수와 애슐리가 멈춰서 로랜드 감독을 본다.

조수: 로랜드, 이분이 애슐리 앤라잇입니다.

애슐리는 긴장해서 로랜드를 보고 미소를 짓는다.

로랜드: (로랜드에게) 안녕하세요.
조수: 야들리에서 온…

중년 영화감독인 로랜드 폴라드가 애슐리 쪽으로 걸어 들어온다.

로랜드: 처음 뵙겠습니다.
조수: 애슐리, 감독님이세요.

로랜드는 조수 옆에 서서 애슐리와 악수를 한다. 조수는 로랜드를 본다.

조수: 시사 준비됐고 시간 여유가 없어요.

- assistant
  조수
- shake hands with
  ~와 악수하다
- screening
  시사, 심사
- set up
  준비하다

Roland nods at the assistant, who walks. Roland gestures toward some sofas.

ROLAND :   (murmuring to Ashleigh) Please.

Roland and Ashleigh walk to the sofas. A maid is working at a table in a kitchenette. Ashleigh gestures excitedly at Roland

ASHLEIGH :   (to Roland) First of all, I'd just like to say that, uh, eh, what an honor this is for me. I just want to say you're by far the most interesting American director. (nervous chuckle)

Ashleigh sits down on a sofa. Roland stops in front of a chair.

ROLAND :   Thank you.

Roland sits down on the chair. The assistant exits through a doorway. Ashleigh, taking out her notebook, gestures at Roland.

ASHLEIGH :   I write on the arts for our paper and I've always put you right up in a class with Renoir and De Sica. (chuckles softly)

The maid picks up a tray and walks with it. Roland starts to fiddle with the lid of a flask in his hands.

ROLAND :   I'm surprised to hear that s—someone your age is familiar with Renoir and De Sica.

Ashleigh gestures at Roland.

ASHLEIGH :   Oh, um...well, film's my total thing. I've seen all the American classics. Particularly the Europeans. Mm. Kurosawa's my favorite.

로랜드는 조수에게 고개를 끄덕이고 조수는 걸어나간다. 로랜드는
소파 쪽으로 손짓을 한다.

로랜드: (에슐리에게 중얼거리며)

로랜드와 애슐리는 쇼파쪽으로 걸어간다. 직원이 작은주방 테이블
에서 일하고 있다. 애슐리는 로랜드에게 흥분해서 손짓을 한다.

개츠비: (로랜드에게) 우선 정말 영광이라고 말씀드리
고 싶어요. 최고로 흥미로운 미국 감독이시
거든요. (긴장하며 웃는다)

애슐리는 쇼파에 앉고, 로랜드는 의자 앞에 멈춘다.

로랜드: 고마워요.

로랜드는 의자에 앉는다. 조수는 복도 쪽으로 나간다. 애슐리는 노
트북을 꺼내며 로랜드에게 손짓을 한다.

애슐리: 전 늘 감독님을 르누아르와 데시카 레벨이
라고 써요. (부드럽게 웃으며)

여직원은 쟁반을 들고 나간다. 로랜드는 손에 음료병의 뚜껑을 가
지고 만지작거리기 시작한다.

로랜드: 그 나이에 그 감독들을 알다니 놀랍네요.

애슐리는 로랜드에게 손짓을 한다.

애슐리: 영화는 제 인생의 전부거든요. 미국 고전 영
화도 다 봤어요. 특히 유럽 영화들. 구로사
와 감독이 제일 좋구요.

- **murmur**
  중얼거리다

- **kitchenette**
  작은 주방

- **first of all**
  우선, 무엇보다도

- **by far**
  훨씬

- **fiddle**
  만지작 거리다

**I'd just like to say that what an
honor this is for me.**
I'd (just) like to say (that) ~ 는 '~라
고 말하고 싶다, 그러니까 내말은' 이라
는 뜻으로 'What I'm trying to say is
(that)의 의미를 지닌다.

Zoom In **I'd just like to say that what an honor this is
for me.**

이것은 나에게 정말 영광이라고 말하고 싶어요.

ROLAND : (frustrated breaths)

ASHLEIGH : Um, (inhales, smacking lips) I?

ROLAND : Ah.

ASHLEIGH : I mean, technically, he's not European. Technically, he's obviously Japanese, but you...

ROLAND : Mm.

ASHLEIGH : ...really speak to my soul.

ROLAND : Um...what college are you from?

ASHLEIGH : Yardley

ROLAND : Oh.

ASHLEIGH : It's small.

Roland finally gets the lid of the flask open and picks up a coffee cup off a coffee table. He stands up and walks to the kitchenette.

ROLAND : I know it well. My first wife went there.

ASHLEIGH : Really?

Roland stops at the table. He puts down the coffee cup, then pours a good amount of liquor in it from the flask.

ROLAND : Yes, a brilliant woman. Long blonde hair and a state-of-the-art overbite. Very sexy, a philosophy major.

Roland puts down the flask, then picks up a coffeepot. He fills the rest of the coffee cup with coffee.

ROLAND : To tell you the truth, I didn't deserve her. And I...didn't end up with her, either, so...

로랜드:	(실망하는 숨소리로)
애슐리:	음, (입술로 쩝쩝소리를 내며) 저는…
로랜드:	아.
애슐리:	물론 유럽인은 아니고 일본인이지만…
로랜드:	음.
애슐리:	암튼 감독님 삭품은 정말 심금을 울려요.
로랜드:	어느 대학에서 왔다고요?
애슐리:	야들리요.
로랜드:	오.
애슐리:	작은 학교죠.

로랜드는 마침내 병의 두껑을 열고 커피잔을 든다. 그는 일어나서 작은 주방쪽으로 걸어간다.

로랜드:	잘 알아요. 첫 번째 아내가 거길 나와서.
애슐리:	정말요?

로랜드가 커피테이블에서 멈춘다. 그는 커피잔을 내려 놓고 병에서 잔으로 상당한 양을 붓는다.

로랜드:	응. 똑똑했지, 긴 금발에 토끼 이빨이 예술이었는데. 아주 섹시하고 철학 전공이었죠.

로랜드는 음료병을 내려 놓고 커피 주전자를 집어 든다. 그는 커피로 커피 커피잔의 나머지를 채운다.

로랜드:	나한테 과분했지 근데 결국 헤어졌으니까 뭐…

■ smack
소리를 내다

■ speak to my soul
심금을 울리다

■ flask
음료 플라스크(병)

■ state-of-the-art
최첨단

■ overbite
피개 교합(아랫니[턱]보다 윗니[턱]가 훨씬 튀어나온 상태), 토끼 이빨

I didn't deserve her.
deserve는 '~을 받을 만하다, 누릴 자격이 있다' 라는 의미로, I didn't deserve her는 '그녀는 나에게 과분했어' 라는 의미이다.

I didn't deserve her.
그녀는 나에게 과분했어.

ASHLEIGH : Oh. Well, uh, that's, uh…neither hither… nor yon, I'd imagine. I guess…it's probably…more yon than hither.

ROLAND : Are you from New York?

Ashleigh shakes her head.

ASHLEIGH : (shaking her head) Mm–mn…Tucson, Arizona.

Roland walks with the cup of coffee.

ROLAND : What does your family do?

ASHLEIGH : Aggh, I was afraid you'd ask. My father owns banks.

Roland sits down on the sofa and looks at Ashleigh.

ROLAND : Is that bad?

ASHLEIGH : Well…I know what you're thinking. You know. Republicans. The one percent. But we're not. We're just, uh…totally Episcopalians who happen to just be rich.

ROLAND : (very softly, nodding) Mm.

ASHLEIGH : That's how my Ashley was.

ROLAND : Well, who's your Ashleigh?

ASHLEIGH : My first wife. The one with the long blonde hair and the state–of–the–art overbite.

Ashleigh looks at Roland with surprise.

ROLAND : Her name was Ashleigh?

ASHLEIGH : A–S–H–L–E–Y.

애슐리: 음, 그건… 이쪽도 저쪽도 아닌… 그런 거겠
죠. 근데 아마도…이젠 저쪽에 가까운…?

로랜드: 뉴욕 출신이에요?

애슐리는 머리를 가로 젓는다.

애슐리: (머리를 저으며) 아뇨, 애리조나주 투손이요.

로랜드는 커피잔을 가지고 걸어간다.

로랜드: 부모님은 뭘 하세요?

애슐리: 그 질문 싫은데… 아빠가 은행들을 갖고 계
세요.

로랜드는 소파에 앉아 애슐리를 쳐다본다.

로랜드: 그게 뭐 나쁜가?

애슐리: 선입견을 갖고 보니까요. 공화당원, 상위 1
퍼센트. 우린 아닌데. 어쩌다 보니 부자가
된 성공회 교도들일 뿐이죠.

로랜드: (아주 부드럽게 고개를 끄덕이며) 음…

애슐리: 나의 애슐리도 그랬는데

로랜드: 감독님의 애슐리요?

애슐리: 내 첫 번째 아내. 긴 금발에 토끼 이빨이 예
술이라는.

애슐리는 놀라서 로랜드를 쳐다본다.

애슐리: 그분 이름도 애슐리예요?

로랜드: A-S-H-L-E-Y

- **hither**
  여기로

- **yon**
  저쪽의 물건[사람]

- **Episcopalian**
  성공회 교도

- **state-of-the-art**
  최첨단

- **overbite**
  피개 교합(아랫니[턱]보다 윗니[턱]가 훨씬
  튀어나온 상태), 토끼이빨

What does your family do?
What do you do?는 '(지금) 뭐하세
요?(What are you doing?)' 가 아니라,
직업을 묻는 말로 '직업이 뭐예요?' 라는
질문이다.

Zoom In

What does your family do?
부모님은 뭐하세요?(직업을 묻는 질문)

Ashleigh looks at Roland with amusement, then shakes her head.

ASHLEIGH : Oh, well...tsk, mine is A–S–H–L–...E–I–G–H.

ROLAND : You use the Forbes Five Hundred spelling.

ASHLEIGH : (giggles)

ROLAND : Since, uh...this is your first meaningful assignment, would you like a scoop?

Ashleigh looks at Roland with confusion.

ASHLEIGH : Of?

ROLAND : Umm...inside information. You've heard the term.

Ashleigh looks at Roland with realization.

ASHLEIGH : Oh, a scoop!

ROLAND : I'd rather share this with you...than some slick, gossip–hungry newspaper hack.

ASHLEIGH : My God.

He drinks from his cup of coffee.

ASHLEIGH : You keep going, I'm liable to have one of my famous psychological hiccup fits.

ROLAND : When I'm nervous, I stammer.

ASHLEIGH : Is that the scoop?

ROLAND : No, that's, that's not the scoop.

ASHLEIGH : Oh, well...the worst, of course, is when I'm sexually conflicted. Then I'll hiccup indefinitely.

ROLAND : Hm.

애슐리는 놀라서 로랜드를 쳐다보고, 머리를 젓는다.

애슐리: 아, 저는…A–S–H–L–E–I–G–H 예요.

로랜드: 포브스지에 실릴 만한 부유층 철자네.

애슐리: (웃는다)

로랜드: 이번이… 뜻 깊은 첫 기사인 만큼 건수 하나
줄까요?

애슐리는 당황해서 로랜드를 쳐다본다.

애슐리: 그게 무슨…

로랜드: 내부 정보 특종 건 말이에요.

애슐리는 깨닫고 로랜드를 쳐다본다.

애슐리: 아, 특종이요!

로랜드: 가십만 쫓는 글쟁이들 말고 기자님 주고 싶
어서.

애슐리: 세상에.

그는 커피를 마신다.

애슐리: 계속하시면 너무 떨려서 제 딸꾹질병 도지
겠어요.

로랜드: 난 떨리면 말을 더듬지.

애슐리: 그게 특종인가요?

로랜드: 아니, 그건 아니고.

애슐리: 전 성적 충동을 느낄 때 더 심해요. 끝도 없
이 딸꾹질이 나죠.

로랜드: 음.

- **Forbes**
  포브즈(미국의 경제 잡지)

- **meaningful**
  의미 있는, 뜻 깊은

- **scoop**
  (신문의) 특종, 기사, 최신정보

- **slick**
  말을 번지르르하게 하는 (=glib)

- **hack**
  기자, 저널리스트

- **be liable to**
  ~하기 쉽다

- **psychological**
  정신(심리)적인

- **hiccup fit**
  딸꾹질 발작

- **stammer**
  말을 더듬다

- **indefinitely**
  무한정으로

I'd rather share this with you
I'd rather ~는 '차라리(훨씬) ~하는 편
이 낫다' 라는 의미로, 이 문장은 '차라리
이것을 너와 함께 하는 게 낫다' 라는 의
미로 쓰인다.

I'd rather share this with you
차라리 이것을 너와 함께 하는 게 낫다.

ROLAND :   The scoop is...I'm not happy with this film.

Ashleigh looks at Roland with surprise.

ASHLEIGH :   You're not?

ROLAND :   I'm thinking of quitting...actually. That's the scoop.

ASHLEIGH :   Well, if I could speak frankly...Mister Pollard... you'll never have mass appeal. You're too original. I mean, you've never once made one single commercial concession. You're a free creative spirit. Like...Van Gogh, or Rothko, or Virginia Woolf. Of course, they all committed suicide.

ROLAND :   That's a very sweet thing to say, Ashleigh.

ASHLEIGH :   You should read me on you. I wrote that your best work is yet to come. I mean, it's only in the, you know, the...Yardley Argus, but...we have a good circulation.

ROLAND :   You...

                ...think that my best work is yet to come.

ASHLEIGH :   I do. I mean, I haven't seen your new film, but I'm willing to bet?

ROLAND :   Would you like to?

Ashleigh reacts with surprise, then looks at Roland.

ASHLEIGH :   I'd love to!

                But I kn-, I know how...secretive you are which I totally respect.

로랜드:	특종은… 이번 영화가 맘에 안 든다는 거.

애슐리는 놀래서 로랜드를 쳐다본다

애슐리:	그래요?
로랜드:	은퇴를 고민 중이에요. 특종은 그거예요.
애슐리:	그럼…솔직히 말씀 드릴게요. 흥행은 절대 안 될 거예요. 너무 독특하시거든요. 한 번도 상업적 타협은 안 하셨잖아요. 자유로운 작가 영혼. 예를 들면 반 고흐, 마크 로스코 버지니아 올프처럼요. 물론 다 자살했지만요.
로랜드:	칭찬 고맙네요.
애슐리:	제가 쓴 감독님 기사 보셔야 되는데. 감독님의 최고작은 아직 안 나왔다고 썼어요. 그래 봤자 학교 신문이긴 하지만 부수가 꽤 많아요.
로랜드:	당신은… 내 최고작은 아직이라고?
애슐리:	네. 신작은 아직 못 봤지만 제 생각엔 분명히…
로랜드:	보고 싶어요?

애슐리는 놀래서 반응하고 로랜드를 쳐다본다.

애슐리:	그럼요. 하지만 보안 철저히 하셔야 하잖아요.

- commercial concession
  상업적 타협

- commit suicide
  자살하다

- be yet to
  아직 …하지 않고 있다

- We have a good circulation
  부수가 많다

- secretive
  비밀스러운

I'm not happy with this.
be happy with~는 ~에 만족하다는 뜻
이므로 이문장은 '나는 이게 맘에 안 들
어, 만족 못해' 라는 의미이다.

I'm not happy with this.
나는 이게 맘에 안 들어, 만족 못해.

ROLAND :   What are you doing now?

ASHLEIGH :   Now?

Ashleigh looks at him. Roland stands up.

ROLAND :   Yes, now. I'm…I'm screening it for Ted Davidoff, who did the script.

ASHLEIGH :   I know who he is. Yeah, he writes all your movies. He's a genius.

Ashleigh puts her notebook back in her pocketbook.

ROLAND :   I'm screening some…last-minute changes. Face-saving changes.

ASHLEIGH :   Well, how long does it run?

Ashleigh stands up and walks. Roland turns and walks alongside her.

ASHLEIGH :   Uh, I guess I–I could shift my lunch plans.

SOHO STREETS
Pedestrian cross a street in a crosswalk. Gatsby enters and strolls across the street.

GATSBY :   (voice over) One thing about New York City you're here or you're nowhere. You cannot achieve this level of anxiety, hostility, and paranoia anywhere else. It's really exhilarating.

A short time later, looking at a display of various cigarette holders, which is outside the front of a corner store. The display copy reads: Stylish and sophisticated, burn proof, Bakelite cigarette holders.

로랜드:　　지금 뭐 해요?
애슐리:　　지금이요?

애슐리는 로랜드를 쳐다보고, 로랜드는 일어난다.

로랜드:　　그래요. 각본 쓴 테드 다비도프와 볼 건데.
애슐리:　　누군지 알죠. 감독님 영화 다 쓰신 분 천재
　　　　　　잖아요.

애슐리는 가방에 노트북을 다시 넣는다.

로랜드:　　막판 수정을 해야 해서. 망작은 피하려면.
애슐리:　　얼마나 길죠?

애슐리는 일어나서 걸어간다. 로랜드는 그녀쪽으로 돌라서 걸어간다.

애슐리:　　점심 약속 변경해야겠네요.

소호거리
보행자들이 횡단보도를 건넌다. 개츠비는 거리를 건넌다.

개츠비:　　(해설)뉴욕에 한번 빠지면 다른 덴 못 간다.
　　　　　　이 정도의 불안, 적대감 불신은 어디에도 없
　　　　　　기에. 이 얼마나 멋진가.

잠시 후에, 모퉁이 가게 앞에 외부에 있는 다양한 담배 파이프 진열
을 보며, 진열대에는 "멋지고 세련된, 화재 내구성있는, 백라이트
담배파이프"라고 쓰여져 있다.

- screen
  (적절한지) 확인하다, 거르다

- last-minute
  마지막 순간의, 막바지의

- face-saving
  체면을 세우기 위한

- hostility
  적대감

- paranoia
  피해망상

- exhilarating
  아주 신나는(즐거운)

How long does it run?
run은 '(얼마의 기간 동안) 계속되다'는
의미로 '얼마나 오래 계속해요?, 얼마나
길죠?'라는 의미로 쓰인다.

How long does it run?
얼마나 오래 계속해요?, 얼마나 길죠?

55

Gatsby steps out of the store onto the sidewalk. He has a new cigarette holder with a cigarette in it in his mouth.

GATSBY : (voice over) Anyhow, I decided to treat myself to a cigarette holder...

Gatsby strikes a match and lights the cigarette with it.

GATSBY : (voice over) ...which makes me look dapper and serves the double duty... of delaying the inevitable onset of cancer or emphysema. I smoke too much.

Gatsby enters from around a corner and walks down the sidewalk.

GATSBY : (voice over) So then who do I meet but one of the most obnoxious and revolting characters from my high school.

TROLLER : Welles?

Alvin Troller, a high school classmate of Gatsby's, turns and walks down the sidewalk toward Gatsby.

TROLLER : Hey.

GATSBY : Troller.

Troller stops and looks Gatsby.

TROLLER : I heard you flunked out of freshman year.

GATSBY : No, no...

Gatsby shakes his head at Troller.

개츠비는 가게에서 나와 보도로 걸어간다. 그는 입에 담배파이프를
물고 있다.

개츠비: (해설)암튼 시가렛 홀더를 사서.

개츠비는 성냥을 켜고 담배에 불을 붙인다.

개츠비: (해설)폼 좀 잡아보기로 했다.

개츠비: (해설)암이나 폐기종 발병도 늦출 겸. 난 너무
많이 피우거든.

개츠비는 모퉁이를 돌아 보도로 걸어간다.

개츠비: (해설)그러다 누굴 만났느냐…고교 동창 중
가장 재수 없는 녀석.

트롤러: 웰즈?

개츠비의 고등학교 동창인 알빈 트롤러는 개츠비쪽 보도로 걸어간
다.

트롤러: 야!
개츠비: 트롤러.

트롤러는 멈춰서 개츠비를 본다.

트롤러: 너 1학년 때 학교에서 쫓겨났다며?
개츠비: 아니야.

개츠비는 트롤러에게 머리를 젓는다.

- **cigarette holder**
  담배 파이프

- **treat oneself to**
  …을 즐기다, …을 큰맘 먹고 사다

- **strike[light] a match**
  성냥을 긋다(켜다)

- **dapper**
  멋부리는 신사

- **inevitable**
  불가피한, 필연적인

- **onset**
  시작

- **emphysema**
  의학 (폐)기종

- **obnoxious**
  아주 불쾌한, 몹시 기분 나쁜 (=offensive)

- **revolting**
  혐오스러운, 역겨운 (=disgusting)

- **Welles**
  게츠비의 성

- **flunked out of**
  성적불량으로 퇴학당하다

I decided to treat myself.
'treat myself' '큰맘 먹고 돈을 썼다' 라
는 뜻으로, 무엇에 돈을 썼는지 언급하려
면 뒤에 전치사 to를 붙인다. I decided
to treat myself to a cigarette holder
라고 하면 자신을 위해 큰맘 먹고
cigarette holder(담배 파이프)를 샀다는
의미이다.

I decided to treat myself.
큰맘 먹고 돈을 썼다.

GATSBY :	...I didn't flunk out. Uh...I transferred up to Yardley because the first place I tried was too unstructured.
TROLLER :	Oh. The word around is "flunked".
GATSBY :	Nope.
TROLLER :	Where the hell is Yardley? Afghanistan? (soft chortle)
GATSBY :	Upstate.
TROLLER :	Hey, you hear about Finletter?
GATSBY :	No.
TROLLER :	He got thrown out of Princeton for passing bad checks.
GATSBY :	No, I didn't hear about that.
TROLLER :	Yeah, but big deal.
TROLLER :	Because of his father, he's got like the all-time golden parachute. He could commit mass murder, he'd still have a cushy job waiting for him.
GATSBY :	That's a weird way to put it.
TROLLER :	And Millstein is marrying Carol Durand! Which...I'll never understand because she resembles Yasser Arafat! (snorts) Not to mention, she's an ice queen
GATSBY :	Yeah, well, you can't believe everything that?
TROLLER :	What are you doin' in town?
GATSBY :	It's my girlfriend. I'm just, uh...showin' her around for the weekend.
TROLLER :	Oh. Who's your girlfriend?
GATSBY :	You wouldn't know her.
TROLLER :	She's got a name, hasn't she?

개츠비:	쫓겨난 거 아냐. 체계가 없어서 야들리로 옮겼지.
트롤러:	소문엔 '쫓겨났다' 였거든.
개츠비:	아냐.
트롤러:	야들리는 어디 붙어있냐? 아프가니스탄? (비웃으며)
개츠비:	뉴욕주 북부.
트롤러:	핀레터 소식은 들었냐?
개츠비:	아니.
트롤러:	부도 수표 남발하다 프린스턴에서 쫓겨났어.
개츠비:	전혀 몰랐어.
트롤러:	그게 뭐 대수냐.
트롤러:	아버지 덕에 퇴직금도 빵빵하게 받을 텐데. 대량 학살을 하고도 돈 잘 벌 놈이야.
개츠비:	말이 좀 그러네.
트롤러:	또 밀스틴은 캐롤과 결혼해. 어떻게 야세르 아라파트 닮은 여자애랑 결혼하냐(코웃음치며). 인정머리도 없는 앤데.
개츠비:	그런 걸 다 믿을 순 없으니…
트롤러:	뉴욕엔 웬일이냐?
개츠비:	주말에 여친한테구경 좀 시켜주려고.
트롤러:	누군데?
개츠비:	말해도 몰라.
트롤러:	이름은 있을 거 아냐.

- transfer
  (장소를) 옮기다

- get thrown out of
  쫓겨나다

- big deal
  큰일, 큰 대수

- golden parachute
  고액의 퇴직금

- cushy job
  수월한(편한) 직장

- snorts
  코웃음을 웃다(치다)

- ice queen
  냉정하고 거만한 여자

That's a weird way to put it.
put은 '표현하다' 라는 뜻으로 사용되어,
이 문장은 '그 말이 좀 그러네(이상하네)'
라는 의미로 쓰인다.

That's a weird way to put it.
그 말이 좀 그러네(이상하네).

GATSBY :   Ashleigh.

TROLLER :   Ashley.

GATSBY :   Mm—hm.

TROLLER :   Like Ashley Wilkes in "Gone with the Wind"? That wimp?

GATSBY :   What about Josh Loomis?

TROLLER :   I just saw Josh.
He's shooting a movie on Minetta.

GATSBY :   A movie?

TROLLER :   It's his student film. This...N.Y.U. project. It looked completely stupid to me. You should stop by. He's with Evans and the younger Tyrell.

Troller shakes his head.

TROLLER :   You always liked Josh, that Turner Classic wimp.

Gatsby gestures hesitantly at Troller.

GATSBY :   Did you say Amy's younger sister was there? Is Amy there?

TROLLER :   Amy's...at Vassar. Big deal. I'm impressed. Flat chested. Like two dimes on an ironing board.

GATSBY :   Amy was beautiful.

TROLLER :   Yeah, if you like Grace Kelly! (incredulous chortle)

Gatsby looks down.

TROLLER :   What are you in town for?

개츠비:	애슐리.
트롤러:	애슐리.
개츠비:	음.
트롤러:	'바람과 함께 사라지다'의 애슐리 윌크스? 그 소심이?
개츠비:	조쉬 루미스는?
트롤러:	방금 봤어. 미네타에서 영화 찍고 있더라.
개츠비:	영화?
트롤러:	학교 과제. 뉴욕대 다니잖아 내가 보기엔 엉터리던데. 들러봐, 에반스랑 에이미 동생 트렐도 있어.

트롤러는 고개를 젓는다.

트롤러:	너 조쉬 좋아했잖아 소심이 영화광.

개츠비는 망설이며 트롤러에게 손짓을 한다.

개츠비:	에이미 여동생? 에이미도 있어?
트롤러:	갠 바사대 다녀 별일이지, 깜짝 놀랐다. 절벽 가슴 다리미판에 동전 두 개였잖아.
개츠비:	에이미 예뻤잖아.
트롤러:	그래 뭐 그레이스 켈리가 좋다면. (믿지 못한다는 비웃음으로)

개츠비는 아래를 내려다 본다.

트롤러:	여긴 웬일이라구?

- wimp
  소심이, 겁쟁이

- shooting a movie
  영화를 찍다

- stop by
  잠시 들르다

- wimp
  겁쟁이, 약골 (=weed)

- ironing board
  다리미판

- incredulous
  믿지 않는, 못 믿겠다는 듯한

- chortle
  (기쁘거나 재미있어서) 깔깔거리다

He's shooting a movie on Minetta.
shooting a movie는 '영화를 찍다' 라는 의미이다.

He's shooting a movie on Minetta.
그는 미네타에서 영화 찍고 있어.

GATSBY: Just my girlfriend, uh...she has an interview with Roland Pollard for the school paper.

TROLLER: Who's that?

GATSBY: It's a director. He did "Winter Memories", uh..."Moonglow".

TROLLER: ...yeah!

Troller shakes his head.

TROLLER: I can't stand his flicks. All that...wimpy emotional probing, never a single decent toilet joke.

GATSBY: Yeah, well, uh?

TROLLER: Hey, you should go and watch them shoot.

Gatsby, puffing on his cigarette through the cigarette holder, glances at his wristwatch.

TROLLER: You could be in it. They're lookin' for volunteers. With that cigarette holder, you could be the perfect milquetoast nerd!

GATSBY: Okay, well, I'm runnin' a little bit late.

Troller steps, camera panning with him to reveal Gatsby.

TROLLER: Hey...

Troller stops and turns to Gatsby.

TROLLER: ...I wouldn't trust my girl with a big-time Hollywood director.

GATSBY: Okay, good to know.

개츠비:	여친이 롤란 폴라드와 인터뷰가 있어서.
트롤러:	누구?
개츠비:	영화감독 '윈터 메모리즈', '달빛'
트롤러:	알아!

트롤러는 머리를 젓는다.

트롤러:	난 도통 못 봐주겠더라. 처량한 감정 탐구에 화장실 유머도 없고.
개츠비:	어, 뭐…
트롤러:	촬영장 가봐.

개츠비는 담배파이프를 피우며 손목시계를 쳐다본다.

| 트롤러: | 촬영장 가봐, 출연도 하고 사람 필요한가 보던데. 시가렛 홀더도 있겠다 소심한 괴짜로 딱이네. |
| 개츠비: | 알았어, 그만 가봐야겠다. |

트롤러는 발을 내딛고, 카메라는 개츠비를 비춘다.

| 트롤러: | 야… |

트롤러가 개츠비에게 멈추고 돈다.

| 트롤러: | 나 같으면 유명 감독한테 여친 혼자 안 보낸다. |
| 개츠비: | 충고 고맙다. |

- **flick**
  영화

- **pobing**
  진실을 캐기(조사하기) 위한

- **decent**
  괜찮은

- **milquetoast**
  변변치 못한 남자

- **nerd**
  멍청하고 따분한 사람, 괴짜

I can't stand.
stand는 '서다' 라는 뜻으로 많이 알고 있지만, '견디다, 참다' 라는 뜻으로 쓰여, 이 문장은 '참을 수 없다' 라는 의미이다.

I can't stand.
참을 수 없다.

Gatsby walks, then Troller gestures at Gatsby.

TROLLER :   Hey, you didn't ask me what I'm doin'.

Gatsby gestures back at Troller.

GATSBY :   What are you doing?

TROLLER :   I'm only premed. We have pull with the board in Grenada.

THE WOOSTER/ LOBBY

Past Gatsby, sitting in and reading a newspaper, to Ashleigh, who hurries across the lobby from. People are sitting and walking around the busy lobby. Ashleigh stops and looks at him.

ASHLEIGH: I can't make lunch.

GATSBY :   What? Why not?

Ashleigh walks toward Gatsby and gestures giddily.

ASHLEIGH: I have to see his film!

GATSBY :   You do?

Gatsby stands up, Ashleigh stops and gestures at him.

ASHLEIGH: Oh, it's an unbelievable opportunity. And then we're gonna discuss it after and everything!

Gatsby steps to a coffee table and puts down the newspaper.

GATSBY :   When did this develop? I thought you just had an hour with him.

ASHLEIGH: So did I, but then he started opening up to me.

GATSBY :   He did?

개츠비가 걸어나가고 트롤러는 개츠비에게 손짓한다.

트롤러: 나 뭐 하는진 묻지도 않네?

개츠비는 트롤러에게 다시 손짓을 한다.

개츠비: 뭐 하는데?
트롤러: 겨우 의대 다녀. 세인트 조지 보내주셨거
든.

우스터 호텔 로비
개츠비는 앉아서 신문을 읽고 애슐리는 서둘러 로비로 간다. 사람
들은 바쁜 로비에 앉아있고 걸어 다닌다. 애슐리는 멈춰서 그를 본
다.

애슐리: 나 점심 못 먹어.
개츠비: 뭐? 왜?

애슐리는 개츠비 쪽으로 걸어가고 들떠서 손짓을 한다.

애슐리: 감독님 신작 봐야 돼.
개츠비: 정말?

개츠비는 일어나고 애슐리는 멈춰서 그에게 손짓을 한다.

애슐리: 엄청난 기회인 거지. 영화 보고 얘기도 나누
고.

개츠비는 커피 테이블로 가서 신문을 내려둔다.

개츠비: 어떻게 된 거야? 한 시간만 준다더니.
애슐리: 그랬지, 근데 나한테 마음을 연 거야.
개츠비: 그래?

- **I'm only premed.**
(i.e., 'I am only a premedical
student'

- **premed**
의학부 예과 (학생)

- **We have pull with**
= My family has influence with

- **board**
school board (교육위원회)

- **We have pull with the board in
Grenada.**
트롤리의 가족이 트롤리가 그레나다에 있는
(세인트 조지대학) 의대를 가는데 영향을 주
었다는 의미: '그레나다에 있는 세인트 조
지대학에 보내주셨거든'

- **giddily**
(너무 좋아) 들떠서

- **open up to me**
나에게 마음을 열다
i.e., 'being open about himself with
me'

I can't make lunch.
약속을 정할 때 '안돼, 못가' 라는 의미
로 I can't make it을 쓰는 것과 같이 I
can't make lunch는 '나 점심 못 먹어
(i.e., I can't go to lunch with you.)'
라는 뜻으로 쓰인다.

I can't make lunch.
나 점심 못 먹어.

Ashleigh gestures excitedly at Gatsby.

ASHLEIGH: Yeah. He's going through this real artistic crisis.
There's a real story here.

GATSBY :   Well, we have a lunch reservation.

ASHLEIGH: Yeah, but, well, I mean, you wouldn't want me to
have to say no to the screening. I mean, I'm here
for work. We'll have plenty o'time.

GATSBY :   Well, when? A film's gonna take a couple of
hours.

Ashleigh looks at her wristwatch.

ASHLEIGH: Well, what, I mean...it's one now.

ASHLEIGH: The movie'll probably be over around three, and
then, you know, we'll have all afternoon.

GATSBY :   How'd you get friendly so fast?

ASHLEIGH: Oh. He's going through, on this whole self-
sabotage trip.

Ashleigh nudges Gatsby excitedly with her elbow.

ASHLEIGH: It's a scoop.

Gatsby points at Roland.

GATSBY :   Is that him?

ASHLEIGH: Yes.

Gatsby walks past Ashleigh, camera dollying with him to reveal Roland,
standing at the front desk. Gatsby stops and looks at Roland.

애슐리는 개츠비에게 흥분해서 손짓을 한다.

애슐리: 심한 슬럼프에 빠져있어. 특종이 될 거야.

개츠비: 점심 예약해놨는데.

애슐리: 설마 이 시사를 거절하라는 거야? 취재하러 온 거고. 끝나고도 시간 많잖아.

개츠비: 언제? 영화 두 시간은 할 거 아냐.

애슐리는 손목시계를 쳐다본다.

애슐리: 그래 봤자… 지금 1시고.

애슐리: 3시쯤 끝나면 아직 이르잖아.

개츠비: 어떻게 그렇게 빨리 친해졌어?

애슐리: 엄청난 자기파괴 과정을 겪고 계셔.

애슐리는 흥분해서 팔꿈치로 개츠비를 쿡 찌른다.

애슐리: 특종이라니까!

개츠비는 로랜드를 가리킨다.

개츠비: 저 사람이야?

애슐리: 응.

개츠비는 애슐리를 지나가고 카메라는 프론트 데스크에 서 있는 로랜드를 비춘다. 개츠비는 멈춰서 로랜드를 본다.

■ go through
경험하다, 겪다
i.e., "undergo" 'experience' –
'suffer through'

■ screening
(영화) 시사, 상영(방영)

■ be over
끝나다

■ go through
경험하다, 겪다

■ self-sabotage
자기파괴, 자기 태만

■ nudge
(팔꿈치로 살짝) 쿡 찌르다

■ scoop
(신문의) 특종

I'm here for work.
'I'm here for + 목적' 이 쓰여 '나는 여기 ~하러 왔어' 라는 뜻으로, 예를 들어 'I'm here for travel'은 '나는 여기 여행하러 왔어' 'I'm here for work'는 '나는 여기 일하러 왔어' 라는 의미로 사용된다.

Zoom In

I'm here for work.
나는 여기 일하러 왔어.

GATSBY :	Oh, wow. He's a lot older looking than I thought.
ASHLEIGH:	It's a good look, though, don't ya think? He's a sufferer.
GATSBY :	So what? What's so great about suffering?
ASHLEIGH:	You should hear him talk about the arts. He's so passionate. I can see how all his leading ladies fall in love with him.
GATSBY :	Do you want me to meet him or…?
ASHLEIGH:	Oh, no…no, I wouldn't want you to spook him.
GATSBY :	It's okay.

Gatsby starts to step, but Ashleigh steps toward him and gestures at him, stopping Gatsby.

| ASHLEIGH: | No, he's a very private person, and distraught. Yeah, okay, well… |

Ashleigh starts to walk toward Roland. She looks back at Gatsby and gestures at him.

| ASHLEIGH: | …I'll see you later and I—I'll meet you back at the Carlyle at three. |

Ashleigh turns and hurries to Roland.

| GATSBY: | It's the Pierre. The Carlyle's tonight. |

Ashleigh stops beside Roland. Gatsby turns and walks out.

개츠비: 생각보다 나이가 많네.

애슐리는 개츠비를 쳐다본다.

애슐리: 그래도 잘생겼지? 고뇌하는 영혼.

개츠비: 그게 뭐, 고뇌가 멋져?

애슐리: 예술 얘기할 때 보면 완전 열정적이야. 왜
              여주인공들이 다 사랑에 빠졌는지 알겠어.

개츠비: 가서 인사할까?

애슐리: 아냐, 불편해할 거야.

개츠비: 괜찮아.

애슐리가 걸어나가는데 애슐리는 그 쪽으로 가서 손짓을 하며 개츠
비를 막는다.

개츠비: 아냐, 혼자 있길 좋아하는 데다 심난한 상태
              라.

애슐리는 로랜드쪽으로 걸어가기 시작한다. 그녀는 개츠비를 뒤돌
아보고 그에게 손짓을 한다.

애슐리: 가볼게, 이따 3시에 칼라일에서 봐.

애슐리는 돌아서 로랜드에서 서둘러 간다.

개츠비: 피에르 호텔. 칼라일은 저녁 때 갈 거고.

애슐리는 로랜드 옆에서 멈춘다. 개츠비는 돌아나간다.

- **sufferer**
  고통받는(괴로워하는) 사람

- **passionate**
  열정적인

- **fall in love with**
  ~와 사랑에 빠지다

- **spook**
  겁먹게 하다, 겁먹다

- **distraught**
  (흥분해서) 완전히 제정신이 아닌, 심난한

He's a very private person.
private person은 남에게 본인 이야기
를 거의 안하는 사람으로, he's a very
private person은 '그는 남에게 자기
얘기를 거의 안 하는 사람이다, '그는 혼
자 있기를 좋아하는 사람이다' 라는 의미
이다.

Z   om In

He's a very private person.

그는 남에게 자기 얘기를 거의 안 하는 사람이다.
그는 혼자 있기를 좋아하는 사람이다.

A Rainy
Day in
New York

Movie Talk

Travel NYC With 'A Rainy Day in New York': Lower Manhattan

소호 (SoHo)

　소호 (SoHo)라는 이름은 '휴스턴 가의 남쪽(South of Houston Street)'의 앞 글자를 합성한 것으로, 1970년대 가난한 예술가들이 과거 공장 지역이였던 소호의 높고 넓은 빈 공간을 저렴하게 임대해 들어오면서부터 뉴욕에서 가장 활기찬 문화지역으로 발전했다. 그 후, 1980년대에서 90년대 사이에 고급화 되면서 임대료가 비싸졌고, 현재는 쇼핑몰들이 그 빈자리를 채우고 있다. 하지만 현대 예술의 발원지답게 소호는 여전히 특유의 매력을 갖고 있어 관광객들의 필수 방문 지역으로 손꼽는다. 다음과 같이 영화 속 대화에서 소호에 대한 이야기가 나온다.

GATSBY:	Yeah, we should go, because his hotel's downtown. There might be a little bit of traffic.
ASHLEIGH :	Oh, it's far?
GATSBY:	It's in Soho. You're gonna like Soho.
GATSBY:	It was filled with creative people. Then it got commercial and expensive, so all the creative people moved to Tribeca. But then that got expensive, so they all moved to Brooklyn.

　롤랜드 감독님이 있는 The Bowery 호텔은 다운타운(시내) 소호에 있고, 개츠비는 애슐리가 소호를 좋아할 거라고 말한다. 그러면서 소호의 역사에 대해 아주 간단히 설명한다. 과거 소호는 창의적인 사람들로 가득 차 있었지만, 상업적으로 변하면서 비싸졌고, 그 예술가들은 트라이베카로 옮겨가게 되었다. 하지만 거기도 더 비싸져서 이제는 다들 브루클린으로 이동했다고 말한다. 실제 1900년 초부터 1960년까지 공장과 창고 지역이던 소호는 넓은 공간을 필요로

하던 젊은 예술가들이 이주하면서 뉴욕에서 가장 예술적이고 유명한 문화지역이 된다. 예술가들은 천장이 높고 공간이 넓은 창고를 화랑으로 개조하기 시작했으며, 점차 공장은 사라지고 예술가들이 소호 거리를 점령하게 된다. 그들은 자신만의 예술성을 발휘하여 거리를 예술적으로 만들었으며, 그 분위기는 아직까지도 계속 되어지고 있다. 그 1세대 예술가들은 나이가 들면서, 돈을 벌어 풍족한 생활을 하고, 1980년대부터는 특권층의 삶을 추구하게 된다. 소호 거리에 화려하고 비싼 클럽이 들어서고 식당과 일대 상점들이 고급스럽게 바뀌면서 (gentrification：젠트리피케이션화) 지금의 모습으로 변신하게 된다. 때문에 젊은 예술가들은 치솟는 임대료와 변질되는 분위기를 피해 트라이베카로 옮겨갔고, 이후 똑같은 현상으로 인해 다시 맨해튼 밖의 브루클린으로 옮겨가게 된다. 영화를 통해 개츠비의 시선을 따라 소호 거리를 잠시 감상할 수 있다.

SOHO STREET– Pedestrians cross a street in a crosswalk Gatsby enters and strolls across the street.

GATSBY:　　One thing about New York City you're here or you're nowhere. You cannot achieve this level of anxiety, hostility, and paranoia anywhere else. It's really exhilarating.

　영화 속 개츠비의 혼잣말인 "뉴욕에 한번 빠지면 다른 데는 못 간다. 이 정도의 불안, 적대감, 불신은 어디에도 없기에. 이 얼마나 멋진가."을 통해 뉴욕 시티, 소호 거리가 그만큼 매력적인 도시라는 것을 알 수 있다.

그리니치 빌리지 (Greenwich Village)

17세기에 영국 이주민들이 정착하면서 주택가가 형성된 곳으로, 런던 근교에 위치한 '그리니치'의 명칭을 따서 부르게 되었다. 미국 보헤미안 문화의 중심지로, 독특하면서 자유로운 분위기를 형성하고 있다. 빈티지한 붉은 벽돌의 브라운 스톤의 주택을 비롯해 워싱턴 스퀘어 파크, 뉴욕대학교 등 다양한 명소가 모여있다. 그리니치 빌리지는 '뉴욕의 미로'라고 불리는 곳이다. 바둑판처럼 규칙적으로 구획된 다른 지역과 달리 거리가 불규칙하게 얽혀 있어 길을 잃기 매우 쉽다. 그래서 여행객들은 물론 현지인들도 가끔씩 당황하게 만드는 독특한 동네라 '그리니치 빌리지를 헤매지 않고 마음껏 누빌 수 있어야 진짜 뉴요커' 라는 이야기 또한 있다고 한다. 이곳은 주거지역이라서 특별한 관광지가 있는 것은 아니지만, 주택들의 모양도 디자인도 전부 제 각각이며 그리니치 빌리지만의 고급스럽고 예술적인 분위기가 있어 조용히 산책하고 둘러보기에 좋다고 한다. 미국 유명 드라마, '프랜즈(Friends)'의 모니카, 챈들러, 조이와 레이첼이 살았던 아파트와, '섹스 앤 더 시티(Sex and the City)'의 여주인공 캐리의 집으로 나온 촬영지를 실제로 볼 수 있기 때문에 이를 보기 위해 여행객들이 찾지만, 관광 명소로 유명한 곳은 아니다. 그리니치 빌리지는 특히 뉴욕 현지인들이 골목 골목 숨겨진 맛 집 때문에 많이 찾고, 특유의 분위기 때문에 뉴요커들이 가장 좋아하는 장소 중에 하나로 손꼽히기도 한다.

영화 속 브라운 스톤의 주택가는 다음 대화에서 보듯이 바로 개츠비의 형인 헌터의 집이 있는 곳이며, 개츠비가 미네타 길에서 촬영하고 있는 챈과의 첫 만남 장소이기도 하다. 또한 다양한 명소와 맛집이 모여 있는 지역이다.

Hunter's Brownstone-Gatsby walks down the sidewalk toward the steps of Hunter's brownstone. The rain is now falling much harder.

GATSBY: I wonder what's been bothering Hunter. Something was definitely on his mind when I called him.

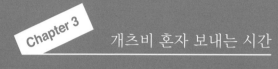

Chapter 3

개츠비 혼자 보내는 시간

Gatsby's day alone

시간 00:17:10 ~ 00:26:06

SOHO STREETS

Gatsby, smoking another cigarette in his cigarette holder, enters and walks down a sidewalk. Pedestrians walk past him on the street.

GATSBY: (voice over) What the hell is it about older guys that seems so appealing to women? Christ, all they are is decrepit. What's sexy about shortterm memory loss?

PASSING PEDESTRIANS: (low and indistinct chatter – continues under following dialogue)

As Gatsby stops and drops the cigarette butt on the sidewalk, then grinds it down with his foot.

GATSBY: (voice over) I don't ever want to get old. Of course, with my smoking habit I'll be spitting blood at forty. Look, if she's gonna get some big inside news story, she, she's gotta put in time with this guy.

Gatsby glances at his wristwatch, then turns and walks down the sidewalk.

소호거리
개츠비는 담배를 피우고 보도로 걸어간다. 보행자는 거리로 그를 지나 걸어간다.

개츠비: (해설) 여자들은 왜 나이든 남자한테 끌릴까? 늙어빠진 게 뭐. 또 건망증은 뭐가 섹시해?

보행자: (낮은 목소리로 분명하지 않은 수다소리)

게츠비는 멈춰서 담배꽁초를 바닥에 던지고 발로 뭉갠다.

개츠비: (해설) 난 절대 늙고 싶지 않다. 물론 지금처럼 피워대다간 마흔에 피를 토하겠지만. 하긴 특종거리를 얻어내려면 당연히 시간을 투자해야겠지.

개츠비는 손목시계를 보고 보도 아래로 걸어간다.

- **pedestrian**
  보행자

- **decrepit**
  노후한, 노쇠한

- **shortterm memory loss**
  건망증

- **grind**
  갈다, 빻다, 뭉개다

GATSBY: (voice over) Meanwhile, it's gonna rain soon.

MINETTA LANE

As Josh Loomis, another of Gatsby's high school classmates, talks to a member of his film crew. More crew members of his student film are carrying a film camera toward a BMW convertible, which is parked at the side of the street. Chandler "Chan" Tyrell, the attractive younger sister of Amy Tyrell, is standing on the sidewalk beside the convertible, her face turned. A makeup artist is putting makeup on her face.

Josh looks up at Gatsby.

JOSH: Hey! Gatsby!

Gatsby enters and walks down the street.

GATSBY: Josh. How are you?

JOSH: Hey, how's it goin', man? Nice to see ya.

GATSBY: It's good to see you.

JOSH: Yeah.

Josh and Gatsby stop and shake hands.

GATSBY: Look, I just ran into Alvin Troller. He told me you were shootin' a short film down here and I thought I'd stop by and say hi.

JOSH: Oh, yeah. Yeah, yeah. Oh, it's just my term project. It's nothin' big, yeah.

GATSBY: Nice, nice.

JOSH: How's, uh…Yardley? Is that where you are?

GATSBY: It's okay, I'm not really liking it too much. I'd rather be goin' to school in the city, but you know my mother.

개츠비: (해설) 그나저나 곧 비가 올 거 같네.

미네타 거리

개츠비의 또 다른 고등학교 동창인 조쉬 루미스가 스테프에게 말한
다. 많은 직원들이 주차되어 있는 BMW 컨버터블 자동차로 영화 카
메라를 이동하고 있다. 에이미 티렐의 매력적인 여동생인, 챈들어
"챈" 티렐이 차 앞 보도에 서 있고 얼굴을 돌린다. 메이크업 아티스
트가 그녀 얼굴에 화장을 해주고 있다.

조쉬는 개츠비를 본다.

조쉬: 이야! 개츠비!

개츠비는 거리로 걸어간다.

개츠비: 조쉬. 잘 지냈어?
조쉬: 헤이. 잘 지냈니? 반갑다.
개츠비: 반갑다.
조쉬: 응.

조쉬와 개츠비는 멈춰서 고개를 젓는다.

개츠비: 방금 트롤러 만났는데 너 여기서 촬영한다
          기에.
조쉬: 별건 아니고 학기 과제야.
개츠비: 좋아.
조쉬: 야들리는 어때? 거기가 너가 있는 곳이지?
개츠비: 괜찮아, 그럭저럭. 난 여기가 좋지만 우리
          엄마 알잖아.

- **run into**
  ~와 우연히 만나다

- **stop by**
  잠시 들르다.

- **term project**
  학기 과제

How's it going?
'잘 지내지? 요즘 어떻게 지내?' 라는 뜻
으로, 안부를 묻는 표현이다.

How's it going?
잘 지내니? 요즘 어떻게 지내?

81

GATSBY: If it's not the perfect image, she bites down on that cyanide capsule she keeps for special emergencies.

JOSH: Oh, yeah? No, I d–, I didn't know that. I?
The only thing I remember about them is they had that, uh, fundraiser for Jeb Bush, right?

GATSBY: Yeah, the fund, right, right, right, yeah, yeah.

JOSH: Yeah, right, yeah, that was?

GATSBY: Tsk.

JOSH: Yeah.

GATSBY: So, listen, how are you? How's life? What, what, uhhh, what's, what's goin' on here? What are you doin'?

JOSH: Uh, you know, just out here tryin' to create a modern film–noir classic, that's all.

GATSBY: Okay. All right.

JOSH: Do you want to be in it?

GATSBY: No.

Josh pats Gatsby on the arm.

JOSH: Come on, man. Look.

GATSBY: No. No, no, no, no.

Josh puts his arm around Gatsby and leads him toward the convertible.

JOSH: No, no, no, no, no, no, no. We're just light on extras, okay?
We have all these people who were no–shows.

GATSBY: Listen, I'm not an actor.

개츠비:	본인 기대에 못 미치면 자살도 불사할 분인 거.
조쉬:	그건 몰랐네, 젭 부시 모금행사 하신 건 기억나.
개츠비:	아, 모금행사… 그래.
조쉬:	그때 참…
개츠비:	쯧.
조쉬:	응.
개츠비:	어떻게 지내? 촬영은 뭘 하는 거야?
조쉬:	현대식 필름 누아르 한번 찍어보려고.
개츠비:	그렇구나.
조쉬:	너도 출연할래?
개츠비:	아니.

조쉬가 개츠비의 팔을 두드린다.

조쉬:	그러지 말구.
개츠비:	아냐, 못 해.

조쉬는 개츠비에 팔에 손을 올리고 컨버터블 차로 데리고 간다.

조쉬:	엑스트라가 모자라.
	펑크낸 인간들이 많아서.
개츠비:	난 배우도 아니잖아.

■ cyanide capsule
청산가리 캡슐

■ fundraiser
모금행사

■ Tsk
쯧 ((못 마땅해서)혀 차는 소리)

What's going on?
친한 친구들 사이에서 할 수 있는 비 격
식적인 표현으로, '무슨 일이야?' 또는
'어떻게 지내니?' 라는 의미로 사용된다.

What's going on?
무슨 일이야?, 어떻게 지내니?

The makeup artist has walked and excited, leaving Chan on the sidewalk on the far side of the convertible.

JOSH:	You don't even have to talk or anything.
GATSBY:	Uhhh... (nervous chuckle)
JOSH:	Seriously. You just get in the car...and then on "Action" you let the girl out. That's it.
GATSBY:	Okay, I don't have to talk?
JOSH:	None.
GATSBY:	Okay.
JOSH:	Zero words.
GATSBY:	All right, I can handle that.
JOSH:	Okay. There we go.
	You remember...Chan, don't ya?

Gatsby enters, then Chan smiles at him.

GATSBY:	Chan Tyrell.
CHAN:	Hi.
GATSBY:	Yeah, you're Amy's little sister, right?
CHAN:	Yeah, good to see you.
GATSBY:	Good to see you.

Chan glances at Josh.

CHAN:	(to Josh) Should we do this?
JOSH:	Yeah, go ahead.

Gatsby opens the convertible door. Josh steps, as he gestures at Chan. The crew members are gathered around the movie camera.

JOSH:	I like that coat, actually. No, keep that on.

메이크업 아티스트는 걸어 나가고, 컨버터블 차 멀리 보도에 챈이
있다.

조쉬:　　　대사도 없어.

개츠비:　　응……(긴장하는 웃음)

조쉬:　　　그냥 차에 타서' 액션' 하면 여자애 내려주는
　　　　　　거야

개츠비:　　오케이

조쉬:　　　한마디도?

개츠비:　　그럼 해볼게.

조쉬:　　　좋아.
　　　　　　너 기억하지? 챈. 그치?

개츠비는 들어가고, 챈은 그를 보고 미소를 짓는다.

개츠비:　　챈 타이렐.

챈:　　　　안녕.

개츠비:　　에이미 동생 맞지?

챈:　　　　반가워.

개츠비:　　반가워.

챈은 조쉬를 본다

챈:　　　　그럼 시작할까?

조쉬:　　　그래.

개츠비는 차 문을 연다. 조쉬는 가면서 챈에게 손짓을 한다. 영화
스테프들이 카메라 주변에 모인다.

조쉬:　　　코트 좋다, 입고 있어.

■ handle
　　다루다

You just get in the car.
get in은 '안에 들어가다' 라는 뜻으로
You just get in the car는 '그냥 차에
타' 라는 뜻이다.

You just get in the car.

그냥 차에 타.

Chan enters and sits down in the passenger seat of the convertible. Gatsby enters and sits down in the driver's seat.

GATSBY: Hey, listen, I hear your older sister's at Vassar now, am I right?

CHAN: Yeah, no, political science major. Can you believe it? I mean, Amy never heard the news that Lincoln was shot.

GATSBY: My God, Chan Tyrell, this is insane. And you were a, a little girl and now you're actually a li–

Chan peers at Gatsby

GATSBY: –a young woman.

CHAN: Ah. Mm, you're not gonna start singing "Gigi", are you?

GATSBY: I'm not gonna start singin' "Gigi", I just meant?

JOSH: (to Gatsby) Uh, so, here's the, the story. She...

Gatsby and Chan look at Josh.

CONVERTIBLE
Josh stands in front of the crew members and gestures at Gatsby.

JOSH: ...is totally mad with lust and she can't let go of you. So, uhh, she kisses you and then she bursts away.

Gatsby sits and looks nervously at Chan

GATSBY: Chan Tyrell.
             Incidentally, I apologize in advance for ruining your scene. I'm...not an actor.

챈은 차 조수석에 앉는다. 개츠비는 들어가서 운전석에 앉는다.

개츠비: 언니는 바사대 갔다며?

챈: 응, 정치학과. 믿어져? 링컨 암살 사건도 몰랐던 언니가.

개츠비: 세상에, 챈 타이렐 기가 막히다. 꼬맹이였었는데 다 커서…

챈은 개츠비를 응시한다.

개츠비: 아가씨가 다 됐네.

챈: 뮤지컬 '지지' 라도 부를 건 아니지?

개츠비: '지지' 안부를거야. 내말은…

조쉬: (개츠비에게) 그래서 여기 이야기에서 그녀는…

개츠비와 챈은 조쉬를 쳐다본다.

컨버터블 차
조쉬는 스텝 앞에 서서 개츠비에게 손짓을 한다.

조쉬: 욕정에 불타서 남자를 안 놔주려는 여자가… 키스하고 황급히 떠나는 장면.

개츠비는 차에 앉아서 챈을 긴장해서 쳐다본다.

개츠비: 챈 타이렐.
네 장면을 망치게 돼 미안. 배우가 아니라서.

- **insane**
  제정신이 아닌

- **lust**
  성욕[욕정]

- **let go of**
  (손에 쥔 것)을 놓다

- **burst away**
  급히 떠나다

I apologize in advance.
in advance는 '미리' 라는 뜻으로, apologize in advance는 '미리 사과할께' 라는 의미이다.

I apologize in advance.
미리 사과할께.

CHAN: Oh, I'm not an actress, either. I'm just helping
            out a friend.

GATSBY: And we kiss?

CHAN: Yeah. That's why I never wanted to be an actress.
            You gotta fake...passion with all kinds of
            weirdos.

GATSBY: Thank you.

CHAN: Yeah, but never mind. Just...kiss me so I can
            really feel it in my toes.

GATSBY: I used to kiss your older sister. She ever say
            anything about that or no?

CHAN: Mmm, I don't know I don't recall. I think maybe
            she said you were a four.

GATSBY: A four?

CHAN: Yeah. I don't know, maybe a six.

GATSBY: She said I was a four?

CHAN: Maybe a six, I can't recall. Just this kiss, I, I want
            it to be...hot. If we're gonna do it, let's...do it
            right.

Gatsby nods his head.

GATSBY: Oh, good work ethic.

CHAN: Thank you.

Josh stands beside the movie camera as the cameraman points it at Chan and
Gatsby.

JOSH: And...action.

챈: 나도 배우 아냐. 그냥 도와주는 거지.

개츠비: 이제 키스해?

챈: 응, 이래서 배우 하기 싫었어. 연기라는
        게… 별별 놈들과 좋은 척해야 하잖아.

개츠비: 고맙다.

챈: 됐고 그냥… 키스해줘, 발끝까지 짜릿하게.

개츠비: 네 언니한테 키쓰했었어. 네 언니가 내 키스
        얘기 안 했어?

챈: 기억 안나. 10점 만점에 4점 줬었나.

개츠비: 4점?

챈: 응, 아니면 6점.

개츠비: 4점이랬다구?

챈: 6점이었나 기억 안나. 암튼 이 키스는 섹시
        하길 바래. 할 거면 제대로 하자구.

개츠비는 고개를 끄덕인다.

개츠비: 프로 정신 좋네.

개츠비: 고마워.

카메라 맨이 챈과 개츠비를 가리키고, 조쉬는 카메라 옆에 서 있다.

조쉬: 액션.

■ weirdo
  괴짜, 별난 사람

■ good work ethic
  프로정신 좋네

If we're gonna do it, let's do it right.
let's do it right는 '올바로(제대로) 하자'
라는 뜻으로, If we're gonna do it, let'
s do it right은 '할거면, 제대로 하자' 라
는 의미로 사용된다.

If we're gonna do it, let's do it right.

할거면, 제대로 하자.

Chan turns and smiles at Gatsby. Chan pulls Gatsby toward her and kisses him passionately. He responds uneasily.

JOSH: Cut.

Chan leans back and looks at Gatsby.

CHAN: Hey…are you gonna keep your mouth closed?

GATSBY: I have a girlfriend, Chan. I don't think I can do this. Uh…I'm sorry, I think I froze.

CHAN: You have a girlfriend? Who's your girlfriend?

GATSBY: Her name's Ashleigh.
She's from Yardley. Well, she's from Tucson, originally.

CHAN: Tucson? You're dating a girl from Arizona.

GATSBY: Do I have your permission?

CHAN: What do you guys talk about, cactus?

GATSBY: Rattlesnakes.

Chan leans back and looks mockingly at Gatsby.

CHAN: Wow. Arizona. That'll be great for your asthma.

GATSBY: Tsk. I don't have asthma.

CHAN: That's funny, when we were kissing, I, I thought I heard you wheezing.

GATSBY: (irritably) You know, I always remembered you as a very snotty kid

Josh stands with the crew members and looks at Gatsby.

JOSH: Uh…ready?

CAMERAMAN: Ready.

챈은 개츠비를 보고 미소를 짓는다. 챈은 개츠비를 그녀 쪽으로 당겨서 열정적으로 키스를 한다. 그는 불안하게 반응한다.

조쉬: 컷.

챈은 상체를 뒤로 젖히고 개츠비를 쳐다본다.

챈: 입 꼭 다물고 키스할 거야?

개츠비: 여친 생각이 나서 못 하겠어. 미안, 얼어버렸어.

챈: 여친이 있어? 누군데?

개츠비: 애슐리라고. 야들리 다녀. 고향은 투손이고.

챈: 투손? 애리조나 여잘 만나?

개츠비: 그럼 안 되냐?

챈: 만나면 무슨 얘기해, 선인장?

개츠비: 방울뱀.

챈은 상체를 뒤로 젖히고 개츠비를 조롱하며 쳐다본다.

챈: 우와, 애리조나라…오빠 천식엔 좋겠네.

개츠비: 나 천식 없거든?

챈: 그래? 키스할 때 식식거리던데.

개츠비: (짜증내며) 그때도 꼬맹이가 참 당돌하더니만.

조쉬는 스테프들과 함께 서있고 개츠비를 쳐다본다.

조쉬: 준비됐어?

카메라맨: 준비됐어.

- **passionately**
  열정적으로
- **uneasily**
  불안 속에, 걱정하여
- **mockingly**
  조롱하며
- **asthma**
  천식
- **wheeze**
  쌕쌕거리다
- **snotty**
  콧물 범벅의, 당돌한

Do I have your permission?
내가 너의 허락을 받아야 해?

Do I have your permission?
내가 너의 허락을 받아야 해?

JOSH:	Mm–hm.
CAMERAMAN:	All right.
GATSBY:	Yeah, well, wh–what are you up to now?
CHAN:	I'm studying design at the Fashion Institute.
GATSBY:	Oh, that's unique.

Josh stands beside the cameraman as he starts the movie camera.

| JOSH: | Rolling. |

Sam, a female member of the crew, steps in front of the camera.

| SAM: | Scene nineteen, take two. |
| JOSH: | Action. |

Chan leans to Gatsby, then clasps him by the cheek and kisses him passionately. He sits there stiffly.

| JOSH: | Uh, cut. It's, uh, better. |

Chan pulls back away from Gatsby, then turns and shakes her head at Josh.

CHAN:	Josh, he's way too uptight to open up his mouth.
	(to Gatsby) Hey, are you still seeing that shrink?
GATSBY:	Gimme a break, all right? I was just takin' a walk, he asked me to help out, all right? I've never acted before.

Sam steps in front of Josh and the cameraman.

| SAM: | Scene nineteen, take three. |
| JOSH: | Action. |

조쉬:	음.
카메라맨:	좋아.
개츠비:	넌 어떻게 지내?
챈:	FIT에서 디자인 공부해
개츠비:	특이하네

조쉬는 카메라맨 옆에 서있고 카메라는 시작한다.

조쉬: 카메라 돌았어.

여자 스테프인 샘은 카메라 앞으로 온다.

샘:	씬 19, 테이크 2.
조쉬:	액션.

챈은 개츠비쪽으로 기대어 그의 볼을 잡고 열정적으로 키스를 한다. 그는 뻣뻣하게 앉아있다.

조쉬: 컷, 아까보단 나아.

챈은 개츠비에게 뒤로 멀어져 조쉬를 보고 머리를 젓는다.

챈:	너무 긴장해서 입을 못 열어!
	(개츠비에게) 아직도 상담 받아?
개츠비:	좀 봐주라. 나는 그냥 걸어가고 있었는데 걔가 나한테 도와 달라고 부탁한거야. 갑자기 연기를 하라니 되나.

샘은 슬레이트를 가지고 조쉬와 카메라맨 앞으로 간다.

샘:	씬 19, 테이크 3.
조쉬:	액션.

- **FIT**
  Fashion Institute of Technology
  뉴욕주립대의 세계적인 패션스쿨

- **uptight**
  긴장한

- **shrink**
  정신과 의사

What are you up to now?
요즘 뭐하고 지내? 지금 뭐하고 있어?

What are you up to now?
요즘 뭐하고 지내? 지금 뭐하고 있어?

Chan leans toward Gatsby and kisses him. This time Gatsby responds, and the kiss lasts a long time.
Gatsby caresses Chan's cheek as they kiss. Raindrops starts to fall on them.

FEMALE CREW MEMBER: Josh, it's, uh, starting to rain.

Josh, Sam, the cameraman and the other crew members, are watching the scene on the camera viewfinder. Josh then looks at Chan and Gatsby.

JOSH: And cut. Great.

CHAN: See? I knew you could do it. And I won't tell your girlfriend.

Josh stands and talks to the cameraman and the other crew members.

GATSBY: Hey, Josh, you liked it? You want a different version? I didn't even?

Josh turns and waves his hand at Gatsby, them makes a "thumbs-up" gesture.

JOSH: That's No, no-no-no-no-no, we're good with that version. That's the version, we're stickin' with that. Okay.

CHAN: All right, well, have fun in Arizona, and whatever you do, don't get lost in the desert and die of thirst.

Gatsby smiles insincerely at Chan.

GATSBY: I'll be sure to bring a canteen.

CHAN: Oh, don't fall in the Grand Canyon...too. It's really deep.

Chan opens the passenger door. She steps out of the car, then walks and exits. Gatsby shakes his head.

챈은 개츠비쪽으로 기대고 그에게 키스를 한다. 이번에는 개츠비가
반응을 하고 오랫동안 키스를 한다.
그들이 키스를 할 때 개츠비는 챈의 얼굴을 어루만진다. 빗방울이
떨어지기 시작한다.

여성스태프: 조쉬, 비 오는데.

조쉬, 샘, 카메라맨과 다른 스태프들은 카메라 파인더에 화면을 지
켜보고 있다. 그리고 나서 조쉬는 챈과 개 츠비를 쳐다본다.

조쉬: 컷! 좋았어.

챈: 거봐, 잘하면서. 여친한텐 안 이를게.

조쉬는 서서 카메라맨과 다른 스태프들과 이야기를 나눈다.

개츠비: 조쉬, 좀 다르게 다시 할까?

조쉬는 고개를 돌리고 개츠비에게 손을 흔들며 엄지척을 한다.

조쉬: 아니, 그대로 좋아.

챈: 애리조나 가서 잘 놀아 사막에서 길 잃어버
리거나 목말라 죽진 말고.

개츠비는 챈에게 성의없이 웃는다.

개츠비: 물통 꼭 챙길게.

챈: 그랜드 캐니언도 조심해. 엄청 깊다더라.

챈은 조수석문을 열고 차에서 내려 밖으로 걸어간다. 개츠비는 고
개를 젓는다.

- caress
  어루만지다

- raindrop
  빗방울

- insincerely
  성의 없이, 불성실하게, 거짓으로

- canteen
  (휴대용) 물통

We're stickin' with that.
'(원래 방식, 계획)을 따르다, 고수하다'
라는 뜻으로 '하던 대로 그대로 하겠다'
는 뜻이다.

We're stickin' with that.
그대로 할게.

SOHO STREETS

Gatsby enters from Minetta lane, then walks across the street. A light rain is still falling.

GATSBY: She always was the pain–in–the–ass kid sister. How could she not be? Amy was gorgeous and so sexually advanced. Word on Amy was she performed oral sex at a bar mitzvah. I think they should make that part of every Jewish holiday. It certainly beats fasting.

Gatsby walks down the sidewalk. The rain starts to fall harder.

GATSBY: It's also a great way to celebrate the Jewish New Year, and what a great Hanukkah gift.

HUNTER'S BROWNSTONE

Gatsby walks down the sidewalk toward the steps of hunter's brownstone. The rain is now falling much harder.

GATSBY: I wonder what's been bothering Hunter. Something was definitely on his mind when I called him.

Gatsby turns and walks up the steps to the front door. He rings the doorbell. Hunter, Gatsby's older brother, opens the front door to reveal Gatsby.

HUNTER: Gatsby!

Gatsby steps into the house and embraces Hunter.

GATSBY: Sur–, surprise.

소호거리
개츠비는 미네타 길로 들어가고, 거리를 걷는다 가벼운 비가 여전히 오고 있다.

개츠비: 옛날에도 싸가지더니 여전하네. 에이미는 매력적이고 자유분방했는데. 소문엔 성인식 때 오럴섹스를 거행했다나. 유대 명절마다 하면 금식보다 인기일 텐데.

개츠비는 보도로 걸어간다. 비가 더 심하게 오기 시작한다.

개츠비: 신년 축하로도 훌륭하고 하누카 선물로도 좋고.

헌터의 브리운 스톤
개츠비는 컨터의 브라운 스톤으로 보도아래로 걸어간다. 이제 비는 훨씬 더 심하게 오고있다.

개츠비: 헌터 형은 뭐가 걱정일까. 통화할 때 목소리가 안 좋던데.

개츠비는 헌터집 앞으로 가고 도어벨을 누른다.
개츠비의 형인 헌터는 문을 열어 개츠비를 본다.

헌터: 개츠비!

개츠비는 집안으로 들어와 형을 껴안는다.

개츠비: 써프라이즈!

* pain-in-the-ass
  골칫거리

* fasting
  금식

* celebrate
  축하하다

* embrace
  포옹하다

Something was definitely on his mind.
on one's mind는 '마음에 걸려, 신경이 쓰여' 라는 뜻으로, '뭔가 분명히 그 마음에 걸렸어' 라는 의미이다.

Something was definitely on his mind.
뭔가 분명히 그 마음에 걸렸어.

A Rainy
Day in
New York

HUNTER:	What? Aaaaw!
GATSBY:	Hey, yeah, I told you I might drop in.
HUNTER:	That's crazy, what? Uh...

Hunter closes the front door.

GATSBY:	Good to see you. Listen, if you got somethin' to do, I can come back another time and take a...
HUNTER:	No! I got nothing to do!

Gatsby embraces Hunter again.

HUNTER:	Okay, then bring it in. It's good to see you.
GATSBY:	How are ya?
HUNTER:	Doin' well.

Hunter steps to the dining room table, Gatsby follows him.

HUNTER:	I'm good, I'm good. You?
GATSBY:	Good, good, no complaints.

Hunter, who is already slightly drunk, picks up a bottle of bourbon off the table. Gatsby stops beside Hunter, who pours bourbon into his mug.

HUNTER:	That's awesome. You come in for Mom's party?
GATSBY:	No. So you can't tell her I'm here, okay?
HUNTER:	Gee.
GATSBY:	It's okay, Hunter. You can pull it off.

Hunter leads Gatsby out of the dining room.

GATSBY:	You're engaged and outta the house now. She's not gonna take your phone away.

헌터:	뭐? 아우…
개츠비:	들를 수도 있댔잖아.
헌터:	이게 웬일이야.

헌터는 앞문을 닫는다.

개츠비:	반가워. 혹시 바쁘면…다음 번에 다시 올 게.
헌터:	아냐, 전혀.

개츠비는 헌터를 다시 껴안는다.

헌터:	이리 와, 반갑다.
개츠비:	잘 지냈어?
헌터:	잘 지냈어.

헌터는 주방으로 가고 개츠비도 따라간다.

헌터:	좋아, 넌?
개츠비:	좋아, 불만 없지.

이미 약간 취한 헌터는 테이블에 버번 술병을 집어든다. 개츠비는
헌터 옆에 서있고, 헌터는 잔에 술을 붓는다.

헌터:	잘됐네, 엄마 파티 온 거야?
개츠비:	아니, 나 온 거 말하지 마.
헌터:	이런.
개츠비:	괜찮아, 형은 숨길 수 있어.

헌터는 다이닝룸 밖으로 개츠비를 리드한다.

개츠비:	약혼해서 독립했으니 이제 엄마가 핸드폰도 못 뺏잖아.

- drop in
  잠깐 들르다

- complaint
  불만

- bourbon
  버번위스키(미국산 위스키)

- engage
  약혼하다

You can pull it off.
pull something off는 '(힘든 것을)해내
다' 는 의미이다.

You can pull it off.
당신은 해 낼 수 있다.

HUNTER: Hmmmm. If Mom finds out, she'll die.

GATSBY: No, she won't, she'll live and she's not gonna find out.

Hunter drinks from his mug.

HUNTER: Yeah, I Well, how come you're in?

GATSBY: Oh, it's Ashleigh, uh, my girlfriend.

Hunter leads Gatsby out of the dining room.

GATSBY: She has to do an interview with Roland Pollard, the film director, for the school paper.

HUNTER: That Ohh.

GATSBY: It's a big coup.

HUNTER: Ashleigh. That is the one that Mom's high on.

GATSBY: She's never even met her.

HUNTER: Okay.

Lily, Hunter's fiance, enters on a staircase and hurries down the steps.

LILY: Hunter, your parents want to…

Seeing Gatsby, Lily reacts with surprise.

LILY: Oh, hey, Gatsby!

GATSBY: Hey.

LILY: It's so good to see you!

GATSBY: It's good to see you. How are you?

Lily and Gatsby hug.

LILY: I'm good. What are you doin' in town?

헌터:	엄마 알면, 죽으려고 할 텐데.
개츠비:	아냐, 안 죽어. 알게 될 리도 없고.

헌터는 그의 잔에 술을 마신다.

헌터:	시내엔 웬일이야?
개츠비:	여친 애슐리 땜에.

헌터는 개츠비를 거실에 소파쪽으로 리드한다.

개츠비:	롤란 폴라드 감독과 신문 인터뷰가 있어서.
헌터:	오.
개츠비:	대박인 거지.
헌터:	애슐리. 엄마가 찜한 애구나.
개츠비:	보지도 않고.
헌터:	오케이.

헌터의 약혼녀 릴리는 계단에서 서둘러 내려왔다.

릴리:	헌터, 자기 부모님이…

개츠비를 보고 릴리는 놀라는 반응을 한다.

릴리:	어머, 개츠비!
개츠비:	안녕.
릴리:	반가워!
개츠비:	반가워, 잘 지냈어요?

릴리와 게츠비는 껴 안는다.

릴리:	난 좋아. 웬일이야?

- ■ big coup
  대성공

- ■ fiancé
  약혼녀

- ■ staircase
  계단

How come you're in?
How come~?은 Why와 같은 의미이
나, How come + 주어 + 동사~?로 쓰
이고 Why + 동사 + 주어 ~?의 형태로
쓰이는 차이가 있다.

How come you're in?
여기는 왜 있어(웬일이야)?

Lily steps back and looks at Gatsby's jacket.

LILY: You're all wet.

HUNTER: See, his girlfriend is interviewing Roland P–, uhh....

LILY: (to Gatsby) Sit.

Lily, Gatsby and Hunter walk toward the sofa.

GATSBY: Okay. Yes, eh, Pollard, he's a film director, but...

...do me, do me a favor and don't tell my mom I'm here, you know, I'm not goin' to her big party tonight, yeah, yeah.

HUNTER: He hates parties! He's Mister Antisocial.

LILY: What?

HUNTER: (to Gatsby) You always hated Mom's literary salons.

GATSBY: It's rich housewives who have the leisure to pursue esoteric culture.

The out–of–work discussing the out–of–print.

HUNTER: She only wanted to make sure that we were exposed to great literature.

GATSBY: Okay, what about Jimmy Cannon, then? All right, what about Tom Adair? It's not all giant insects and madeleines.

HUNTER: Huh.

Lily taps Gatsby on the knee, then he looks back at her.

LILY: Hey, you're not gonna duck out of our wedding, are you?

릴리는 한발 뒤로 물러서서 개츠비의 자켓을 본다.

릴리: 다 젖었어.

헌터: 여친 인터뷰 땜에, 롤란…

릴리: (개츠비에게)앉아.

릴리, 개츠비, 헌터는 소파쪽으로 간다.

개츠비: 오케이. 폴라드, 영화감독이야.
엄마한텐 비밀이야. 오늘 파티 안 갈 거거
든.

헌터: 앤 파티라면 질색해. 우리 '낯가림' 씨지!

릴리: 정말?

헌터: (개츠비에게)엄마 문학 클럽도 싫어했잖아.

개츠비: 돈 많은 아줌마들이 아는 척하려는 모임이
었지.
한물간 분들의 한물간 책 토론.

헌터: 우리도 문학 좀 알라고 그러신 거지.

개츠비: 지미 캐넌 기자도 있었잖아. 작곡가 탐 아데
어는? 문학명작들만이 아니었어.

헌터: 응.

릴리는 개츠비의 무릎을 치고 개츠비는 그녀를 쳐다본다.

릴리: 우리 결혼식에도 잠수 탈 건 아니지?

- **Do me a favor**
  부탁하나 들어줘.

- **antisocial**
  반사회적인 사람

- **leisure**
  여가

- **esoteric**
  소수만 이해하는(즐기는)

- **The out-of-work discussing the out-of-print.**
  한물간 분들의 한물간 책 토론

- **It's not all giant insects and madeleines.**
  문학작품 "The Metamorphosis"에서 한
  사람이 깨어나보니 거대한 곤충으로 변해있
  었다는 내용과 "In Search of Lost Time"
  에서 작가의 어린 시절의 기억을 떠 올리게
  하는 것이 마들렌이었다는 의미로 말한 것
  으로, 유명한 문학작품이 반드시 고전소설
  일 필요는 없다는 것을 조롱하듯 말한 것.

You're not gonna duck out of our wedding, are you?
duck out of는 '숨기다, 피하다' 는 의미
이다.

You're not gonna duck out of our wedding, are you?

우리 결혼식에 잠수 탈건 아니지? (숨고 안 나타나지 않겠지?)

Hunter gestures at Lily.

HUNTER: How can he? He's the best man! Come on. He cries at weddings. He...well, he's not so tough as he makes out. He cries at weddings and funerals.

GATSBY: Same reason.

LILY: All right, um, I'm gonna go take a shower, but there's coffee.

GATSBY: Sure.

LILY: I'm so glad you're here.

GATSBY: Hey, it's nice being here!

Lily runs upstairs to take a shower.
Gatsby walks to the dining room table.

GATSBY: (to Hunter) I always liked her.

Gatsby pours himself a cup of coffee. Hunter stands up.

HUNTER: Gatsby?

GATSBY: What's the matter?

HUNTER: Gatsby

HUNTER: I don't want to go through with this wedding.

GATSBY: What?

HUNTER: I can't do it. I can't.

HUNTER: And I can't pull out now. It'll kill her. There's two hundred guests invited. They booked...the Century Club. They booked an orchestra.

Hunter sits down in a chair, then looks down despondently.

헌터는 릴리에게 손짓을 한다.

헌터: 안 되지, 들러리인데. 앤 결혼식 때도 울어.
평소엔 센 척하는데 결혼식, 장례식 다 울
어.

개츠비: 결혼은 장례식과 동급이야.

릴리: 난 이제 샤워해야겠다. 커피는 저기 있어.

개츠비: 물론.

릴리: 정말 반가워.

개츠비: 나도.

릴리는 샤워하러 계단으로 뛰어간다.
개츠비는 다이닝 룸으로 걸어간다.

개츠비: (헌터에게) 형수 참 좋아.

개츠비는 커피를 잔에 따른다. 헌터는 일어선다.

헌터: 개츠비.

개츠비: 왜 그래?

헌터: 개츠비.

헌터: 나 이 결혼 못 할 거 같아.

개츠비: 뭐?

헌터: 못 하겠어.

헌터: 근데 취소할 수도 없어 릴리 쓰러질 거야.
근데 취소도 못해. 쟤 쓰러질 거야. 손님이
200명에 장소도…센추리 클럽이야. 교향악
단도 불렀어.

헌터는 의자에 앉아서 실망스럽게 아래를 본다.

- **go through st**
  ~을 거치다

- **pull out**
  철수하다, 취소하다

- **despondently**
  낙담하여, 실망하여

I'm gonna go take a shower.
am gonna는 am going to의 대화제 표
현으로 '~할거야' 라는 의미이고, take
a shower는 '샤워하다' 라는 의미이다.

I'm gonna go take a shower.
나 샤워할 거야.

HUNTER:	Oh, God, save me!
GATSBY:	Okay, all right, what...what happened?
HUNTER:	You'll think I'm so stupid.
GATSBY:	I'm not gonna think you're stupid. Just tell me what happened.
HUNTER:	I can't. It's too stupid.
GATSBY:	I, I– Y–Y–You're making me anxious. I want to hear this fascinating piece of stupidity.
HUNTER:	Uh, well, she's, she's bright.
GATSBY:	Mm–hm.
HUNTER:	Gatsby, she's nice, she's kind.
GATSBY:	So?
HUNTER:	I can't stand the way she laughs.
GATSBY:	What?
HUNTER:	Yeah, I can't take her laugh.
GATSBY:	Her laugh?
HUNTER:	Yes.

Gatsby stands up.

HUNTER:	Yeah, her laugh. Her laugh!
GATSBY:	Hunter, that's probably the most idiotic thing I've ever heard in my life.
HUNTER:	I told you you'd think it's stupid.
GATSBY:	What's wrong with her laugh?
HUNTER:	Listen to it. It's a total turnoff.
GATSBY:	How much do you love her?
HUNTER:	But I do! I love her, I love her! It's just her laugh!
GATSBY:	If you love her, then get over it.

헌터:	어떡해. 살려줘.
개츠비:	알았으니까 얘기 좀 해봐.
헌터:	바보 같다고 할걸.
개츠비:	안 그럴게, 말해봐.
헌터:	못해. 너무 황당해서.
개츠비:	답답해 죽겠네! 얼마나 바보 같은지 들어보자.
헌터:	릴리는 똑똑해.
개츠비:	응.
헌터:	좋은 여자야, 착하고.
개츠비:	근데?
헌터:	웃음소릴 못 참겠어.
개츠비:	뭐?
헌터:	웃음소리가 끔찍해.
개츠비:	웃음소리?
헌터:	응.

개츠비는 일어난다.

헌터:	그래, 웃음소리!
개츠비:	이렇게 바보 같은 소린 처음 들어.
헌터:	그럴 거라고 했잖아.
개츠비:	웃음소리가 어떤데?
개츠비:	들어봐, 확 깨.
개츠비:	사랑하긴 해?
헌터:	그럼, 사랑해! 단지 웃음소리가 문제야.
개츠비:	사랑하면 극복해.

- **Save me.**
  살려줘

- **turnoff**
  (성적인) 흥미를 잃게 하는
  sexually unattractive characteristic

- **get over**
  극복하다
  i.e., 'learn to accept it'

I can't stand the way she laughs.
stand는 '참다, 견디다'라는 뜻으로
tolerate, endure의 의미로 사용된다.

I can't stand the way she laughs.
웃음소리를 못 참겠어.

HUNTER:	I can't. I've tried. I've tried, I've tried.

Hunter stands up and walks toward him. Hunter stops and gestures at Gatsby.

HUNTER:	Last night, we were talkin' in bed, and she laughed and I couldn't m—make love to her.
GATSBY:	What?!
HUNTER:	I couldn't.
GATSBY:	Just?
HUNTER:	I was impotent.
GATSBY:	From her laugh?
HUNTER:	It's happened before.
GATSBY:	Hunter, you gotta see a shrink.
HUNTER:	What?
GATSBY:	I'm serious, you gotta see?
HUNTER:	I don't need a shrink, I know what the problem is. She has a fatal laugh!
HUNTER:	It—it, uh, it, uh, a cross between Dad's sister Betty and...Lennie in "Of Mice and Men".

Hunter turns and walks on Gatsby. He walks toward Hunter.

GATSBY:	I've never heard of a problem like that before.
HUNTER:	Well, you're young, Gatsby. The world is full of tragic little deal—breakers.
GATSBY:	Haven't you been seeing Lily for over a year? Wh—wh—why is this comin' up now?
GATSBY:	Have you talked to her about it?
HUNTER:	Uhh, (inhales, then exhales between closed lips) yeah, I...

헌터: 그게 안 돼. 노력해봤는데 안 돼.

헌터는 일어나서 그쪽으로 걸어간다. 헌터는 멈춰서 개츠비에게 손
짓을 한다.

헌터: 어제도 침대에서 얘기하다 웃으니까 할 수
          가 없었어.
개츠비: 뭐?
헌터: 할 수가 없었어.
개츠비: 그냥…
헌터: 서질 않더라구.
개츠비: 웃음소리 땜에?
헌터: 처음이 아냐.
개츠비: 형 상담 받아야겠다.
헌터: 뭐?
개츠비: 진짜로.
헌터: 상담 필요 없어. 웃음소리 땜에 그렇다니
          까.
헌터: 꼭 베티 고모 웃음하고… '생쥐와 인간' 의
          레니 웃음을 합쳐놓은 거 같아.

헌터는 개츠비쪽으로 돌아 걸어간다. 개츠비는 헌터쪽으로 간다.

개츠비: 이런 고민은 처음 들어봐.
헌터: 네가 어려서 그런데 세상엔 뜻밖의 결정적
          인 걸림돌이 많아.
개츠비: 만난 지 1년 넘었잖아? 왜 이제 와서 그래?
개츠비: 얘기는 해봤어?
헌터: 어… (닫힌 입술사이로 숨을 쉬며) 나는…

- impotent
  무력한, 발기불능의

- shrink
  정신과 의사

- deal-breaker
  걸림돌

- seeing
  = dating

You gotta see a shrink.
gotta는 have got to의 비격식 표현으로
'~해야 한다' 는 의미이다.

You gotta see a shrink.
상담 받아야 겠어.

Gatsby walks into the dining room. Hunter is preparing to pour more bourbon into his mug.

HUNTER: ....brought it up, tactfully, but I d–, I don't think she realizes how serious it's gotten.

Hunter pours bourbon into his mug, then shrugs at Gatsby.

HUNTER: I love her. But I can't marry her, Gatsby.

HUNTER: I won't be able to have sex with her.

GATSBY: No, no, you mean you don't want to marry her...so you're focusing on this laugh insanity.

HUNTER: Come on. Oh, please, spare me the fruits of your Upper East Side talking cure. Listen to her laugh. When she comes down, we'll get her to laugh. You'll s–...see what I mean.

개츠비는 주방으로 걸어간다. 헌터는 잔에 술을 더 마시기 위해 준비하고 있다.

헌터: 조심스레 꺼내봤는데 심각성을 모르는 거 같아.

헌터는 잔에 술을 딸고, 개츠비에게 어깨를 으쓱한다.

헌터: 사랑하지만 결혼은 안 되겠어.

헌터: 섹스를 못 하겠는걸.

개츠비: 아냐, 결혼하기가 싫은 거야. 그래서 웃음소릴 트집 잡는 거지.

헌터: 어쭙잖은 상담 치료는 됐구. 한번 들어봐. 내려오면 웃겨볼게. 들으면 알아.

■ **tactfully**
눈치 있게, 약삭빠르게

■ **this laugh insanity**
i.e., 'this insane aversion you have to her laugh'

■ **insanity**
미친짓, 어리석은 짓(folly)

Spare me the fruits of your Upper East Side talking cure.
spare me the fruits of는 빈정거리는 말투로 '배운 지식으로 나를 실험하지 마라'는 의미(i.e., 'Don't subject me to the wisdom you have acquired from —said sarcastically)이고, Upper East Side는uptown Manhattan으로 의사와 심리상담소가 많다는 의미로 사용되며, talking cure는 '대화치료'를 말한다.

Zoom In **Spare me the fruits of your Upper East Side talking cure.**

어쭙지 않은 상담 그만둬.

Chapter 4

비오는 날

Starting to rain

시간 00:26:07 ~ 00:32:23

SCREENING ROOM

Ashleigh sits in the darkened room and looks intently at the movie screen as Roland, sitting, rubs his head. Ted Davidoff, the handsome middle-aged screenwriter of the film, is sitting and watching the movie with them and a projectionist is sitting at a desk. Roland shakes his head with dismay.

ROLAND: (groaning miserably) Oh…agh…aaggh, agh-agh-agh. I can't…mm?

Ashleigh looks at Roland, who starts to sit up.

ROLAND: I, I can't do this, I'm sorry.

Ted reacts with exasperation.

ROLAND: I know. I, I, I'm, I'm sorry, Ted.
TED: Rollie, come on.
ROLAND: It's just actually, it's physically…
TED: Don't do this.

Roland stands up.

상영실
애슐리는 어두컴컴한 방에 앉아 화면 밖의 영화를 열심히 보고 있다. 그 동안 롤랜드는 앉아서 머리를 비빈다. 중년의 멋진 시나리오 작가인 테드 데이비드오프는 그들과 함께 앉아서 영화를 보고 있고, 프로젝션리스트는 책상에 앉아 있다. 롤랜드는 실망감을 느끼며 고개를 젓는다.

롤랜드: (비참하게 신음) 으… 나는… 음…

애슐리가 자세를 고쳐 앉고 있는 롤랜드를 바라본다.

롤랜드: 나 못하겠어. 미안해.

테드는 분노하며 반응을 한다.

롤랜드: 미안해, 테드.
테드: 롤리.
롤랜드: 진짜.
테드: 이러지 마.

로날드가 자리에서 일어난다.

- exasperation
  분노, 격노

- physically
  물리적으로, 신체적으로

ROLAND: ...making me sick. I have to?

TED: Don't do this.

Roland walks.

ROLAND: It's humiliating.

TED: It's a process, Rollie.

Ashleigh and Ted stand up. Roland's face enters as he walks toward the door.

ROLAND: ...changes are shit.

TED: Rollie, sit down.

ROLAND: Everything that I did is shit.

Ted steps toward Roland and grabs him by the arm, trying to stop him.

TED: They're not shit. Different, different.

Ashleigh also stops beside Roland.

ASHLEIGH: Mister Pollard.

TED: Not all the changes work, but some are good.

Roland gestures at Ashleigh.

ROLAND: Thank you for coming, Ashleigh. I need to get a little air.

TED: Come and sit down.

Roland walks toward the door.

ROLAND: I need time.

TED: Don't do this.

롤랜드:	토할 거 같아.
테드:	이러지 마.

로날드가 걷는다.

롤랜드:	굴욕적이야.
테드:	다들 거치는 거야.

애슐리랑 테드가 일어난다. 로날드가 문 쪽으로 걸어나가면서 그의 얼굴이 등장한다.

롤랜드:	수정한 것도 거지 같고.
테드:	롤리, 앉아.
롤랜드:	전부 거지 같아.

테드가 롤랜드 쪽으로 걸어가서 그를 멈추려고 팔을 붙잡는다.

테드:	거지 같지 않아. 달라졌어.

애슐리도 롤랜드 뒤에서 멈춘다.

애슐리:	폴랜드 감독님.
테드:	몇 군데는 나아졌어.

롤랜드가 애슐리에게 손짓한다.

로날드:	와줘서 고마워요, 애슐리. 난 바람 좀 쐬어야겠어.
테드:	와서 앉아, 이러지 마.

롤랜드가 문을 향해 걸어간다.

로날드:	생각할 시간이 필요해.
테드:	이러지마.

- humiliating
  굴욕적인, 면목 없는

- shit
  'terrible(끔찍한)' 의 속어

- Rollie
  'Roland' 의 줄임말

- grab
  잡다

Ted grabs him by the arm.
'전치사 + the +신체 일부분' 이 나오는 경우 정관사 the는 소유격 대신에 쓰인 것으로, grab his arm의 의미로 사용된다.

Ted grabs him by the arm.
테드는 그의 팔을 붙잡는다.

Roland opens the door, then stops and gestures back at Ted and Ashleigh.

ROLAND: (inhales) I need to think. I'm— (inhales and exhales)

Ted steps toward Roland and gestures at him.

TED: Don't— No booze. Please, no booze.

Roland gestures at Ted.

ROLAND: You just watched two hours of an existential steaming shit pile and that's all that you can say to me?

Ted turns and walks, shaking his head.

TED: It's a process. We?
ROLAND: Ted?
TED: We—we do this every time.
ROLAND: Ted?

Ted stops, then turns and gestures at Roland.

TED: Rollie, come on back.

Roland walks out of the screening room, then walks down a hallway and exits.

TED: Don't drink! Oh, God.

Ashleigh, shakes her head at Ted.

ASHLEIGH: Well, shouldn't we go after him?

롤랜드가 문을 열더니, 멈추고 테드와 애슐리를 향해 다시 몸짓한다.

롤랜드: (숨을 들이 마시며) 나 생각 좀 해야겠어. 나는…
(숨을 들이마시고 내뱉는다)

테드가 롤랜드를 향해 걸어가서 손짓한다.

테드: 술은 안 돼. 술은 마시지 말라구.

롤랜드가 테드를 향해 손짓한다.

롤랜드: 2 시간짜리 실존주의 쓰레기를 봐놓고 그 소리가 다야?

테드가 머리를 흔들며 뒤돌아서 걷는다.

테드: 과정이야. 우리가…
롤랜드: 테드?
테드: 매번 하는 거잖아.
롤랜드: 테드!

테드가 멈추고, 뒤돌아 롤랜드에게 손짓한다.

테드: 롤리, 들어와.

롤랜드가 상영실 밖으로 나가고, 복도를 지나 밖으로 나간다.

테드: 술 마시지 마! 못 말려.

애슐리가 테드를 향해 머리를 흔든다.

애슐리: 가봐야 되는 거 아녜요?

- **No booze**
  booze는 '술(liquor)'이라는 뜻으로 '술 금지(Don't drink liquor-Don't get drunk)' 의미

- **existential**
  실존주의

- **steaming**
  몹시 화가 나는

- **Come on**
  Please - Don't do this의 의미

- **go after**
  따라가다

That's all that you can say to me.
That's all은 '그게 전부이다' 라는 의미로 '그게 너가 나에게 말할 수 있는 전부이다' 라는 뜻으로 사용된다.

Zoom In

That's all that you can say to me.
그게 너가 나에게 말할 수 있는 전부다.

TED: That's the sure sign he is gonna drink. Hey, you go. You can go. I, I, I have to watch it all...to, to be able to talk to him intelligently about it.

Ted steps and sits back down in his seat.

ASHLEIGH: Oh, well...No, I...I love...

Ashleigh walks back toward her seat and exits.
Ted looks at Ashleigh with surprise. Ashleigh reenters as she sits down and looks over her shoulder at him.

TED: You do?

ASHLEIGH: I do.

Ashleigh turns and looks back at the movie screen. Ted turns and gestures at the projectionist.

TED: (to projectionist) Let's go back.

HUNTER'S BROWNSTONE/ LIVING ROOM
Past hunter, sitting in a chair, to Gatsby, who sits on the sofa and looks at him. Hunter pours more bourbon into his mug.

HUNTER: There's a high-stakes card game later at the Freemont Hotel. I can't make it, but I know you love that kinda thing. You want me to call Joe Cohen, say you'll take my chair?

GATSBY: I would love a high-stakes card game, I'm loaded right now, but, uh...

HUNTER: (chuckling) Yeah.

GATSBY: ...Ashleigh and I, we have plans tonight.

HUNTER: I'm dying to meet Ashleigh.

테드:　술 마시러 간 거예요. 그만 가봐도 돼요. 난 끝까지 보고 현명한 얘기를 해줘야 하니.

테드가 다시 자리에 앉는다.

애슐리:　아뇨, 영화 너무 좋아요.

애슐리도 다시 자리로 간다. 테드가 화면 밖의 애슐리를 놀란 눈으로 본다. 애슐리는 자리에 앉으며 재등장하고 자신의 어깨너머로 테드를 쳐다본다.

테드:　그래요?
애슐리:　네.

애슐리가 돌아서 화면 밖의 영화를 본다. 테드는 뒤를 돌아 영사 기자에게 손짓한다.

테드:　(영사 기자에게) 다시 돌려줘요.

헌터의 브라운 스톤/ 거실
의자에 앉아있는 헌터를 지나 쇼파에 앉아있는 개츠비는 헌터를 바라본다. 헌터는 그의 머그잔에 버번 위스키를 더 따른다.

헌터:　이따 프리몬트 호텔에서 큰 포커 판이 열려. 난 못 가는데, 너도 좋아하잖아. 전화해서 네가 대신 간다고 해줘?
개츠비:　큰 판 좋아하지. 총알도 충분하고… 근데…
헌터:　(웃으며) 응.
개츠비:　애슐리와 갈 데가 있어.
헌터:　애슐리 빨리 보고 싶다.

- **intelligently**
  총명하게

- **high-stakes**
  (도박 따위에 거는) 큰 돈

- **You'll take my chair**
  내 대신에 가
  my chair : i.e., 'my place at the game'

- **I'm loaded.**
  'I have a lot of money' 의 구어체

- **loaded**
  장전된, 준비가 된

- **I'm dying to**
  ~하고 싶어 죽겠어
  (I'm dying : i.e., 'I am very eager')

I can't make it.
make it은 '(어떤 곳에 간신히) 시간 맞춰 가다' 라는 뜻으로, 여기 내용상 I can't make it 은 'I can't go to the game' 의 의미로 사용된다.

I can't make it.
(어떤 곳에 간신히) 시간 맞춰 가지 못할 것 같다. 난 못가.

GATSBY: I know. I don't know where she is right now.

Hunter puts the bottle of bourbon on an end table and sips from his mug.

HUNTER: (sipping drink) Hm.

GATSBY: I was supposed to show her the city today.

HUNTER: Well, you better take an umbrella.

Lily, wearing a robe and with a towel on her head after her shower, enters and walks down the stairs. Hunter looks at Gatsby.

HUNTER: (quietly to Gatsby) Watch, I'll make her laugh.

Hunter stands up and walks toward the stairs, camera dollying in with him.

HUNTER: (loudly to Lily) Oh! Hey! (quick breath) I was just tellin', uh, Gatsby, Larry Nash told me a great joke.

Camera continues to dolly in as Lily stops on the stairs and Hunter stops in front of her.

HUNTER: (quick breath) Two cannibals are eatin' a comedian and one says, "Hey, do you taste somethin' funny?".

Camera holds in as Lily looks at hunter without amusement.

LILY: That is so unfunny.

HUNTER: D– Umm...okay.

GATSBY: Okay! That's my cue.

Gatsby enters and walks toward the front of the Brownstone.

GATSBY: ...lovely to see you, as always.

HUNTER: Uhhh, so great to see you.

개츠비: 그러게, 나도 어디 있는지 몰라.

헌터가 버번 위스키 병을 테이블 끝 쪽에 올려놓고 머그잔을 홀짝댄다.

헌터: (술을 홀짝거리며) 흠…
개츠비: 시내 구경시켜주기로 했는데.
헌터: 우산 꼭 챙겨라.

릴리가 샤워 후에 샤워가운을 입고 머리에 수건을 감은 채로 등장해서 계단을 내려온다. 헌터가 개츠비를 쳐다본다.

헌터: (개츠비에게 조용하게) 봐, 내가 웃겨볼게.

헌터가 일어나서 계단을 향해 걸어간다. 카메라는 헌터와 함께 서서히 다가간다.

헌터: (큰 소리로) 방금 (짧은 숨) 래리가 해준 웃긴 얘기 중이었는데.

카메라는 릴리가 계단에서 멈추고 헌터가 그녀의 앞에 멈출 때까지 계속해서 다가간다.

헌터: (짧은 숨) 식인종 둘이 개그맨을 먹다 한 명이 그랬대, '야, 맛이 좀 웃기지 않냐?'.

릴리가 헌터를 재미없게 쳐다보는 동안 카메라는 멈춘다.

릴리: 완전 안 웃기거든.
헌터: 음… 그래.
개츠비: 자, 난 그만 퇴장해야겠다.

개츠비가 등장해서 브라운스톤 앞쪽으로 걸어간다.

개츠비: 형, 반가웠어.
헌터: 응 나도 반가웠어.

- cannibals
  식인종

- That's my cue
  그럼 난 이만!
  i.e., 'That's my cue to leave'

- as always
  늘 그렇듯

I was supposed to show her the city today.
be supposed to+ 동사원형은 '~할 예정이다, ~할 것이다'는 의미이다.

I was supposed to show her the city today.
오늘 시내 구경시켜 주기로 했다.

GATSBY: (to Lily) Lily, thank you for the coffee.

Lily blows a kiss and waves at Gatsby.

LILY: (blows kiss) It was so good to see you.

Hunter gestures at Gatsby.

HUNTER: Wait. I heard one more.

Hunter turns and looks at Lily.

HUNTER: (to Lily) A homeless man stopped a Jewish mother on the street and said...

Gatsby puts down his cup of coffee and walks quietly toward the front door, camera dollying with him.

HUNTER: ... "Lady, I haven't eaten in three days," and she said, "Force yourself."

Camera holds as Gatsby turns back toward Lily, listening to the awfulsounding laughter with disbelief.

HUNTER'S BROWNSTONE
Gatsby, holding an umbrella, opens the front door and looks up at the rain, which is pouring down. He opens the umbrella and closes the front door. He walks down the stairs to the sidewalk, camera dollying back and tilting down with him. His cell phone rings. Camera holds in as he stops on the sidewalk, then takes the cell phone out of his pocket and talks into it.

GATSBY: (into cell phone) Hello? Ashleigh, what's goin' on? You said you were gonna call me thirty minutes ago.

개츠비: (릴리에게) 커피 고마워요.

릴리가 개츠비에게 키스를 날리고 손을 흔든다.

릴리: (키스를 날린다) 만나서 반가웠어.

헌터가 개츠비에게 손짓한다.

헌터: 잠깐, 하나 더 있어.

헌터가 릴리를 쳐다본다.

헌터: (릴리에게) 노숙자가 지나가던 유대인한테…

개츠비가 커피잔을 내려놓고 조용히 현관 문을 향해 걸어간다. 카메라도 따라간다.

헌터: '3일이나 굶었어요' 하니까 그 여자가 대답하길 '굶지 말고 좀 먹어요'.

개츠비가 뒤를 돌아 화면 밖의 릴리를 쳐다보며, 믿을 수 없다는 듯이 릴리의 소름끼치는 웃음소리를 듣고있다.

헌터의 브라운 스톤
개츠비가 우산을 들고 현관 문을 열어 쏟아지는 비를 쳐다본다. 그는 우산을 펴고 현관 문을 닫는다. 계단을 내려가 인도로 간다. 카메라는 기울여 개츠비와 함께 따라간다. 개츠비의 전화가 울린다. 개츠비가 도보에서 멈춰 전화기를 주머니에서 꺼내서 받는다. 카메라는 멈춘다.

개츠비: (전화기에) 애슐리, 어떻게 된 거야? 30분 전에 걸기로 해놓고.

- **homeless man**
  노숙자

- **awful sounding**
  소름 끼치는 소리

- **disbelief**
  믿기지 않음, 불신감

- **pour**
  마구 쏟아지다

- **tilt**
  기울다

Force yourself.
'억지로 (무리해서라도) 해보다' 라는 뜻으로 이 내용에서는 "Force yourself to eat something (굶지 말고 좀 먹어요)" 라는 의미이다.

Force yourself.
억지로 (무리해서라도) 해봐.

SCREENING ROOM/PROJECTION BOOTH – Ashleigh, standing beside an editing bench, talks excitedly into her cell phone.

ASHLEIGH:　(inhales, then speaking quietly) I know. The film got delayed. I'm, uh, I'm up at this, uh, screening room place.

HUNTER'S BROWNSTONE
Gatsby talks into the cell phone.

GATSBY:　It's fine, just meet me at the Museum of Modern Art, it's on Fifty–third Street. We'll grab a bite to eat there and then we're gonna go see the Weegees.

SCREENING ROOM/PROJECTION BOOTH
Ashleigh gestures as she talks into the cell phone.

ASHLEIGH:　I, I can't. I can't.

HUNTER'S BROWNSTONE
Gatsby talks into the cell phone.

GATSBY:　What do you mean? Why not?

SCREENING ROOM/PROJECTION BOOTH
Ashleigh talks into the cell phone.

ASHLEIGH:　Because I'm onto a real story here. This is a seventy–million–dollar movie and Rollie's very unhappy with it.

HUNTER'S BROWNSTONE
Gatsby reacts with dismay as he talks into the cell phone.

상영실/상영 부스
애슐리가 편집 벤치 옆에 서서 흥분되어 전화기에 말한다.

애슐리: (숨을 마쉬고, 조용히 말한다) 상영이 지연돼서, 아
직 시사실에 있어.

헌터의 브라운스톤
개츠비가 전화에 대고 말한다.

개츠비: 알았고, 현대미술관에서 만나. 53번가에 있
어. 거기서 간단히 먹고 위지 사진전 보자.

상영실/상영 부스
애슐리가 전화를 하며 손짓한다.

애슐리: 안 돼, 못 가.

헌터의 브라운 스톤
개츠비가 전화에 대고 말한다.

개츠비: 왜?

상영실/상영 부스
애슐리가 전화에 대고 말한다.

애슐리: 특종 취재해야 돼. 7천만불짜리 영화인데
롤리가 아주 못마땅해 해.

헌터의 브라운 스톤
개츠비가 실망하여 전화에 대고 말한다.

- I'm onto
  I am pursuing
  계속하다, 뒤쫓다

- real story
  특종

- dismay
  실망

We'll grab a bite to eat.
bite는 '한입(물기)' 라는 뜻으로 grab a
bite는 '간단히 한입 먹다' 라는 의미로,
이 내용에서는 'We'll have a small
meal there – meaning lunch' 라는
의미로 사용된다.

We'll grab a bite to eat.
간단히 먹을게.

GATSBY: (dismayed) You call him Rollie?

SCREENING ROOM/PROJECTION BOOTH
Ashleigh gestures excitedly as she talks into the cell phone.

ASHLEIGH: (quick breath) Yeah, and Ted and I, we have to find him. We have to find him and talk with him before he has one of his crazy fits and then re-edits the whole thing and ruins it.

HUNTER'S BROWNSTONE
Gatsby talks into the cell phone with confusion.

GATSBY: Who's Ted?

SCREENING ROOM/PROJECTION BOOTH
Ashleigh, glancing toward the screening room, talks into the cell phone.

ASHLEIGH: Gatsby, I–I–I can't talk right now, but I'll call you as soon as I'm through. And, um, if, uh…I'm running late, I'll just meet you back at the Plaza.

HUNTER'S BROWNSTONE
Gatsby, walking down the sidewalk, talks into the cell phone.

GATSBY: It's not the Pla – It's the Carlyle! It's the, it was the bar and the piano for tonight!

SCREENING ROOM/PROJECTION BOOTH
Ashleigh stands as ted enters through a doorway, then stops and gestures at her, camera dollying in.

개츠비: (실망스럽게) 이제 롤리라고 불러?

상영실/상영 부스
애슐리가 흥분해서 전화에 대고 말한다.

애슐리: (가쁜 숨) 응, 테드하고 내가 그분을 찾아야
해. 그분이 미쳐서 영화 망쳐놓기 전에 테드
하고 찾아서 얘기해야 돼.

헌터의 브라운 스톤
개츠비가 혼란스러워 하며 전화에 대고 말한다.

개츠비: 테드는 또 누구야?

상영실/상영 부스
애슐리가 화면 밖의 상영실 쪽을 슬쩍 보며 전화에 대고 말한다.

애슐리: 지금 통화 오래 못 해. 끝나자마자 다시 걸
게. 그리고 혹시… 내가 늦으면, 다시 플라
자 호텔에서 만나.

헌터의 브라운 스톤
개츠비가 도보를 걸어 내려가며 전화에 대고 말한다.

개츠비: 플라자가 아니라 칼라일! 거기 피아노 바 가
기로 했잖아!

상영실/상영 부스
애슐리가 서 있을 때 테드가 출입구를 통해 들어섰을 때 멈춰 서서
그녀에게 손짓을 한다. 카메라는 서서히 따라간다.

- crazy fits
  미친 듯한 발작

- confusion
  혼란

- I'm through.
  끝났어.

- I'm running late.
  늦어

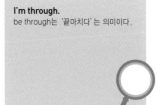

I'm through.
be through는 '끝마치다' 는 의미이다.

Zoom In

I'm through.
끝났어.

TED:	Well, he's not at the hotel, and…he didn't show up for the press interview, so… he's wallowing in self-loathing somewhere, drinking Courvoisier, thinking up new ways to screw up our work.
ASHLEIGH:	Oh, I thought the film was full of wonderful things.
TED:	Me, too. Tell him. You– Tell him, tell Rollie, because hearing that from me won't mean anything. I'm always at…this end of the argument. But you, a fresh, honest, new-generation woman, especially a pretty one, maybe….

Ashleigh starts to hiccup.

ASHLEIGH:	(hiccups) Oh….
TED:	He may– Come on, let's find him.
ASHLEIGH:	(hiccups again, then chuckles softly in embarrassment)

Ted gestures at Ashleigh with concern.

TED:	You okay?
ASHLEIGH:	Yeah.
TED:	Come on.

Ted walks toward the door and Ashleigh follows him.

GREENWICH VILLAGE STREETS
Gatsby, holding the umbrella over his head, walks down a sidewalk in the rain.

GATSBY:	(voice over) He doesn't like her laugh? Now, Ashleigh's laugh is perfect.

테드:	호텔에도 없고, 기자회견에도 안 나타났으니… 어딘가에서 코냑 마시면서 자기혐오에 **빠져있을** 거야. 우리 영화를 망칠 새로운 방법을 궁리하면서.
애슐리:	영화 정말 잘 나왔는데.
테드:	그러게요. 롤리한테 말해줘요. 내 말은 듣지도 않아. 난 늘 좋다고 그냥 두자는데… 하지만 신선하고 솔직한 요즘 세대 아가씨가… 그것도 미인이라 먹힐지도…

애슐리가 딸꾹질을 하기 시작한다.

애슐리:	(딸꾹질) 아..
테드:	자, 찾으러 가요
애슐리:	(다시 딸국질을 하고, 부끄러움에 살짝 웃는다)

테드가 걱정스럽게 애슐리에게 손짓한다.

테드:	괜찮아요?
애슐리:	네.
테드:	가요.

테드가 문을 향해 걸어가고 애슐리는 따라간다.

그린위치 빌리지 거리
개츠비, 우산을 머리 위로 들고, 빗속에서 보도를 걷는다.

| 개츠비: | (해설) 웃음소리가 싫다구? 애슐리는 웃음소리도 완벽한데. |

- **wallow**
  젖어[빠져] 있다

- **self-loathing**
  자기혐오

- **screw up**
  망치다

- **hiccup**
  딸꾹질

He didn't show up.
show up 은 arrive as expected(나타나다)의 뜻이고, show off 는 brag(자랑하다)는 뜻이다.

He didn't show up.
그는 안 나타났다.

Gatsby walks down the sidewalk, camera dollying back in with him.

GATSBY: (voice over) Let's go, Ashleigh. We're blowing the day, and it's so moody out. We could be on the ferry...or the top of the Empire State Building...in black and white.

BAR
Ted and Ashleigh look across the bar at a bartender. Bar patrons are sitting at tables around the bar.

BAR PATRONS: (low and indistinct chatter – continues under following dialogue)

TED: He was here?

BARTENDER: ...yeah, he was here. He seemed very distraught. He knocked back a couple of brandies.

Ted shakes his head with exasperation.

BARTENDER: Mumbled somethin' about heading out to the studio.

Camera continues to dolly in, off the bartender, on Ted and Ashleigh.

TED: (sighs) Okay. (inhales)

Camera holds in as ted, turns toward Ashleigh.

TED: Let's get my car and it's out to Queens.

ASHLEIGH: (reacting nervously) Oh, Queens.

TED: Yeah, it's a big...film studio. You still want to come?

Ashleigh gestures excitedly at Ted.

개츠비가 보도를 걷는다. 카메라는 천천히 따라간다.

개츠비: (해설) **빨리 끝내, 애슐리. 시간이 없어, 날도
쓸쓸하고. 우리는 지금 쫌 유람선… 아니면
엠파이어스테이트 빌딩 꼭대기도 좋은데.**

바
테드랑 애슐리가 바를 가로질러 바텐더를 쳐다본다. 바 단골 손님
들은 바의 테이블에 앉아있다.

바 단골 손님들: (낮고 희미한 말 소리- 대화 중에도 계속 들린다)

테드: 여기 왔었나요?

바텐더: 네, 왔었어요. 아주 심란한 얼굴로 브랜디
두 잔 원샷하고,

테드는 분노해서 고개를 젓는다.

바텐더: 스튜디오로 간다고 웅얼거린 거 같아요.

카메라가 바텐더에서, 테드와 애슐리 차례로 보여준다.

테드: (한숨 쉰다) **알았어요.** (숨을 들이 마신다)

테드가 애슐리를 향해 돌 동안 카메라는 멈춘다.

테드: 차 갖고 퀸즈로 가요.

애슐리: (긴장되어 반응하며) 아 퀸즈요.

테드: 대형 영화 촬영장. 같이 갈래요?

애슐리가 기쁘게 테드에게 손짓한다.

- **indistinct**
  또렷하지 않은, 흐릿한, 희미한

- **distraught**
  완전히 제정신이 아닌, 심난한

- **knock back**
  (특히 술을) 급히 마시다
  'drink in one gulp'

- **exasperation**
  격분, 분노

- **it's out to**
  운전하고 나가다 i.e., 'we drive out to'

> **We're blowing the day, and it's
> so moody out.**
> blow the day는 '하루가 떠나다(사라지
> 다) 로 'We're losing the day we had
> planned' 의미이고, moody는 '쓸쓸
> 한, 서글픈' 이라는 뜻이다.

Zoom In

We're blowing the day, and it's so moody out.
시간이 없고 날도 쓸쓸해.

ASHLEIGH: Oh, definitely.

TED: When, when Rollie gets drunk and morose, he likes to wander around the soundstages and pretend he's Norma Desmond.

TED: (to Bartender) Thanks.

BARTENDER: Sure.

Ted and Ashleigh hurry Ashleigh looks back at the bartender and waves at him.

ASHLEIGH: (waving to Bartender) Thanks.

BAR

Ted opens an umbrella as he and Ashleigh walk out of the bar into the pouring rain. He holds the umbrella above their heads as they turn and walk down the sidewalk.

NEW YORK STREETS

Through the windshield to Ted, who drives his car down a street in the pouring rain. Ashleigh, sitting in the passenger seat, opens her notebook. Ashleigh gestures at Ted.

ASHLEIGH: Could I ask you a few questions, um, since I am on assignment?

TED: Oh, sure. What's your favorite film of Rollie's?

ASHLEIGH: Oh, "Winter Memories". The one in Venice.

TED: And when did you first see it?

ASHLEIGH: Um...it was with Gatsby, actually. It was on our very first date. (soft chuckle and breath)

TED: Hm.

Ashleigh shakes her head at ted.

ASHLEIGH: The dialogue made me want to kiss him.

애슐리: 물론이죠.

테드: 롤리는 취해서 시무룩해지면, 촬영장을 헤매면서 노마 데즈먼드 흉내를 내거든.

테드: (바텐더에게) 고마워요.

바텐더: 별 말씀을요.

테드랑 애슐리가 급히 나간다. 애슐리가 화면 밖의 바텐더를 뒤 돌아보고 손을 흔든다.

애슐리: (바텐더에게 손을 흔들며) 감사해요.

바
애슐리랑 테드가 바에서 쏟아지는 빗속으로 걸어 나가며 우산을 펼친다. 테드는 애슐리와 함께 돌아 인도로 걸어가면서 우산을 그들의 머리 위로 쓴다.

뉴욕 거리
자동차의 앞 유리를 통해 쏟아지는 빗속에서 거리를 운전하는 테드가 보인다. 애슐리는 조수석에 앉아 그녀의 공책을 편다. 애슐리는 테드에게 손짓한다.

애슐리: 질문 몇 개만 해도 돼요? 취재 중이니까.

테드: 그럼요. 롤리 영화 중에 뭐가 제일 좋아요?

애슐리: 아. '윈터 메모리즈' 베니스에서 찍은 거요.

테드: 언제 처음 봤어요?

애슐리: 개츠비와 봤어요. 첫 번째 데이트 때요. (살짝 웃고 숨을 쉰다)

테드: 흠…

애슐리는 테드를 향해 고개를 젓는다.

애슐리: 대사 때문에 키스하고 싶어졌죠

- **morose**
  시무룩한, 뚱한 (=gloomy)

- **wander around**
  방황하다

- **soundstage**
  촬영장

- **dialogue**
  대사, 대화

The dialogue made me want to kiss him.
make는 사역동사로 'make + 사람 + 동사원형'이 쓰이면 '~가 …하게 하다'는 사역의 의미를 지닌다.

The dialogue made me want to kiss him.
대사는 내가 그와 키스를 하고 싶게 했어.
(대사 때문에 키스하고 싶어졌어).

TED:	Hm.
ASHLEIGH:	(inhales and exhales excitedly) That line about love and death being two sides of the same coin. (inhales and exhales blissfully)
TED:	Hm. Did you understand it?
ASHLEIGH:	Um... no.
	(embarrassed chuckle) Uh...I got confused and felt insecure, and like I wanted to just be held and kissed.

Ted looks up thoughtfully, then looks at Ashleigh.

TED:	You ever been to Venice?
ASHLEIGH:	No. But Gatsby has.

Ted glances at Connie, then reacts with shock.

TED:	(seeing something) Oh, my God.

TED'S CAR

Ashleigh sits as Ted, turns the car around a corner. Connie, Ted's wife, walks across an intersection. Connie is wearing a yellow raincoat and holding an umbrella.

ASHLEIGH:	What?
TED:	Oh, I...I knew it. I knew it, I knew it!
ASHLEIGH:	Are you okay?

Ted drives the car toward the curb.

TED:	Oh, God!
ASHLEIGH:	You, um, you turned all white.

테드:	흠…
애슐리:	(숨을 들이 마시고 흥분하여 내쉰다) 사랑과 죽음은 동전의 양면 같다는 대사요. (흐뭇하게 숨을 들이 마쉬고 내쉰다)
테드:	이해가 됐어요?
애슐리:	아뇨. (부끄러운 웃음) 그냥 혼란스럽고, 불안해져서… 날 안고 키스해줬으면 했어요.

테드가 사려깊게 올려다 보다가 애슐리를 본다.

테드:	베니스엔 가봤어요?
애슐리:	아뇨, 개츠비는 가봤어요.

테드가 화면 밖의 코니를 슬쩍 보더니 충격에 휩싸인다.

테드:	(무언가를 보곤) 세상에.

테드의 차
애슐리는 앉아있고, 테드는 갓길에 차를 세운다. 테드의 부인 코니는 교차로를 건넌다. 코니는 노란 우비를 입고 우산을 들고 있다.

애슐리:	왜요?
테드:	그럼 그렇지. 내 저럴 줄 알았어!
애슐리:	괜찮으세요?

테드는 차를 연석쪽으로 운전했다.

테드:	이럴 수가!
애슐리:	얼굴이 창백해졌어요.

- line
  대사

- blissfully
  흐뭇하게

- insecure
  불안한

- thoughtfully
  생각이 깊게

- intersection
  교차로

- I knew it
  그럴줄 알았어.

- curb
  (차도 가의) 연석, 도로 경계석

- all white
  온통 창백한

I got confused and, and, and felt insecure.
feel 은 다음에 형용사(insecure)가 오는 2형식동사로 쓰인다.

I got confused and, and, and felt insecure.
혼란스럽고, 불안해졌어.

Ted stops the car. Connie reenters as she walks down the sidewalk.

Lipshitz's building
Through the windshield to Ted, who looks angrily at Connie.

TED: I knew it! She was lying!

Through the windshield to Ashleigh, who looks at Connie.

ASHLEIGH: Who?
TED: Connie, my wife!

Through the windshield to Ted, who looks at Ashleigh. He then turns and gestures at Connie.

TED: She's seeing Lipshitz!
ASHLEIGH: Who's Lipshitz?

Through the windshield to Ted, who gestures at Ashleigh.

TED: ...she was going shopping with her sister in Connecticut, but...

He gestures at the building.

TED: ...she's walking (quick breath) into Lipshitz's building!

Through the windshield to Ashleigh, who looks at the building.

ASHLEIGH: Oh, is Lipshitz a spy?
TED: What?

Ashleigh looks at Ted.

Through the windshield to Ted, who gestures at Ashleigh.

테드가 차를 세운다. 코니가 도보를 건너며 재등장한다.

립쉬츠 빌딩

앞유리를 통해 코니를 분노가 가득한 눈으로 바라보는 테드가 보인다.

테드:　　　날 속이는 줄 알고 있었다고!

앞 유리를 통해 화면 밖의 코니를 바라보는 애슐리가 보인다.

애슐리:　　누가요?

테드:　　　코니, 내 아내!

앞유리를 통해 화면 밖에 있는 애슐리를 바라보는 테드가 보인다. 그리고 그는 돌아서 화면 밖의 코니에게 손짓한다.

테드:　　　립쉬츠를 만나다니!

애슐리:　　립쉬츠가 누군데요?

앞유리를 통해 테드가 보이고, 그가 화면 밖에 있는 애슐리를 향해 손짓한다.

테드:　　　언니랑 코네티컷에 쇼핑하러 간다더니…

화면 밖의 빌딩을 향해 손짓한다.

테드:　　　립쉬츠 건물로 걸어들어가네!

앞 유리를 통해 화면 밖의 빌딩을 바라보는 애슐리가 보인다.

애슐리:　　아 립쉬츠라는 사람이 스파이 같은 분이에요?

테드:　　　뭐라고?

애슐리가 테드를 본다.

앞유리를 통해 화면 밖에 있는 애슐리에게 손짓하는 테드가 보인다.

■ see
(애인으로)만나다
i.e., 'have a love affair with'

> **She is going shopping with her sister.**
> go-ing는 '~하러 가다'는 의미로, go shopping은 '쇼핑하러 가다'는 뜻이다.

She is going shopping with her sister.
그녀는 언니와 쇼핑하러 갈 거야.

TED: No, Larry Lipshitz! My friend, my best friend!

Ted looks at the building.

TED: My best friend! I can't believe it. She must – I mean, they're having an affair.

ASHLEIGH: Oh, God. (inhales worriedly)

TED: (distressed exhalation)

ASHLEIGH: Are…are you okay? You're clutching your heart.

Through the windshield to Ted, who holds his hand over his heart and closes his eyes.

TED: Okay, here's what we do.

Ted opens his eyes, then gestures at Ashleigh.

TED: We sit here, w–, uh, we wait until she comes out, and then I'll confront her.

Through the windshield to Ashleigh, who looks nervously at Ted.

ASHLEIGH: (exhaling nervously) Uhhh…I hope there's not a gun in your glove compartment like in your movies. (inhales nervously)

Through the windshield to Ted, who gestures at Ashleigh.

TED: You'd better go. You go.

Through the windshield to Ashleigh, who looks at Ted.

ASHLEIGH: No, I can't leave you alone! You're all white and shaky.

테드: 아니, 래리 립쉬츠! 내 제일 친한 친구!

테드가 빌딩을 바라본다.

테드: 둘이 바람을 피우다니.

애슐리: 어떡해. (걱정하며 숨을 들이 마신다)

테드: (괴로워하는 숨을 내쉰다)

애슐리: 괜찮으세요? 가슴을 움켜잡고 계신데.

차의 앞 유리를 통해 손을 가슴위에 올리고 눈을 감고 있는 테드가
보인다.

테드: 이렇게 합시다.

테드가 눈을 뜨고 화면 밖의 애슐리에게 손짓한다.

테드: 나올 때까지 기다렸다가, 내가 가서 잡는 거
         야.

앞 유리를 통해 화면 밖의 테드를 긴장되어 바라보는 애슐리가 보인
다.

애슐리: (긴장된 숨을 내쉰다) 작가님 영화에서처럼 차에
         총은 없길 바래요. (긴장된 숨을 들이마신다)

테드가 화면 밖의 애슐리에게 손짓한다.

테드: 그만 가요.

애슐리가 화면 밖의 테드를 본다.

애슐리: 어떻게 그래요! 하얗게 질려서 떨고 계신데.

- distressed
  괴로워하는, 고통스러워하는

- clutch
  움켜잡다

- clutching
  꽉 움켜쥐는

- confront
  맞서다

- glove compartment
  (자동차 앞좌석 앞에 있는) 사물함

- white and shaky
  창백하고 불안한

They're having an affair.
have an affair는 '~와 관계를 갖다, 바
람을 피우다' 라는 의미이다.

They're having an affair.
그들이 바람을 피우고 있다.

TED: (controlled exhalation)

Ted leans back in his seat with his eyes closed.

TED: Breathe. Deeply. Breathe. (exhales and inhales) Deeply. Doctor Ross said breathe. (inhales)

Ashleigh also starts to take deep breaths.

TED: Breathe. Breathe.

Through the windshield to Ted, who turns and looks at Ashleigh.

TED: No, not you. Me.

Ted leans back against the seat and closes his eyes again.

TED: Oh, God.

테드: (절제된 숨)

테드가 눈을 감고 자리에 기댄다.

테드: 숨 쉬어… 심호흡 하자… (숨을 들이 마시고 내.는
        다) 로스 박사가 숨 쉬랬어… (들이 마신다 – 씬이
        끝날 때 까지 쭉) 심호흡…

애슐리도 심호흡을 한다.

테드: 진정하고 호흡… 심호흡…

테드가 화면 밖의 애슐리를 본다.

테드: 아가씨 말고 나.

테드가 뒤로 기대고 다시 눈을 감는다.

테드: 아이고.

■ controlled
    절제된

■ lean
    기대다

**Ted leans back in his seat with
his eyes closed.**
with 분사구문은 'with + 명사 + 분사'
의 형태로 '~한 채로'라는 의미로, with
his eyes closed는 '눈을 감은 채로'라
는 의미이다.

Ted leans back in his seat with his eyes closed.

테드는 눈을 감은 채로 자리에 기댄다.

A Rainy
Day in
New York

Movie Talk

Travel NYC With 'A Rainy Day in New York': Upper East Side & Central Park

북동부지역(Upper East Side)

  뉴욕 맨해튼 가운데 위치한 센트럴 파크의 동쪽 업다운 지역이 어퍼 이스트 사이드이다. 어퍼 이스트 사이드는 미국의 최상류층을 위한 고급 주택들이 모여있는 곳이다. 한국으로 치면 청담동과 성북동 같이 고급 주택들과 명품 거리가 있는 곳이다. 특히 센트럴 파크를 앞에 둔 5번가와 파크 애비뉴는 과거 케네디 일가와 밴더빌트, 라커펠러, 카네기, 루즈벨트 등 유서깊은 가문들의 타운하우스가 있어 가장 집값이 높은 지역으로 손꼽힌다. 이곳의 타운하우스 주택은 '레이니 데이 인 뉴욕'의 감독인 우디 앨런을 포함해 마돈나, 도널드 트럼프 등의 유명 인사들이 대거 살고있다. 또, 매디슨 애비뉴는 명품 부티크들로 가득 차 있어 이 지역의 부와 권력을 잘 보여주고 있다. 실제로 어퍼이스트 사이드에 거주하는 엄마들의 사치와 현실을 고발하는 옌스 데이 마틴의 '파크 애비뉴의 영장류'라는 책과 이들의 이야기를 담은 전설의 미드 '가십걸'을 통해 어퍼 이스트 사이드는 0.1%의 상류층이 사는 부촌이라는 것을 확인할 수 있다. 또한, 메트로폴리탄 미술관 뿐만 아니라 구겐하임, 휘트니, 맨하탄 뮤지엄, 누 갤러리 등 뮤지엄 마일도 있어 문화의 중심지 역할을 하고 있다.

  19세기 5th Ave.에 미국인들이 존경하는 철강왕 피츠버그 앤드류 카네기, 자산가 헨리 클래이프릭를 포함한 부유한 자본가들이 스타일리시한 고급 맨션과 타운하우스와 센트럴 파크를 짓기 시작했고, 미국 모피상인 아스터와 라인랜더 일가가 부동산 투자를 하기 시작했다. 자본가 록펠러 가, 정치 명가 루즈벨트 가와 케네디 가, 원래 부유한데다 경마로 더 큰 돈 벌은 휘트니 가, 미국 듀크 대학의 설립자인 듀크 가, 미국 브로드웨이 뮤지컬계의 초기 작곡가인 죠지거쉰이 살던 곳이다.

이곳이 친숙한 이름처럼 느껴지는 이유는 카네기홀, 록펠러 빌딩, 휘트니뮤지엄, 프릭컬렉션등 뉴욕의 여러 빌딩, 대학, 뮤지엄에 붙여진 이름에다가 미국 대통령의 이름들이다. 메트로폴리탄 뮤지엄을 필두로 휘트니 뮤지엄 오브 아메리칸 아트, 프릭 컬렉션이 왜 5th Ave.에 몰려있나 했더니만 그 궁금증이 풀렸다. 이 부자들 대부분이 예술을 사랑해서 또는 정부로부터 면세 받기 위해 예술작품을 사들이고 뮤지엄을 세웠기 때문이다. 사업가이자 뉴욕시장이었던 마이클 블룸버그, 포브스 선정 세계80위 갑부인 주식 투자자 조지 서러스, 미국을 대표하는 저널리스트이자 방송인 바바라월터스, 영화감독 우디 앨런, 패션 디자이너 도나 카렌, 랄프로렌, 켈빈클라인 등이 살고 있으며 은수저들고 태어난 애들이 다니는 미국내에서 최고로 손꼽히는 세인트버나드, 버클리 남자사립학교, 채핀, 스펜스, 브레어리 여자사립학교가 있다. 90th St.이상부터는 할렘으로 여기며 해 저물면 그 쪽으로 들어가지 않는다.

칼라일, 피에르와 플라자 호텔(The Carlyle, The Pierre, and The Plaza Hotels)

애슐리와 개츠비는 피에르 호텔을 숙소로, 칼라일 호텔의 베멜 망스 바에 가는 멋진 하루를 계획했다. 피에르 호텔과 칼라일 호텔 은 어퍼이스트 사이드에 있는 럭셔리 호텔들로 손꼽힌다. 중간에 애 슐리가 헷갈려 하며 "플라자 호텔로 갈게." 라고 하는 장면도 등장한 다. 칼라일, 피에르, 그리고 플라자 호텔은 맨해튼에서 모두가 머물 고 싶어 하는 상류계급의 럭셔리 호텔들이다.

GATSBY: Okay. Look, I'm gonna make a reservation at the Carlyle. That's the place I'm always tellin' you about with the...

ASHLEIGH: (very soft chuckle)

GATSBY: ...the piano player at the bar. He sings those old Broadway tunes. And, uh, I'll take you out for lunch and dinner. How does that sound? Maybe I'll show you around the city?

GATSBY: ...and then after dinner we're gonna go to the Carlyle, we'll go to the bar, and, a-a-a-and spend some time there. It's, it's very old New York. Uh, uh, I, I really love it.

ASHLEIGH: (very softly, nodding) Uh-huh.

GATSBY: The murals are by (quick breath) Ludwig Bemelmans.

칼라일 호텔은 전설적인 고급 카바레로 유명한 카페 칼라일 (Cafe Carlyle)과, 세련된 피아노 바인 베멜만스 바 (Bemelmans Bar)로 유명하다. 베멜만스 바 (Bemelmans Bar)는 Madeline이라는 동화의 유명한 삽화가인 Ludwig Bemelmans가 호텔의 이 공간에 뉴욕 Central Park를 묘사한 벽화를 그려, 그의 이름이 붙여졌다. 이 벽화는 Ludwig Bemelmans의 작품 중 유일하게 일반인들에게 오픈된 작품이라고 한다. 베멜만스 바 (Bemelmans Bar)는 세련되고 교양있는 피아노 바로 많은 유명인사, 정치가, 셀럽들이 애정하는 곳이다. 우디 앨런의 영화에 많이 등장하였으며, 개츠비가 뉴스에서 베가와 애슐리를 보고 온 술집이며, 영화가 끝나갈 무렵 애슐리와 개츠비의 재회가 이루어지는 바로 그 곳이다. (개츠비가 바에서 피아노를 치고 있고 트렌치 코트를 입고 다 젖은 애슐리 옆에 서 있는 장면)

GATSBY: And actually, now that I'm thinking about
             it, we can't stay at the Carlyle, it's too
             close to my parents' house…
ASHLEIGH: (very softly, nodding) Oh.
GATSBY: …but I want you to have a park view
GATSBY: (snapping fingers) You know what?
GATSBY :   We're gonna stay at the Pierre.
GATSBY :   That way you can have a park view.

피에르 호텔은 센트럴 파크의 시작 지
점에 위치하고 있기 때문에 도시적인 느
낌(시티뷰)과 동시에 자연 경관(파크뷰)
을 바라볼 수 있다. 이 호텔은 디자이너
가브리엘 샤넬, 입생로랑과 존 에프 케네
디의 부인 등이 살았던 호텔이다. (일반
객실은 하룻 밤에 55만원 선, 스위트룸은
약 6500만원….)

ASHLEIGH: (into cell phone) Gatsby, I-I-I can't talk
             right now, but I'll call you as soon as I'm
             through. And, um, if, uh…I'm running
             late, I'll just meet you back at the Plaza.
She hangs up the cell phone.

GATSBY: (into cell phone) It's not the Pla-It's the
             Carlyle! It's the, it was the bar and the
             piano for tonight!

플라자 호텔은 맨해튼 센트럴 파크 바로 앞에 위치한 호텔이다. 1907년에 건축되었었고, 너무 유명한 만큼 주인도 수차례 바뀌었었다. 한때는 도널드 트럼프가 사서 자신의 부인에게 사장 자리를 준 적도 있었다. 사람들은 플라자 호텔을 〈나 홀로 집에2〉의 촬영지로 많이들 기억한다. 뉴욕 플라자 호텔은 플라자 합의가 채택된 역사적인 장소이기도 하다.

Daniel

'다니엘' 은 프랑스계 셰프 다니엘 블뤼 (Daniel Boulud)라는 세계적인 셰프의 레스토랑이다. 1993년 맨해튼 어퍼이스트에 자리잡은 그의 레스토랑 다니엘은 그의 유명세와 함께 순식간에 세계 Top 10 레스토랑, 최고의 셰프 등 각종 차트에 올랐고, 뛰어난 요리 솜씨와 함께 창의적이고 예술적인 플레이팅으로 '일레븐 매디슨 파크' 와 'Per Se' 와 같은 레스토랑과 함께 파인다이닝의 교과서로 불린다.

최고의 파인 다이닝 식당인 만큼 복장 제한과 함께 최소한 한달 전 예약은 필수이다.

Metropolitan Museum of Arts

　미국에서 'Metropolitan Museum of Arts'를 줄여서 메트 (The Met)라고 불린다. 미국에 매년 수 많은 유명인사들이 화려한 의상을 입고 모이는 뉴욕 패션계 최고의 모금 행사 "멧 갈라 (Met Gala)" 역시 메트로폴리탄 미술관을 줄여서 부른 것이다. 메트로폴리탄 미술관은 유럽 미술관에 비해 역사가 짧지만, 많은 기증품, 구입품 등 학문적으로 가치가 높은 소장품들이 모여 '세계 4대 박물관' 이라는 명성을 얻게 되었다. 메트로폴리탄 미술관 정문은 그 안의 미술품들 만큼이나

유명하다. 많은 관광객들과 매체들이 이 정문을 뉴욕, 맨해튼의 상징처럼 여겼기 때문이다. 200개가 넘는 전시실은 고대 오리엔트 미술, 그리스, 로마 미술, 유럽 회화, 미국 회화, 이슬람 미술, 아시아 미술, 아프리카 미술 등 20개 분야로 나뉘어 전시되어 있다.

Chapter 5

챈과의 재회

Meeting Chan again

시간 00:32:24 ~ 00:42:53

GREENWICH VILLAGE STREETS.
Gatsby, walking down a sidewalk with his umbrella above his head, looks at taxi.

GATSBY: Taxi!

Gatsby hurries down the sidewalk.

GATSBY: Taxi!

Gatsby hurries to reveal a taxi, on the street, and Chan, she is hurrying across the street toward the taxi. Gatsby opens the rear passenger door and sits down in the back of the taxi, camera craning down. Camera holds as Chan, opens the rear driver's door. Camera dollies in as Gatsby and Chan look at one another with surprise.

GATSBY: Oh, my God, Chan! What are you doing here?
CHAN: Hey, I'm just–

Camera holds as Gatsby starts to slide toward the doorway.

GATSBY: Hey, you take it. I'll get the next one!

그린위치 빌리지 거리.
개츠비가 자신의 우산을 머리 위로 들고 인도를 걷는다. 화면 밖 택시를 본다.

개츠비:　　택시!

개츠비가 서두르며 인도를 걸어 내려온다.

개츠비:　　택시!

개츠비가 거리에서 택시를 가리키며 서두르고 있고, 챈, 그녀는 택시 쪽으로 건너편에서 급히 오고 있다. 개츠비는 뒷좌석 승객용 문을 열고 택시 뒤에 앉는다. 카메라가 내려온다. 챈이 운전자 뒷좌석 문을 열때 카메라는 멈춘다.
개츠비와 챈이 서로를 놀라는 눈으로 바라볼때 카메라는 다가가서 찍는다.

개츠비:　　챈! 여긴 웬일이야
챈:　　　어, 오빠!

개츠비가 문 방향으로 미끄러지기 시작할 때 카메라는 멈춘다.

개츠비:　　타, 난 다음 거 탈게!

- rear
  후방의

- passenger door
  조수석 문

- take it
  택시를 타다: ride this taxi

Chan starts to get in the taxi.

CHAN: No, no, get in. I'll– Let's go.

GATSBY: Are you sure?

CHAN: I'll drop you.

Chan sits down in the rear driver's seat and Gatsby settles down in the rear passenger seat.

GATSBY: Hey, where you goin'?

CHAN: Oh, you remember. The same Fifth Avenue joint.

GATSBY: I remember your apartment well from my days with Amy.

The taxi starts to move.

TAXI
Chan turns and looks at Gatsby. The taxi moves down a street through the rain.

CHAN: ···I remember you calling for her. My parents kept warning her about you.

GATSBY: Warning? Why the hell would they be warning her?

CHAN: Because on a first date you took her walking in the rain and she got bronchial pneumonia.

GATSBY: For Chrissake, I'm never gonna get over this. You can't get it from being wet!

Chan, shrugs at him.

CHAN: …yell at me, I thought it was romantic.

챈이 택시에 탄다.

챈:	아니, 타. 내가... 가자.
개츠비:	정말로?
챈:	내가 내려줄게.

챈이 운전자 뒷 자석에 앉고 개츠비는 조수석 뒷자리에 앉는다.

개츠비:	어디 가는데?
챈:	5번가 옛날 그 아파트.
개츠비:	에이미와 사귈 때 자주 갔지.

택시가 움직이기 시작한다.

택시 안에서.
챈이 돌아서 개츠비를 본다. 택시가 비를 뚫고 길을 따라 내려간다.

챈:	언니 부르던 거 기억나. 부모님이 오빠 조심 하랬는데.
개츠비:	내가 조심할 게 뭐가 있다고.
챈:	첫 데이트 때 비 맞혀서 언니 기관지 폐렴 걸렸다고.
개츠비:	그 소린 죽을 때까지 듣겠네. 젖어서 걸리는 게 아냐!

챈은 개츠비에게 어깨를 으쓱한다.

챈:	나한테 화내지 마. 난 로맨틱하다고 생각했 어.

- **from my days with**
  ~와의 나날로부터

- **bronchial pneumonia**
  기관지(氣 管支)폐렴

- **For Chrissake**
  'For Christ's sake' 의 변이형

- **get over**
  극복하다

I'll drop you.
drop은 보통 '떨어지다'로 알고 있는데 '(어디로 가는 길에)내려 주다'로도 쓰인 다.
i.e., 'I'll have the taxi drop you off at your location first.

I'll drop you.
내가 내려줄게.

GATSBY: That's because it is romantic. It's a romantic gesture.

CHAN: That's what I'm saying.

GATSBY: I always tell that to Ashleigh. She thinks I'm nuts.

CHAN: Who's Ashleigh? The rodeo queen you're dating?

GATSBY: She's not a cowgirl.

She comes from one of the biggest banking families in Tucson. She, she was a debutante, actually. She came out.

CHAN: She came out? Is she gay?

GATSBY: No, she's not gay. She's charming and beautiful, and we're supposed to have this...goddamn weekend in the city together, and suddenly she's bogged down with all these interviews for the school paper.

CHAN: She's ambitious. You should find that admirable.

Gatsby, stares at her, then gestures at her.

GATSBY: It's one, it was supposed to be one little, (quick breath) one...tiny little lousy hour interview. Instead...you know...lost the whole goddamn weekend.

Gatsby shakes his head, rubbing his chin agitatedly.

CHAN: Will you just relax? I don't really know why—

Gatsby gestures at chan.

개츠비:	그래, 로맨틱한 상황이었어.
챈:	내 말이.
개츠비:	나는 애슐리한테 항상 그 말을 하는데, 애슐리는 내가 미쳤다고 생각해.
챈:	애슐리가 누구야? 오빠가 만난다는 미스 로데오?
개츠비:	걔 카우걸 아냐. 투손에서 제일 큰 은행 집 딸이야. 사실 사교계에 데뷔도 했었지, 커밍아웃 했어.
챈:	커밍아웃? 동성애자야?
개츠비:	아니, 게이 아니야. 애슐리는 매력적이고 예뻐. 시내에서 멋진 주말을 보내기로 했는데 갑자기⋯ 학교신문 인터뷰가 계속 길어져서⋯ 꼼짝 못하고 있어.
챈:	야심이 있네. 칭찬할 일이야

개츠비는 챈을 쳐다보고, 손짓한다.

개츠비:	원래 겨우 한 시간짜리 작은 인터뷰였는데 (짧은 숨) 일이 꼬여서⋯ 그 대신에 주말 다 망치게 생겼잖아.

개츠비가 고개를 젓고, 불안하며 턱을 문지른다.

챈:	진정 좀 하지? 나는 왜 너가 이러는지⋯

개츠비가 챈에게 손짓한다.

■ nut
미친 사람

■ debutante
처음 사교계에 나가는 상류층 여성

■ coming-out (come out)
사교계 정식 데뷔, 동성애자임을 공식적으로 밝히는 일

■ ambitious
야심이 있는

■ admirable
존경할 만한

■ lousy
보잘것 없는, 사소한: insignificant

■ agitatedly
불안해하며, 동요하게

She's bogged down with all these interviews.
be bogged down with는 '⋯으로[에 빠져] 꼼짝 못하게 되다(preoccupied)'는 의미이다.
i.e., 'preoccupied'

She's bogged down with all these interviews.
그녀는 인터뷰로 꼼짝 못하고 있어.

GATSBY: Look, I, I'm havin' a hard time relaxing, Chan, 'cause this was gonna be a...a special weekend. Instead I'm out here in the...you know, wandering the streets like Hagar in the goddamn desert or something!

Chan shakes her head at Gatsby.

CHAN: Well, don't tell me, tell her. Tell her to get her priorities straight.
You want to drink some wine, walk in the rain and give her bronchitis.

He smiles at her insincerely.

GATSBY: Mm. (inhales irritably)

Gatsby, rubs his hands together and tries to calm down.

GATSBY: Okay, (exhaling) look. She's apparently onto a very big story. She takes her job very seriously, all right?

CHAN: Fine, then get over it.

Gatsby nods his head hesitantly.

GATSBY: I, I, um...I'm in the process of getting over it.

CHAN: Unless you're worried somebody's hitting on her.

GATSBY: What the hell does that mean?

CHAN: I don't know. Is she interviewing attractive men?

GATSBY: I, I haven't really thought about it. I don't know.

개츠비: 챈. 나 진정이 잘 안 돼. 얼마나 기대한 주말
인데. 대신에 난 지금 광야의 하갈처럼 거리
를 헤매고 있다니까!

챈이 개츠비를 향해 고개를 젓는다.

챈: 나 말고 여친한테 말해. 우선순위 바로잡으
라고.
와인도 한잔하고, 빗속을 걷다 폐렴도 걸리
자고.

개츠비가 대충 웃는다.

개츠비: 흠. (불편한듯 숨을 들이 마신다)

개츠비는 손을 비비며 간장을 가라 앉히려고 노력한다.

개츠비: 그래. (숨을 내쉬며) 봐봐. 걘 지금 특종 취재
중이고, 워낙 프로니까, 그치?
챈: 그럼 신경 꺼.

개츠비가 망설이는 태도로 고개를 끄덕인다.

개츠비: 그래…신경 끄는 중이야.
챈: 누가 꼬실까 봐 걱정인 게 아니라면.
개츠비: 그게 무슨 소리야?
챈: 글쎄, 인터뷰 상대들이 멋져?
개츠비: 깊이 생각 안 해봤어, 모르겠네.

- bronchitis
  기관지염

- insincerely
  성의 없이, 불성실하게; 거짓으로

- apparently
  보아하니

- take something very seriously
  ~을 매우 진지하게 받아들이다

- get over
  극복하다

- process
  과정

- hit on somebody
  (성적으로 끌리는 사람에게) 수작을 걸다
  'flirting with' – 'trying to seduce'

- attractive
  매력적인

**Tell her to get her priorities
straight.**
get something straight는 '(어떤 상황
에 오해가 없도록)분명히 밝히다, 확실히
하다' 라는 의미이다.

Tell her to get her priorities straight.
우선순위를 바로 잡으라고 해.

Gatsby shrugs at Chan.

GATSBY: Some might say they're interesting?

CHAN: Well...then maybe you'd better step in and assert yourself.

GATSBY: Oh, you think I gotta be more demanding?

CHAN: I would.

GATSBY: These are like movie big shots she's hangin' out with. Like...

CHAN: Suits?

GATSBY: Yeah, it's a director and a screenwriter.

CHAN: (nodding) Artists.

Chan smiles insincerely, then shakes her head.

CHAN: They're usually passionate.

Past Chan, to Gatsby, who rubs his face agitatedly.

GATSBY: Oh, Jesus Christ.

Gatsby takes his cell phone out of his pocket and dials it.

GATSBY: Okay, you're right, I gotta call her now.

CHAN: I mean, the sooner the better. I—

GATSBY: You think there's that much of a rush?

CHAN: (shrugging) I don't know.

GATSBY: Aw, Christ, all right.

Gatsby raises the cell phone to his mouth, then gestures at Chan.

개츠비가 챈을 향해 어깨를 들썩인다.

개츠비: 흥미롭다고들 하려나?
챈: 그럼 나서서 확실히 해.
개츠비: 아, 더 세게 나가라고?
챈: 나라면.
개츠비: 그래. 상대가 영화계의 잘나가는 유명인사들인데… 음.
챈: 거물들?
개츠비: 응, 감독과 각본가.
챈: (고개를 끄덕이며) 예술가들…

챈이 대충 웃고, 고개를 젓는다.

챈: 열정적이잖아.

개츠비가 불안하게 얼굴을 비빈다.

개츠비: 아, 미치겠다.

개츠비가 주머니에서 핸드폰을 꺼내서 전화를 건다.

개츠비: 그래, 맞아. 지금 당장 전화해봐야겠어.
챈: **빠**를수록 좋지.
개츠비: 그렇게 긴급이야?
챈: (어깨를 으쓱거리며) 모르지.
개츠비: 그래, 바로 건다.

개츠비다 핸드폰을 얼굴에 가져다 대고 챈에게 손짓한다.

- **demanding**
  요구가 많은

- **big shot**
  거물, 유명인사
  important and highly influential people

- **hang out**
  ~와 어울리다: 'socializing'

- **suit**
  거물

- **screenwriter**
  각본가

- **passionate**
  열정적인

- **The sooner the better.**
  빠르면 빠를수록 좋다

- **shrug**
  어깨를 으쓱하다

- **Christ**
  걱정(worry)의 감탄사

You'd better step in and assert yourself.
step in은 '(문제를 해결하기 위해) 나서다' (intervene)라는 의미이고, assert oneself는 '(자신의 권리들) 확고히 하다' 라는 뜻이다.

You'd better step in and assert yourself.
나서서 확실히 해.

GATSBY:	All right, it's your idea. What do, so, what, what, uh…what do you think I should say?
CHAN:	Well, there's nothing you can say.
GATSBY:	What do you mean?
CHAN:	Without sounding possessive, it's, ugh…
GATSBY:	Christ, Chan, you just encouraged me to call her! Now I'm asking for your help and you're just, you're tellin' me there's nothin' I can say?
CHAN:	You're so wishy-washy! I mean, now that I see your M.O., I know exactly why Amy eighty-sixed you.
GATSBY:	Oh, no, no, no. Amy didn't dump me. Eh, I got sick o'. seein' her.

Chan nods dubiously at Gatsby.

CHAN:	Yeah. Because every time you'd call and I'd say it was you on the phone… she'd wave her arms and say, (hushed) "I'm not in, not in."

LIPSHITZ' S BUILDING
Through the windshield to Ashleigh, who is sitting in the passenger seat of Ted's car. She talks into her cell phone.

ASHLEIGH:	Hey, Gatsby?
GATSBY:	(chuckling nervously) Hey, Ashleigh. (quick breath) Listen, um…look, I know you're very busy. That's why we came to New York, right? And no one has more respect for honest ambitions than I do.

개츠비: 너 생각이니까… 걸어서 뭐라고 해?

챈: 딱히 할 수 있는 말은 없어.

개츠비: 뭐라구?

챈: 뭐라고 해도 집착 같아보이니까…

개츠비: 챈! 너가 실컷 전화 걸게 해놓고, 이제 도와 달라고 하니까 내가 할 수 있는 말은 없다 구?

챈: 거 참 우유부단하기는! 지금 패턴을 보니 언 니가 왜 찼는지 정확히 알겠다.

개츠비: 오, 아니거든? 에이미가 아니라 내가 찼던 거야.

챈이 개츠비에게 의심스럽게 끄덕인다.

챈: 그래, 그래서 오빠 전화 올 때마다 언니가 (속삭이듯이) '나 없다 그래!' 한 거구나.

립쉬츠 빌딩
자동차의 앞 유리를 통해 조수석에 앉아 있8는 애슐리가 있다. 핸 드폰으로 전화를 하고 있다.

애슐리: 개츠비?

개츠비: (긴장된 웃음) 애슐리, (짧은 숨) 있잖아…일하는 중인 거 알고, 그러려고 뉴욕에 온 것도 아 는데. 또 그 의욕, 누구보다 존경하는데…

- **sound**
  ~처럼 들리다

- **possessive**
  소유욕이 강한, 집착하는

- **M.O**
  modus operandi의 약자로 어떤 작업의 방식, 절차 라는 뜻임. 여기에서는 개츠비 가 여성을 대하는 태도를 말한다.

- **eighty-six**
  거절하다, 제거하다('got rid of')의 속어

- **dump**
  (애인을) 차다
  leave – end the relationship with

- **get sick of ~**
  ~에 질리다 sick: tired

- **I'm not in**
  i.e., I'm not here

- **ambition**
  야망

You're so wishy-washy.
wishy-washy는 '미온적인, 우유부 단한, 확고하지 못한('indecisive' – 'irresolute' – usually describing a person who keeps changing their mind)의 의미이다.

You're so wishy-washy.
너는 참 우유부단하다.

CHAN: Do I have to listen to this without an airsick bag?

ASHLEIGH: Uh, I can't talk to you right now. I'm, I'm kind of involved in a situation.

Ashleigh glances at Ted.

TAXI
Chan sits as Gatsby talks into his cell phone.

GATSBY: We had a number of things planned for today.

ASHLEIGH: I–I'm just, I–I'm very busy right now, but I–I...I really, I can't explain it over the phone.

GATSBY: Ashleigh, we were talkin' about one movie interview. What could possibly be so secretive about that? Eh, wh–what's so C.I.A.?

Chan leans toward gatsby.

CHAN: Unless there's some funny business going on.

Gatsby, nodding at Chan, repeats the line to Ashleigh.

GATSBY: Unless there's some funny business goin' on.

LIPSHITZ'S BUILDING
Through the windshield to Ashleigh, who talks into the cell phone.

ASHLEIGH: I–I'll talk to you later. Uh...bye, Gatsby.

Ashleigh hangs up the cell phone.

GATSBY: (angrily) All these goddamn cell phones are–!

CHAN: I don't know. To me, it sounds dubious to the max.

챈:　　　나 참, 어디 멀미 봉투 없나?

애슐리:　　지금 상황이 통화하기 좀 그래.

애슐리가 화면 밖에 있는 테드를 힐끔 본다.

택시
챈은 앉아있고 개츠비는 통화하고 있다.

개츠비:　　우리 오늘 하기로 한 일들이 있잖아.

애슐리:　　지금 너무 바쁜데 통화론 설명할 수가 없어

개츠비:　　감독 인터뷰 하나 하면서 무슨 비밀이 그렇게 많아? 무슨 첩보 영화 찍어?

챈이 개츠비 쪽으로 기댄다.

챈:　　　무슨 구린 일이 있지 않고서야.

개츠비, 챈을 향해 고개를 끄덕이고 애슐리에게 그 말을 그대로 반복한다.

개츠비:　　무슨 구린 일이 있지 않고서야.

립쉬츠 빌딩
유리 사이로 보이는 통화하는 애슐리

애슐리:　　나중에 통화해, 끊을게.

애슐리가 전화를 끊는다.

개츠비:　　(화나서) 암튼 이놈의 핸드폰은!

챈:　　　내가 보기엔 완전 수상하네.

- **airsick bag**
  멀미봉투

- **glance**
  힐끗 보다

- **secretive**
  비밀스러운

- **funny business**
  의심스러운 태도(suspicious behavior)
  를 설명하는 대화체 표현

- **dubious**
  수상쩍은

- **to the max**
  최대한도로, 말할 수 없이, 완전히(to the maximum)

I'm kind of involved in a situation.
That's a very situation은 '상황이 아주 심각해' 라는 의미로 사용되고, I'm kind of involved in a situation은 '관련된 상황에 있다' 라는 의미로 '상황이 곤란해' 라는 의미로 쓰인다.

I'm kind of involved in a situation.
상황이 곤란해.

A Rainy
Day in
New York

A Rainy
Day in
New York

A Rainy
Day in
New York

GATSBY: Yeah, it sounds dubious to you because you have a sinister mind.

Chan smiles slightly.

CHAN: You must really love her.

Gatsby looks down and shakes his head.

GATSBY: I do, she's a breath of fresh air. She's charming and delightful. She's pretty. She's sexy somehow, at the same time. She's witty. She sings very nicely, she plays the flute.

CHAN :   Hey, I don't know how to break this to you...but I'm sick of hearing about her, okay?

Chan nods her head, then looks away from Gatsby.

LIPSHITZ'S BUILDING
Through the passenger window to Ashleigh, who sits and looks thoughtfully Ted, visible through the windshield, turns and looks at her.

TED: Was that your boyfriend?

ASHLEIGH: Mm. Gatsby? Yeah. Are you still dizzy?

TED: Nah, I'm okay. What's...Gatsby do?

ASHLEIGH: He goes to Yardley, too. Which he refers to as Forest Lawn University.

TED: Is he a journalist, too?

ASHLEIGH: No. He's not really focused professionally. I think, uh, in his wildest dreams he'd like to be Sky Masterson.

TED: A Broadway bookie?

개츠비: 그야 네가 악의를 품고 보니까 그렇지.

챈이 살짝 웃는다.

챈: 푹 빠져있나 보네.

개츠비는 아래를 보며 고개를 젓는다.

개츠비: 그래, 상큼 그 자체라구. 매력 있지, 사랑스럽지, 예쁘지. 그러면서 섹시하기도 해. 재치도 있고, 노래도 잘하고, 플룻도 연주해.

챈: 이런 말 하기 뭐하지만 더는 못 들어주겠다.

챈은 고개를 끄덕이며 계츠비에서 먼 곳을 본다.

립쉬츠 빌딩
조수석 창문을 통해 애슐리가 보인다. 애슐리는 왼쪽에 앉아서 생각이 깊어보인다. 테드는 오른쪽 앞 유리를 통해 볼 수 있고, 테드는 돌아서 그녀를 본다.

테드: 남자친구예요?

애슐리: 개츠비요? 네. 아직 어지러워요?

테드: 아니, 괜찮아요. 개츠비는 무슨 일 해요?

애슐리: 같이 야들 다녀요. 걘 우리 학교가 포레스트 론 공원묘지 같대요.

테드: 남친도 기자예요?

애슐리: 아뇨. 직업엔 그닥 관심이 없어요. 스카이 매스터슨을 꿈꾸긴 하는 거 같은데.

테드: 뮤지컬 속 도박꾼?

- **sinister mind**
  사악한 마음, 악의

- **charming**
  매력적인, 멋진, 애교있는

- **delightful**
  기분 좋은

- **witty**
  재치있는

- **be sick of**
  지겹다

- **look away**
  시선을 돌리다

- **Nah**
  No의 대화체

- **Forest Lawn**
  포레스트 론 공원묘지
  (LA에 밖에 위치해 있는 거대한 공동묘지. 화려한 정원으로 유명)

- **focus professionally**
  직업 쪽으로 열중하다

- **Sky Materson**
  브로드웨이 뮤지컬 주인공. 도박꾼

- **Bookie**
  'bookmaker'의 은어. 불법 마권업자

I don't know how to break this to you.
break this to you는 '솔직히 말해서(reveal this to you; tell you this truth)'라는 의미이다.

I don't know how to break this to you.
이 사실을 어떻게 말할 지 모르겠다.

ASHLEIGH:	Yeah.
TED:	Ha-ha.

Ashleigh wiggles her hand at Ted.

ASHLEIGH:	He's a little eccentric.
TED:	In what way...eccentric?
ASHLEIGH:	Well... I think it has to do with the fact that he and his mom never really hit it off, you know? Uh, (quick breath) she was always forcing him to read everything and learn piano and...I mean, he is really smart. Yeah, he's one of those students who he doesn't have to study for a test and then he just, you know, aces it.
TED:	Sounds like me.
ASHLEIGH:	To tell you the truth, I'm... Don't tell anybody, but... I think he has a touch of Asperger's.

TYRELL APARTMENT BUILDING
The taxi stops at the curb in front of the apartment building on fifth avenue. Chan enters from the taxi, then walks under the awning in front of the building.

CHAN:	(ducking rain) Whoo!
GATSBY:	Hey, you know what, Chan? I'm gonna get out here...too.

He closes the taxi door. Chan walks toward the door and Gatsby follows her.

GATSBY:	What are you doing now?
CHAN:	Why?

애슐리: 네.

테드: 하하.

애슐리가 테드를 향해 손을 흔든다.

애슐리: 좀 별나요.

테드: 어떤 면에서?

애슐리: 음… 엄마와 사이가 안 좋아서 그런 것 같아
요. (짧은 숨) 어머니께서 늘 뭐든 읽게 하고,
피아노도 억지로 시키고… 아니, 정말 똑똑
하긴 해요. 왜 공부 안 하고도 시험 잘 보는
애들 꼭 있잖아요.

테드: 나랑 비슷하네.

애슐리: 솔직히 말하면… 비밀인데… 아스퍼거 증후
군이 살짝 있는 거 같아요.

타이렐 아파트 빌딩
택시가 아파트 앞 5 번가 커브의 오른쪽에 멈춘다. 챈이 택시에서
부터 등장하고 건물 앞에 있는 차양막의 왼쪽 아래를 걷는다.

챈: (비를 피하며) 우!

개츠비: 챈, 나도 여기서 내릴래.

개츠비가 택시 문을 닫는다. 챈이 문 쪽으로 걸어가고 개츠비가 그
녀를 따라간다.

개츠비: 이제 뭐 해?

챈: 왜?

■ eccentric
괴짜인, 별난, 기이한

■ hit it off with somebody
…와 사이좋게 지내다(=get along well
with somebody)

■ has a touch of
살짝 ~의 기미가 있다.

■ Asperger's
아스퍼거 증후군(발달장애의 일종)

He just aces it.
aces it은 '노력없이 완벽하게 (무엇
을) 해내다' 라는 의미의 속어로, 여기
서는 '완벽한 점수를 받다(i.e., 'gets
aperfect score')는 의미로 사용되었다.

He just aces it.
그는 그냥 시험을 잘 봐.

| GATSBY: | Uh, why? Because I got a little bit of time to kill and I...thought about goin' to the Modern Museum, look at the Weegee exhibit. |
| CHAN: | Oh, I see. You've got nothing better to do, so you want me to keep you company? |

Gatsby steps toward the taxi, then steps back and gestures at Chan.

GATSBY:	You know what? Forget it. I dated your older sister. You always had a little bit of an attitude. Okay, I'm not looking for any trouble.
CHAN:	I've got to check out some paintings at the Met for fashion class, if you want to keep me company.
GATSBY:	(shaking his head) I don't know why you couldn' ta just, uh... Fine. It'll be fun. We can get on each other' s nerves.
CHAN:	All right, let me change.

Chan Leads Gatsby, Camera dollying with them to reveal doorman.

| CHAN: | I'm soaked. Are you hungry? I'd give you an Arizona lunch, but we're all out of beef jerky. |
| GATSBY: | Ahh. |

The doorman holds the door open for them

TYRELL APARTMENT/FOYER
The light turns on in the foyer of the luxurious apartment. Chan enters then walks and puts down her bags at the side of the room. Gatsby enters and strolls, looking around at the apartment.

| GATSBY: | Ohh, boy. This brings back a lotta memories. |

개츠비:	시간이 좀 남아서 모던 미술관에 위지 사진 전 보러 갈까 하는데.
챈:	아, 할일 없으니까 나 보고 놀아달라?

개츠비가 택시 쪽으로 갔다가 다시 돌아와 챈에게 몸짓한다.

개츠비:	아니다, 전 여친 동생에 까칠한 애랑 뭘 하겠다고. 괜히 문제 만들라.
챈:	수업 땜에 미술관에 갈 건데 원하면 같이 가든가.
개츠비:	(머리를 저으며) 글쎄, 그러는 게… 그래, 재밌겠다. 서로 갈구면서.
챈:	일단 옷 좀 갈아입고.

챈이 개츠비를 이끌고 카메라는 서서히 다가가 도어맨을 보여준다.

챈:	나 완전 젖었어. 배고파? 육포가 떨어져서 애리조나식은 못 해주겠네.
개츠비:	아.

문지기가 문을 열고 잡아준다.

타이렐 아파트/포이어
호화로운 아파트의 포이어에서 불이 켜진다. 챈이 걸어 들어가고 그녀의 가방을 방 한쪽에 내려놓는다. 개츠비는 아파트를 둘러보며 들어가서 거닌다.

개츠비:	옛날 생각 난다.

- **time to kill**
  'idle time' – 'time with nothing to do'의 대화체

- **exhibit**
  전시회

- **I see.**
  =I understand.

- **keep company**
  ~의 곁에 있어 주다(친구가 되어 주다)

- **Met**
  Metropolitan Museum of arts의 줄임말

- **get on a person's nerves**
  신경을 건드리다, 신경질나게 하다
  We can get on each other's nerves.
  서로 신경을 건드리다, 신경질나게 하다
  ('We can annoy one another' – said humorously)

- **beef jerky**
  쇠고기 육포 (애리조나 주 출신 애슐리 놀리는 것)

This brings back a lotta memories.
bring back은 '~을 기억나게 하다, 상기시키다'라는 의미이고, lotta는 lot of 나 lots of의 대화체의 발음을 쓴 것이다.

This brings back a lotta memories.
이게 옛날 생각 나게 한다.

Gatsby stops, then Chan stops and turns toward him.

CHAN: Oh, my folks are in East Hampton for the weekend.

Chan takes off her jacket and drops it on top of the bags. Gatsby turns and strolls.

GATSBY: Yeah? How come you didn't go?

CHAN: I've got a date tonight.

GATSBY: You?

Gatsby walks into the living room as Chan turns and walks toward a hallway.

CHAN: Don't be so startled. It turns out I'm desirable.

Chan exits into the hallway. Gatsby walks into the living room, camera dollying in.

GATSBY: Oh, yeah? Who's the unfortunate victim?

CHAN: You wouldn't know him. He's a girlfriend's...

Chan, drying her hair with a towel, reenters then stops and looks at him.

CHAN: ...dermatologist.

GATSBY: that's romantic. Hm. Don't forget to show him those three irregular black moles on your back. I'm...sure they're nothing.

Chan shakes her head. Gatsby walks back into the foyer, camera dollying back with him.

CHAN: I really hope I don't regret not going to the Hamptons. The beach is so pretty in the rain, too.

개츠비가 멈추고, 챈이 멈추어 개츠비 쪽으로 돈다.

챈: 부모님은 주말이라 이스트 햄튼 가셨어.

챈이 외투를 벗어 가방 위에 놓는다. 개츠비는 돌아서 걷는다.

개츠비: 넌 왜 안 갔어?
챈: 오늘 데이트 있거든.
개츠비: 네가?

개츠비가 거실로 들어가고 챈은 돌아 복도 쪽으로 걷는다.

챈: 놀라는 척은. 나도 인기 좀 있거든.

챈이 복도 쪽으로 나간다. 개츠비가 거실로 들어가고 카메라는 서서히 다가간다.

개츠비: 그래? 비운의 희생양은 누구야?

개츠비가 거실에서 멈추고 카메라는 가만히 있는다.

챈: 말해도 몰라. 그는 친구의…

챈이 수건으로 머리를 말리며 다시 등장한다. 그리고 멈춰서 개츠비를 본다.

챈: 피부과 의사.
개츠비: 로맨틱하기도. 등의 까만 점들 꼭 보여줘. 피부암은 아닐 거야.

챈이 고개를 젓는다. 개츠비는 다시 현관 입구로 걸어가고, 카메라는 개츠비와 함께 서서히 다가간다.

챈: 햄튼 안 간 걸 후회하게 되지 않길. 비 오는 바닷가도 예쁘잖아.

- How come ~ ?
  어째서 왜(…인가)?

- hallway
  복도

- desirable
  호감 가는

- unfortunate
  비운의

- victim
  피해자

- dermatologist
  피부과의사

- mole
  (피부 위에 작게 돋은 진갈색) 점

- foyer
  로비, 현관(입구)

**I really hope I don't regret not
going to the Hamptons.**
regret not -ing는 '~하지 않은 것을
후회하다' 라는 의미이다.

I really hope I don't regret not going to the Hamptons.
햄튼에 안 간걸 후회하게 되지 않길 바래.

GATSBY:	Would you have to be with your parents?
CHAN:	So what? I...love my parents. You, you know them. Yeah, they're fun. Don't you have fun with your parents?
GATSBY:	Nah, fun's not the word I would use.
CHAN:	All right, I'll be right back.
GATSBY:	Hey, listen, can I play your piano?
CHAN:	Yeah, go ahead. It's a family heirloom.

Gatsby turns and walks into the living room, camera dollying in to the living room with him. He walks to an antique grand piano, camera panning with him. Camera holds in as Gatsby sits down at the piano, then turns on the lamp beside it.

TYRELL APARTMENT/ CHAN'S BEDROOM
Chan stops at a dresser and rubs her hair with the towel. Gatsby starts to play an old standard on the piano.

Chan opens a drawer on the dresser, then takes out some socks and tosses them on her bed.

TYRELL APARTMENT/LIVING ROOM
Gatsby plays piano.

CHAN: That's pretty.

Gatsby, looking up at Chan, continues to play the piano.

GATSBY: I love a cocktail lounge piano...outside, a drizzle...grey...New York City enveloped in a light mist. Two lovers have a date to meet at six o'clock.

개츠비:	부모님이랑 있고 싶니?
챈:	왜? 난 부모님 좋은데. 알잖아, 유쾌한 분들인 거. 부모님 재미없어?
개츠비:	재미란 말은 안 나오네.
챈:	금방 올게.
개츠비:	피아노 좀 쳐도 돼?
챈:	그래, 우리 가봐야.

개츠비가 돌아서 거실로 걸어 간다. 카메라는 개츠비와 함께 거실로 서서히 걸어 들어간다. 그는 오래된 그랜드 피아노로 다가간다. 카메라는 같이 다가간다. 개츠비가 피아노 앞에 앉고, 옆에 있는 램프를 켠다. 카메라는 멈춰있다.

타이렐 아파트
챈의 침실 – 챈이 옷장앞 에 서서 수건으로 머리를 비빈다. 화면 밖에서는 개츠비가 피아노로 오래된 곡들을 치기 시작한다.

챈이 옷장의 서랍을 열고, 양말을 꺼내서 자신의 침대에 던진다.

타이렐 아파트/ 거실
개츠비는 피아노를 친다.

챈:	좋다.

개츠비가 첸을 올려다보며 계속 피아노를 친다.

개츠비:	난 라운지 바 피아노가 좋아 바깥은 우중충, 비가 보슬보슬, 옅은 안개에 싸인 뉴욕 시내. 여섯 시에 만나기로 한 두 연인.

- have fun
  즐겁다
- heirloom
  (집안의) 가보
- dresser
  옷장
- drawer
  서랍
- toss
  던지다

I'll be right back.
금방 올게.

I'll be right back.
금방 올게.

CHAN: At Grand Central Station. Under the clock, like in the movie.

GATSBY: I love that movie, but...I see it outside

Chan walks idly across the room toward the windows, camera dollying with her.

CHAN: Mm–uh...at the East River? Where the tugboats are on the water. I love tugboats.

GATSBY: Almost. You're in the right ballpark.

Chan continues to walk. Chan stops, then turns back and gestures at Gatsby.

CHAN: I know! I know. Under the clock.

She turns and walks toward a window.

GATSBY: Which clock?

Chan glances back over her shoulder at Gatsby.

CHAN: The Delacorte Clock, where all the animals go around in Central Park.

GATSBY: Ahh. I love it. It's very old movie.

Chan stops at the window and looks out at the falling rain. Camera dollies in as she turns and looks at Gatsby.

CHAN: My mom and I used to watch old movies together all the time. She would study the decor.

Gatsby stops playing the piano. Chan sits down on the window sill.

CHAN: I don't know, they're so fabulously escapist.

챈 : 그랜드센트럴역 시계아래에서, 영화처럼…
개츠비 : 그 영화좋아, 근데… 난 바깥이면 좋겠어.

챈은 방 건너편 창문을 향해 느릿느릿 걸어간다. 카메라는 그녀를
따라 서서히 다가간다.

챈: 이스트 강? 물 위엔 예인선들. 난 예인선이
좋아.
개츠비: 거의, 비슷하게 갔어.

챈이 계속해서 걷는다. 챈이 멈추고, 뒤로 돌아 화면 밖의 개츠비에
게 손짓한다.

챈: 알았다! 알았어, 시계 아래.

챈이 돌아서 창문 쪽으로 걸어간다.

개츠비: 무슨 시계?

챈이 어깨 너머로 화면 밖의 개츠비를 본다.

챈: 델라코트 시계 센트럴 파크의 동물상 돌아
가는…
개츠비: 완전 좋아 옛날 영화 스타일.

챈이 창문에서 멈춰서 내리는 비를 쳐다본다. 챈이 돌아서 화면 밖
의 개츠비를 볼 때 카메라는 서서히 다가간다.

챈: 엄마랑 옛날 영화 자주봤거든. 엄마는 실내
장식 공부하느라…

개츠비가 피아노를 치던 것을 멈춘다. 챈이 창문 틀에 앉는다.

챈: 옛날 영화는 참 현실도피적이지.

- tugboat
  예인선

- décor
  실내장식

- window sill
  창문 틀

- fabulously escapist
  엄청나게 현실도피의

You're in the right ballpark.
ballpark는 '야구장' 이라는 뜻으로 많이
알려졌지만 '거의 정확한 것(one is in
close approximation to the correct
answer)' 이라는 뜻으로도 쓰여, 여기
서는 개츠비가 East River 와 거의 같
은 곳을 상상하고 있다(meaning that
Gatsby is imagining a location very
much like the East River)는 의미로 사
용되었다.

Zoom In

You're in the right ballpark.
거의 비슷해.

GATSBY: In my version, he's waiting...the music plays...and she never comes.

Gatsby looks down wistfully.

GATSBY: Or she's waiting...and he chooses the other woman.

CHAN: Can't they just kiss in the rain? That sounds pretty good to me, even if it is commercial.

GATSBY: Picture yourself.

Chan folds her arms and nods at Gatsby.

CHAN: Okay.

GATSBY: It's one minute to six...you're pacing up and down...raindrops are just startin' to fall ...you're at your Delacorte Clock in Central Park...

Chan smiles slightly and nods her head.

GATSBY: ...expecting your dermatologist!
But he's just diagnosed a carcinoma on his own lip. It's metastasizing as you wait.

Chan shakes her head.

CHAN: All right, will you give me a break? In my version, everything's fine. He...meets me and holds me...kisses me. (soft breath) It's lovely. Nobody needs a biopsy.

개츠비: 내 상상 속엔 남자가 기다리고 있고, 음악이 흐르고있고, 여잔 나타나지 않아.

개츠비가 서글프게 아래를 내려본다.

개츠비: 아님 여잔 기다리고 있는데, 남자가 다른 여자를 택해.
챈: 그냥 빗속에서 키스하면 안 돼? 좀 뻔하지만 좋잖아.
개츠비: 상상해봐.

챈이 팔짱을 끼고 화면 밖의 개츠비에게 고개를 끄덕인다.

챈 : 알겠어.
개츠비: 시간은 여섯 시 1 분 전. 막 떨어지기 시작한 빗방울 아래… 넌 서성이고 있어. 장소는 센트럴 파크의 델라코트 시계 아래.

챈이 살짝 웃으며 고개를 끄덕인다.

개츠비: 기다리고 있는 상대는… 피부과 의사! 하지만 그는 방금 입술에서 암을 발견했고 전이되는 중.

챈이 고개를 젓는다.

챈: 분위기 좀 그만 깨. 내 상상에선 다 잘 돼. 그가 나타나 날 안고 키스한다구. (옅은 숨) 사랑스럽게. 조직검사가 웬 말이야.

- wistfully
  (지난일을) 애석해하는
- even if it is commercial
  뻔하더라도.
- commercial
  상업적인
- Picture yourself.
  상상해봐
- fold one's arms
  팔짱 끼다
- pacing up and down
  위아래로 서성거리는
- diagnose
  진단하다
- carcinoma
  상피성 암, 암종
- metastasize
  전이하다

Will you give me a break?
Will you stop kidding의 대화체 표현으로 '이제 그만 좀 해' 라는 의미이다.

Will you give me a break?
이제 그만 좀 해.

매트로 폴리탄 미술관

Metropolitan Museum of Art

시간 00:42:57 ~ 00:52:48

Lipshitz's building

Looking at the front door of the building as the rain continues to fall. The awing reads: The Albert.

Connie, visible through the glass door, walks to the front door. Connie opens the door and walks out of the building.

TED: Connie!

Connie looks up with surprise as Ted hurries toward her.

TED: Connie!

CONNIE: Ted.

TED: Is this...how you're shopping with Judy in...in Connecticut?

CONNIE: What are you doing here?

Ted gestures at the car.

TED: Oh, I happened to see you out the window...from the car...by sheer chance.

Connie looks at the car, then nods with disbelief.

립쉬츠 빌딩
비가 계속 오고 립쉬츠 건물 밖 차양천막에 The Albert 라고 쓰여
져 있다.
보이는 유리문을 통해 코니가 건물 앞문으로 걸어온다. 코니가 문
을 열고 건물 밖으로 나온다.

테드: 코니!

테드가 서둘러 그쪽으로 올 때 코니는 놀라서 쳐다본다.

테드: 코니!
코니: 테드.
테드: 주디랑 코네티컷에 쇼핑 간다더니.
코니: 여기서 뭐 해?

테드는 차 쪽으로 손짓을 한다.

테드: 차에서 우연히 봤어. 완전 우연히.

코니는 차를 보고 못 믿겠다는 듯 고개를 젓는다.

- **happened to**
  우연히 ~하다

- **sheer chance**
  순전히 우연

- **disbelief**
  불신

CONNIE: (chuckling dubiously) Oh–h–h, really? Well, that's awkward, isn't it?

TED: Awkward? Awkward? You've been sleeping with him for months...haven't you?

CONNIE: Look, we were gonna tell you.

TED: When? When, when, when, when we moved to London?

Connie looks down and shakes her head.

CONNIE: No.

TED: Your dream...that we'd move to London?

CONNIE: Look, it just happened, Ted. We, we both fought it.

TED: (sarcastically) Yeah, I'm sure you fought it. In every hotel room, on every mattress. In the backseat of ...?

CONNIE: You know, this isn't about sex.

TED: It's...always about sex. Everything's about sex. The economy's about sex.

CONNIE: Okay, you know what? I can't have this outburst with you on the street.

TED: You...with my best friend...is such a cliché. I can't believe it.

CONNIE: Don't get down on Larry. He adores you. He identifies with you.

TED: I know. He uses my aftershave...and my wife.

코니: (의심스럽게 웃으며) 그래? 거 참 별일이네.

테드: 별일이야? 바람 피운 지 (벌써) 몇 달은 된 거
　　　　 지?

코니: 말하려던 참이야.

테드: 언제? 영국에 이사 가고?

코니는 아래를 보고 고개를 젓는다.

코니: 아니.

테드: 나랑 런던 가는 게 꿈이라며.

코니: 그렇게 됐어. 둘 다 애썼지만…

테드: (빈정거리며) 애썼겠지. 호텔 방에서, 침대 위
　　　　 에서. 차 뒷자리에서…

코니: 섹스 때문이 아냐.

테드: 아니긴, 모든 건 섹스 때문이야. 경제도 섹
　　　　 스로 돌아가는데.

코니: 암튼 길에서 이러고 싶지 않아.

테드: 내 절친과 바람이라니 너무 뻔하지 않아? 믿
　　　　 을 수가 없어.

코니: 친구 욕하지 마, 당신 좋아하고 자기 자신처
　　　　 럼 생각해.

테드: 그러게, 내 화장품도 쓰고 와이프도 쓰고.

- **sleeping with him**
  i.e., 'having sex with Larry Lipshitz

- **outburst**
  (감정의) 폭발(분출): sudden argument

- **cliché**
  상투적인 문구[생각]

- **identifies with**
  ~와 동일시 하다

Don't get down on Larry.
get down on은 '…을 비난하다' 라는 뜻
으로 judge harshly의미로 사용된다.

Don't get down on Larry.
래리 비난하지마.

Connie points at Ashleigh.

CONNIE: Who is she?

ASHLEIGH: (calling from across the street) Ted! Is everything okay?

Ted looks at Ashleigh, Then gestures at Connie.

TED: Oh, what's that got to do with anything?

CONNIE: Who is she?

Ashleigh has gotten out of the car and is walking across the street.

TED: (to Ashleigh) No, no...everything's fine. Stay there, Ashleigh. Keep dry.

Ashleigh hurries across the street and onto the sidewalk. She looks at Connie.

ASHLEIGH: (to Connie) Um...I'm with the, uh, Yardley Argus.

CONNIE: The what?

ASHLEIGH: The Yardley Argus.

TED: She's a reporter doing a piece on Rollie.

Connie glares at Ted as Ashleigh takes out her notebook.

CONNIE: On Rollie? Well, then what is she doing with you following me?

TED: Don't try and turn this around.

CONNIE: (chuckling) I'm not turning–

TED: Don't try and turn this around– you've been caught.

CONNIE: (inhales after laughing)

TED: You were caught.

코니는 애슐리를 가리킨다.

코니: 저 여잔 누구야?

애슐리: (길건너서 부르며) 테드! 괜찮은 거예요?

테드는 애슐리를 보고, 코니에게 손짓을 한다.

테드: 지금 그게 문제야?

코니: 누구냐구?

애슐리가 차에서 내려 길을 건너고 있다.

테드: (애슐리에게) 괜찮아요, 차에 있어요. 젖지 말
고.

애슐리는 서둘러 길을 건너 보도로 왔다. 그녀는 코니를 쳐다본다.

애슐리: (코니에게) 야들리 아거스에서 나왔어요.

코니: 어디요?

애슐리: 야들리 아거스요.

테드: 롤리 취재하는 기자야.

코니느 테드를 쏘아보고 애슐리는 노트를 꺼낸다

코니: 롤리? 근데 왜 당신이랑 날 미행해?

테드: 말 돌리지 마.

코니: (웃으며) 말 돌리긴…

테드: 말 돌리지 말라구. 당신 딱 걸렸어.

코니: (웃고 숨을 내쉰다)

테드: 당신 딱 걸렸어.

■ Stay there
거기 있어.

■ be caught
들키다, 걸리다: exposed in the act

Don't try and turn this around.
turn around는 '방향을 바꾸다(reverse
the point of the argument)로 여기서
는 '너에 대해서 말고 나에 대해서 말해'
라는 의미로 사용되었다.

Don't try and turn this around.

말 돌리지 마.

Connie points back accusingly at Ted. Ashleigh starts to make notes in her notebook.

CONNIE: When? You, you who make a fool of yourself over every young ambitious starlet and, and model and?

TED: No, whoa, whoa, what are you talking about? What are you talking about? You've been having an affair with Larry Lipshitz.

CONNIE: Yeah, and you were spying on me with who... your fifteen-year-old concubine?

TED: She's a journalist.

ASHLEIGH: Tsk, oh, I'm twenty-one.

TED: She's twenty-one.

CONNIE: Oh, she's twenty-one.

TED: She's a journalist.

Ashleigh starts to reach into her purse.

ASHLEIGH: I have proof of age, actually.

TED: (to Ashleigh) No, you don't need to show?

CONNIE: (to Ashleigh) Oh, really?

TED: You don't need to do that.

ASHLEIGH: This always happens in bars.

Connie looks mockingly at Ted.

TED: You've been caught.

Connie gestures at Ashleigh, who holds up her driver's license.

코니는 테드에게 비난하든 손가락질 한다. 애슐리는 노트에 적기 시작한다.

코니:	그러는 당신은 신인 여배우 모델마다 껄떡대잖아.
테드:	무슨 소리야. 립쉬츠와 바람피운 주제에.
코니:	당신은 15 살짜리 첩이랑 날 미행했고.
테드:	기자라니까.
애슐리:	저 21 살이에요.
테드:	21 살이야.
코니:	21 살이셔?
테드:	기자이고.

애슐리는 가방으로 손을 넣는다.

애슐리:	신분증 있어요.
테드:	(애슐리에게) 그럴 필요 없어요.
코니:	(애슐리에게) 오 정말?
테드:	그럴 필요 없어요.
애슐리:	바에서도 늘 걸려요.

코니는 테드를 조롱하듯이 쳐다본다.

테드:	당신은 걸렸다구.

코니는 애슐리에게 손짓을 하고 애슐리는 그녀의 운전면허증을 집어 든다.

- accusingly
  비난하듯

- make a fool of yourself
  바보 같은 짓을 하다(웃음거리가 되다)
  act foolishly and stupidly

- starlet
  신인 여배우

- concubine
  (과거 일부 사회에서 존재하던) 첩

I have proof of age.
of age는 성년의(of my age' : 'of how old I am)라는 뜻으로, I have proof of age는 '성년의 증거, 즉 신분증이 있다'라는 의미이다.

I have proof of age.
신분증 있어요.

CONNIE:	As long as you're a reporter, I would like to, uh, make a press release about my husband.
TED:	Oh, really?
CONNIE:	Yeah.

Ashleigh hurriedly puts away her license.

ASHLEIGH:	Oh, can I, uh, write this down?
CONNIE:	Sure. Go ahead.
TED:	Ashleigh, please.

As Ashleigh opens her notebook, Connie points accusingly at Ted.

CONNIE:	Ask him how many times he has been unfaithful to me.
TED:	No, you're demented. (to Ashleigh) She's demented. (to Connie) You're demented.

Ashleigh writes in her notebook.

CONNIE:	His secretary.
TED:	Wrong.
CONNIE:	The actresses.
TED:	Wrong.
CONNIE:	Oh! The poetess?
TED:	(chuckling) The poetess?

Ashleigh looks at Ted.

ASHLEIGH:	(to Ted) Uh, were all these women for pleasure? Or were you researching a project?

코니:	기자라니 잘됐네. 남편 기사 좀 내보내죠.
테드:	정말?
코니:	그래.

애슐리는 그녀의 운전면허증을 급히 넣는다.

애슐리:	그럼 적을까요?
코니:	네, 그래요.
테드:	애슐리, 제발.

애슐리가 그녀의 노트를 열었을 때, 코니는 테드를 비난하듯 손가락질한다.

코니:	날 몇 번이나 속였는지 물어봐요.
테드:	제정신이 아녜요. (애슐리에게) 제정신이 아냐.
	(코니에게) 제정신이 아냐.

애슐리는 노트에 적는다.

코니:	비서.
테드:	아니.
코니:	배우들.
테드:	아니.
코니:	아! 여류시인도 있었지.
테드:	(웃으며) 여류시인?

애슐리는 테드를 쳐다본다.

애슐리:	(테드에게) 재미 삼아서였나요. 아님 조사차 그랬나요?

- **press release**
  보도자료

- **accusingly**
  비난하듯

- **unfaithful**
  외도를 하는, 바람을 피우는

- **dement**
  미치게 하다

Can I write this down?
write down은 '적다, 기록하다 ' 라는 의미로 write + 대명사(this)+ down은 가능해도 write down + 대명사(this)로 쓰지 않는다.

Zoom In

Can I write this down?
적을까요?

Ted gestures toward the street.

TED: (calling out) Taxi!
                She–Stop filling her head with lies.

Ted takes Ashleigh's pen and notebook away from her

TED: Ashleigh, come here.

A taxi stops on the street. Ted writes in the notebook.

TED: Take this... address to the studio, okay? Find
                Rollie.

Ted hands the notebook and pen back to Ashleigh .

TED: Come on. Find Rollie.

Ted pulls Ashleigh toward the taxi.

ASHLEIGH: Oh, I–I–I, I don't know my way around New
                York.

A Taxi passenger gets out of the taxi. Ted and Ashleigh step toward the taxi.

TED: It's okay. Tell the cab driver. Find Rollie.

Connie reenters, then looks at Ashleigh.

CONNIE: Ask him if he ever slept with Samantha Leroy.
TED: (to Connie) Stop.
ASHLEIGH: You know, the Argus is not a tabloid.
CONNIE: Yeah, there are no papers that are not tabloids.

테드는 거리쪽으로 손짓을 한다.

테드:　(소리지르며) **택시!**
　　　　거짓말 그만해.

테드는 애슐리의 펜을 잡고 노트도 애슐리에게서 가져온다.

테드:　　**애슐리, 이리 와요.**

택시는 멈추었다. 테드는 노트에 쓴다.

테드:　　**촬영장 주소예요. 롤리를 찾아요, 알았죠?**

테드는 노트와 펜을 다시 애슐리에게 건네준다.

테드:　　**롤리를 찾아요.**

테드는 애슐리를 택시쪽으로 이끈다.

애슐리:　　**저 뉴욕 잘 모르는데.**

택시에서 승객이 내린다. 테드와 애슐리는 택시쪽으로 다가간다.

테드:　　**괜찮아요. 기사한테 줘요.**

코니는 다시 와서 애슐리에게 묻는다.

코니:　　**사만사 리로이와 잤는지 물어봐요.**
테드:　　(코니에게) **그만해.**
애슐리:　　**저희 신문은 가십 신문이 아녜요.**
코니:　　**요즘 안 그런 신문이 어딨어.**

■ get out of
　내리다

■ tabloid
　타블로이드 신문(때로 흥미위주의 선정적인
　내용을 다룸)

Stop filling her head with lies.
Stop filling her head with lies.
'거짓말 그만해' 라는 뜻으로, 여기에
서는 'Stop telling all these lies to
Ashleigh' 의 의미로 쓰였다.

Stop filling her head with lies.
거짓말 그만해.

Ashleigh sits down in the back of the taxi, then Ted gestures at her.

TED: (to Ashleigh) Encourage him about the movie so he doesn't mangle it and ruin it, okay?
Please, don't print any of this!

ASHLEIGH: Oh, don't worry. We always protect everybody.

TED: I'm, I'm sure.

Ted closes the taxi door. Ted hurries to Connie, walking down the sidewalk.

TED: Connie! Connie!

METROPOLITAN MUSEUM OF ART
The rain continues to fall and people walk up and down the front steps of the museum. Chan and Gatsby walk up the steps. Chan holds an umbrella over their heads.

GATSBY: You know, the first time I kissed your sister was in this museum.

CHAN: I know, she told me. She said that you were looking at a Hieronymus Bosch and it made you feel romantic, so then you kissed her. That's when she knew your shrink wasn't helping you.

GATSBY: Yeah, well, don't tell me she thought the kiss was a four.

CHAN: If she quoted you a figure higher, I'd have her audited.

Chan hands the umbrella to Gatsby. Chan exits into the museum, then Gatsby closes the umbrella.

애슐리는 택시 뒷 자석에 앉고, 테드는 그녀에게 손짓을 한다.

테드: (애슐리에게) 영화 칭찬해줘요. 다 망쳐버리지
않게.
방금 얘긴 절대 싣지 말고.

애슐리: 걱정 마세요, 지켜드릴게요.

테드: 그래요.

테드는 택시문을 닫는다. 테드는 보도로 내려가 코니에게 서둘러
간다.

테드: 코니! 코니.

메트로 폴리탄 박물관
비가 계속 오고 사람들이 박물관의 앞 계단을 오르고 내린다.
챈과 개츠비는 계단위로 올라간다. 챈은 그들의 머리위로 우산을
들고 있다.

개츠비: 여기서 네 언니와 첫 키스 했었는데.

챈: 들었어. 히에루니무스 보스 그림 볼 때 로맨
틱해져서는 키스했다며. 그때 오빠 상담이
소용없다는 걸 알았대.

개츠비: 설마 그 키스도 4점이었다고 하진 않았겠
지?

챈: 더 높게 매겼으면 내가 감사팀 보냈을걸.

챈은 우산을 개츠비에게 준다. 챈은 박물관으로 들어가고 개츠비는
우산을 접는다.

- **mangle**
  심하게 훼손하다

- **shrink**
  상담

- **audit**
  회계를 감사하다

- **hand**
  건네주다.

It made you feel romantic.
make는 사역동사로 '~를 …하게 하다'
라는 의미로 make you feel romantic
은 '너를 낭만적으로 느끼게 만든다' 라
는 의미이다.

It made you feel romantic.
그건 너를 로맨틱하게 했어.

METROPOLITAN MUSEUM OF ART.
Looking down a gallery where John Singer Sargent paintings are on display along the walls. Chan and Gatsby enter through a doorway and walk toward the paintings on a wall. Camera tilts up on Sargent's 1884 painting "Madame X", a full-length portrait of a socialite in a black dress.

CHAN: There's something charming about that elegance.

Gatsby and Chan stand in the middle of the gallery and look at the painting of "Madame X"

GATSBY: My mother would have liked Sargent to have painted her in just that pose.

A short time later, another gallery Auguste renoir's 1888 painting, "The daughters of catulle mendes" is displayed on the wall. The picture shows the three daughters wearing dresses and learning piano and violin.

CHAN: They dressed so beautifully in Paris back then.
GATSBY: I could see movin' to Paris.
CHAN: Mm, I never really asked you—what are your future plans, Gatsby?

People are walking around in the other galleries. Gatsby follows Chan.

GATSBY: I don't know, I'm floundering.
CHAN: What does that mean?
GATSBY: I don't know what I want to be. I just...know what I don't want to be. Is that terrible?

Chan stops and turns back to Gatsby.

CHAN: So you've got no game plan.

메트로 폴리탄 막물관

쥰 싱어 사전트 그림이 전시되어 있는 갤러리를 따라간다. 챈과 개
츠비는 복도를 통해 벽에 그림들 쪽으로 걸어간다. 카메라는 검정
드레스를 입고 있는 사교계 명사의 전신 초상화인 사전트 1884 그
림 "마담 엑스" 의 그림을 비춘다.

개츠비: 우아하면서 참 매력 있어.

개츠비와 챈은 갤러리 중간에 서서 마담엑스의 그림을 보고있다.

개츠비: 우리 엄만 저 포즈만으로도 사전트를 좋아
했을 거야.

잠시 후에 또 다른 갤러리 어거스트 르노와르 1888 그림, " 꼬들리
에 멘데스의 딸들"이 전시되어 있다. 그림은 세 명의 딸들이 드레스
를 입고 피아노와 바이올린을 배우고 있다.

챈: 저 때 파리에선 옷을 참 예쁘게 입었어.
개츠비: 파리에 가서 살고 싶다.
챈: 오빠 꿈이 뭔지 물어본 적이 없네.

사람들은 다른 갤러리 주변을 걷는다. 개츠비는 챈을 따라간다.

개츠비: 모르겠어. 허우적대는 중이야.
챈: 무슨 뜻이야?
개츠비: 뭐가 되고 싶은진 모르겠고 되기 싫은 것만
알겠어.

챈은 멈추고 개츠비에게 몸을 돌린다.

챈: 아직 전략이 없는 거네.

- socialite
  사교계 명사

- flounder
  (어쩔 줄 몰라서) 허둥대다

You've got no game plan.
game plan은 '전략(작전): strategy for
achieving an objective' 의미이다.

You've got no game plan.
전략이 없는 거네.

GATSBY: Well, I know I don't want to be a, a–a test pilot…
…or a clergyman or a proctologist, so I ruled those out.

Gatsby walks. Chan glances over his shoulder at Gatsby and nods at him.

CHAN: I get it. You don't fit in.
That's why I always had a crush on you when you dated Amy.

GATSBY: You had a crush on me?

CHAN: I did. Isn't that weird?
I don't know, maybe it's because you took her to do oddball things–like you took her to those divey piano bars where no one else ever took her.

GATSBY: I did take her to her first crap game.

CHAN: I know, and I loved that. I loved hearing every detail. I was hoping she would get serious with you, because… you were not like all the other idiots she dated.
I thought you were a special idiot.

Chan walks and stops to look at another painting.

GATSBY: Well, I'm glad I impressed you, Chan.

CHAN: I remember Amy came home and she told me that you took her to the boat basin in Central Park…and made love to her.

GATSBY: She told you about that?

CHAN: Every moist detail.

GATSBY: Well, now I'm embarrassed.

개츠비:	시험비행 조종사는 싫어.
	성직자나 항문과 의사도 싫으니까 그것들은 빼고.

개츠비는 걸어가고 챈은 개츠비 어깨 넘어로 보고 고개를 끄덕인다.

챈:	틀에 박힌 건 싫은 거네.
	그래서 언니랑 만날 때 내가 반했었지.
개츠비:	나한테 반했었어?
챈:	응, 웃기지?
	언니를 이상한 데에 데리고 다녀서 그랬나봐. 나른한 피아노 재즈바에 처음으로 데려가고.
개츠비:	주사위 도박장에도 데려 갔었지.
챈:	알아, 너무 좋았어. 다 자세히 들었지. 오빠랑 잘되길 바랐는데 딴 놈들은 다 멍청이 같아서.
	오빠 좀 특별한 멍청이 같았거든.

챈을 걸어가고 또 다른 그림을 보려고 멈춘다.

개츠비:	특별하게 보였다니 기쁘네.
챈:	이 얘기도 기억난다. 센트럴 파크 호수 정박지에서 사랑을 나눈 거.
개츠비:	그 얘기도 했어?
챈:	축축한 디테일까지.
개츠비:	이건 좀 민망하다.

- **proctologist**
  항문과 의사

- **rule out**
  제외하다

- **I get it**
  이해해
  i.e., 'I understand

- **oddball**
  괴짜: strange

- **divey**
  나른한
  shabby or sleazy

- **crap game**
  주사위 도박장

- **embarrassed**
  민망한, 쑥스러운

That's why I always had a crush on you.
crush는 '반함, 심취(brief but intense infatuation)' 라는 의미로 have a crush on는 '~에게 홀딱 반하다' 라는 의미이다.

Zoom In

That's why I always had a crush on you.
그게 내가 너에게 반했던 이유야.

CHAN: Don't be. That night she gave you a six.

GATSBY: (whispering in frustration) She gave me a six. Amy.

CHAN: With an asterisk. She said you were a little...tense...

Gatsby walks into another gallery. Chan is standing and smiling at him.

GATSBY: Yeah, well, Central Park can be a little dangerous at two A.M.

CHAN: ...but very romantic. And then it started to rain.

GATSBY: Yeah, that was the best part. Her, her hair got wet, her... clothes started to cling to her body.

CHAN: She started sneezing.

GATSBY: Yeah, I don't really remember that part. Tsk.

Chan sits down on a beach in the middle of the gallery. Gatsby sits down on the bench.

GATSBY: Now that I think of it, Chan, you, you...you always were around...givin' me the fish-eye.

Chan looks at Gatsby with disbelief.

CHAN: You're just realizing this now?

GATSBY: Mm-hm.

CHAN: "Mm-hm?" That's all you got to say? You didn't...think I was cute or attractive, anything?

GATSBY: Yeah, you seemed fine.

CHAN: (sarcastically) You...mean I had no physical deformities. I didn't have acromegaly...or a hunchback.

챈: 아냐, 그건 6점 줬는걸.

개츠비: (좌절하며 속삭이며) 6점? 에이미.

챈: 약간 긴장해서였을 거라는 부연설명은 있었어.

개츠비는 또 다른 갤러리 쪽으로 걸어간다. 챈은 그를 서서 보고 웃는다.

개츠비: 그야 새벽 2시 센트럴 파크는 위험할 수 있으니까.

챈: 하지만 아주 로맨틱했대. 그러다 비가 왔고

개츠비: 맞아, 그때가 최고였지. 에이미의 머리가 젖고 옷이 젖어 달라붙고.

챈: 재채기를 시작했지.

개츠비: 그건 잘 기억 안 나네.

챈은 갤러리 중앙 벤치에 앉는다. 개츠비도 벤치에 앉는다.

개츠비: 이제 와 생각해보니 넌 늘 주변에 있었어. 멍한 눈으로.

챈은 못믿는다는 눈으로 개츠비를 쳐다본다.

챈: 그걸 이제 알았어?

개츠비: 음…

챈: 음… 그게 다야? 내가 귀엽거나 매력적이진 않았구?

개츠비: 괜찮아 보였어.

챈: (비꼬는 투로) 신체적 결함은 없어 보였다? 말단 비대증이나 꼽추는 아니었다는?

- **cling to**
  ~에 달라붙다
- **sneeze**
  재채기하다
- **disbelief**
  불신감
- **sarcastically**
  비꼬는 투로, 풍자적으로
- **deformity**
  기형
- **acromegaly**
  (머리·손·발이 비대해지는) 말단 비대증
- **hunchback**
  곱사등이, 꼽추

You always were around giving me the fish-eye.
fish-eye는 (대화체 표현으로)멍한 눈으로(suspicious or unfriendly look)라는 의미이다.

 **You always were around giving me the fish-eye.**
너는 늘 멍한 눈으로 내 주변에 있었어.

GATSBY: You know what, Chan...I wasn't really paying attention, 'cause I was a little tense in front of your parents and, I, I mean, Amy, Amy would make her entrance lookin' like goddamn Miss America.

CHAN: I'm sure Ashleigh's a beauty queen type.

GATSBY: (snorting) Sh–, she is...ac–, well, she was an actual first–place winner at her high school in Tucson.

CHAN: Four–H, right?

GATSBY: Yeah. How'd you, how'd you guess?

CHAN: Ink it in. Let's get outta here.

She stands up.

A short time later, looking down a gallery of ancient Egyptian sculptures, which show the female pharaoh Hatshepsut and her retinue. Gatsby and Chan enter through a door.

GATSBY: Look at these crazy Egyptians. They put all their money on an afterlife.

CHAN: Listen, Gatsby. Let me tell you, you only live once. But once is enough if you find the right person.

GATSBY: Hey, listen, you think she's givin' me the runaround today? I'm, uh...yeah, I'm strugglin' to keep my spirits up.

CHAN: Boy, you really are hooked on her, aren't you?

개츠비: 사실 잘 못 봤어 너희 부모님 앞이라 긴장했고 . 미스 아메리카 같은 에이미 보느라.

챈: 애슐리도 미인대회 1 등 같겠지?

개츠비: (코웃음치며) 실제로 투손에서 학교 미인대회 1 등이었어.

챈: 농촌 청소년 후원 대회?

개츠비: 응, 어떻게 알았어?

챈: 뻔하지, 나가자.

챈은 일어난다.

잠시 후에, 고대이집트의 갤러리를 쳐다 보는데 그것은 여왕 파라오와 그녀의 수행원들이다. 개츠비와 챈은 복도를 통해 들어간다.

개츠비: 미친 이집트인들. 사후세계에 다 쏟아 붓다니.

챈: 개츠비, 인생은 한 번뿐 이라지만 운명적 상대를 만나면 한 번으로 충분해.

개츠비: 걔 지금 나 놔두고 딴짓하는 걸까? 자꾸 그 생각만 나.

챈: 세상에, 진짜 푹 빠졌네.

- snorting
  코웃음치는

- Four- H
  농촌 청소년 후원대회

- ink st in
  (연필이 아니라) 펜으로 덧쓰다(누가 봐도 명확한 것을 말할 때 '뻔하다'는 의미로 사용)

- retinue
  (중요 인물의) 수행원들, 수행단.

- runaround
  속임수
  deceiving or distracting me'

- hooked on
  ~에 중독되어 있는, 빠져있는

I'm strugglin' to keep my spirits up.
keep one's spirits up은 정신을 바짝 차리다(to maintain an optimistic, upbeat attitude)는 의미이다.

om In

I'm strugglin' to keep my spirits up.
정신을 차리려고 안간힘을 쓰고 있다.

They walk out.
A short time, later, Chan and Gatsby stroll through another gallery featuring a large Egyptian tomb. Museum visitors are walking around the busy gallery.
Gatsby walks past the end of a wall at the front of the tomb, then sees aunt Grace and uncle Tyler. He immediately ducks back behind the wall.

GATSBY: Oh, my God!

Chan stops. Aunt Grace and uncle Henry are standing at the side of the gallery, looking at some Egyptian potter.

GATSBY: That's my aunt and uncle. They're here for my mother's party.
CHAN: What party?

Gatsby gestures frantically at Chan.

GATSBY: (inhales in panic) They're here for my mother, they, my mother's party tonight! They're gonna tell her I'm here!
CHAN: Okay.
GATSBY: I can't discuss this, I've gotta hide. I've, I, I, uh?
CHAN: Why don't you duck into the mummy case? I'll get some white tape.

Gatsby dashes into the tomb. He hides in a nook.
Aunt Grace and uncle Tyler walk to the entrance to the tomb.
Gatsby, hiding behind a wall in one of the many chambers in the tomb, peeks toward the tomb entrance. His cell phone rings and he quickly answers it.

GATSBY: (into cell phone) Hello?

그들은 걸어 나간다.
잠시 후에 챈과 개츠비는 커다란 이집트 무덤을 특징으로 하는 또
다른 갤러리 쪽으로 걸어간다. 박물관 방문객들은 바쁜 갤러리 주
변을 걸어가고 있다.

개츠비는 무덤 앞에 벽 쪽을 지나 걸어간다. 그때 바로 그레이스 이
모와 삼촌 타일러를 본다. 그는 바로 벽 뒤에 숨는다.

개츠비: 어떡해!

챈은 멈춘다. 그레이스 이모와 헨리 삼촌이 몇몇 이집트 도자기를
보면서 갤러리 측면에 서있다.

개츠비: 우리 숙모랑 삼촌이야. 엄마 파티 땜에 오셨
나 봐.

챈: 무슨 파티?

개츠비는 극도로 흥분하여 챈을 보고 손짓을 한다.

개츠비: (허둥지둥하며 숨을 들이 쉬며)그들은 우리 엄마를
위해 여기 온 거야, 오늘 저녁 파티, 그들은
내가 여기 있다고 말할거야.

챈: 응.

개츠비: 이걸 토론할 수 없어, 숨어야 돼.

챈: 미라 관에 숨어, 내가 흰 붕대 가져올게.

개츠비는 무덤으로 달려간다. 그는 구석에 숨는다.
그레이스 이모와 헨리 삼촌이 무덤의 입구쪽으로 걸어간다. 무덤의
많은 방중에 하나에 숨어서 개츠비는 무덤 입구쪽을 힐끗 본다. 그
의 휴대폰이 울려서 빠르게 그것을 잡는다.

개츠비: (전화기에 대고) 여보세요?

- **pottery**
  도자기

- **frantically**
  극도로 흥분하여

- **panic**
  (크게 우려하여) 허둥지둥함

- **nook**
  (아늑하고 조용한) 곳(구석)

**Why don't you duck into the
mummy case?**
Why don't you~?는 '~하는게 어때' 라
는 제안의 뜻으로 How/what about ~?
과 같은 의미로 사용된다. duck in은 '숨
다(quickly enter)' 의 뜻이다.

Z om In

Why don't you duck into the mummy case?

미라관에 숨지 그래?

Ashleigh, sitting in the back of the taxi as it moves toward Queens, talks into her cell phone.

ASHLEIGH: (into cell phone) Gatsby! Yeah, I finally got alone. Um, where are you?

GATSBY: (into cell phone) Let me put it this way. Have you heard o' King Tut?

Ashleigh, reacts with confusion as she talks into her cell phone.

ASHLEIGH: (into cell phone) You're where? Wait, what are you doing?

Gatsby hurries behind another wall in the tomb.
Aunt Grace and uncle Tyler, who walk down another corridor in the tomb. Aunt Grace gestures at the walls.

ASHLEIGH: (into cell phone) Hello? Gatsby, hello?

Uncle Tyler and aunt Grace enter through a doorway and Gatsby enters through another doorway in the tomb. Gatsby spins around, trying to find an escape.

UNCLE TYLER: Gatsby!

GATSBY: Goddamn it.

Gatsby turns to face his aunt and uncle and stops.

UNCLE TYLER: Gatsby, what a surprise! Wha—

AUNT GRACE: I was about to call your mother.

KAUFMAN ASTORIA STUDIOS
The taxi moves through the front gate of the film studio in Queens. A guard steps out of a guard booth and steps toward the taxi.

애슐리는 퀸즈로 가면서 택시 뒤에서 그녀의 폰으로 통화한다.

애슐리: (전화기에 대고) **개츠비! 드디어 혼자야. 어디야?**

개츠비: (전화기에 대고) **힌트로 알려줄게. 투탕카멘 알지?**

애슐리는 통화를 하면서 당황해서 반응한다.

애슐리: (전화기에 대고) **어디라고? 뭐 해?**

개츠비는 또 다른 무덤 뒤로 서둘러서 숨는다
그레이스 이모와 헨리 삼촌은 무덤에 또다른 복도로 걸어간다. 그레이스 이모는 벽에 손짓을 한다

애슐리: (전화기에 대고) **여보세요? 개츠비!**

그레이스 이모와 헨리 삼촌은 복도로 들어가고, 개츠비는 또 다른 복도를 통해서 들어간다. 개츠비는 탈출구를 찾으려고 애쓰면서, 주변을 돈다

타일러 삼촌: 개츠비!

개츠비: 이런.

개츠비는 이모와 삼촌 쪽으로 고개를 돌리고 멈춘다.

타일러 삼촌: 이게 웬일이니!

그레이스 이모: 네 엄마한테 전화하려던 참인데.

카우프만 아스토리아 스튜디오 앞
택시가 퀸즈 영화 스튜디오 앞문으로 이동한다. 경비원이 부스에서 나와서 택시 쪽으로 간다.

- **with confusion**
  당황해서

- **spins around**
  주변을 돌다

- **be about to**
  막 ～하려고 하다

Let me put it this way.
put은 '표현하다, 말하다'라는 의미이고, let me 동사원형은 '내가 ～할게'라는 뜻으로 사용된다.

om In

Let me put it this way.
이런식으로 알려 줄게.

FILM STUDIO BUILDING/ CORRIDOR

A studio guard sits in a chair against a wall. Some people are sitting and walking in a corridor, which has a wall lined with photographs from classic movies. Ashleigh enters and walks toward the studio guard.

STUDIO GUARD: Hi. Uh, can I help you?

ASHLEIGH: I'm looking for Roland Pollard.

STUDIO GUARD: Roland Pollard. Right, right. He was here earlier. Uh, I'm not sure if he's still back there.

METROPOLITAN MUSEUM OF ART

Gatsby, walking toward the front of the tomb, talks into his cell phone. Aunt Grace and uncle Tyler follow him and Chan stands in front of the wall, checking messages on her cell phone.

GATSBY: (into cell phone) Mom, it was all planned, okay? Ashleigh and I wanted to surprise you tonight.

Gatsby walks out of the tomb. Aunt Grace and uncle Tyler continue to follow him.

GATSBY: (into cell phone) I happened to run into Uncle Tyler and Aunt Grace, okay? But don't worry, we're gonna be there for dinner. It's gonna be a great time. I just, I thought it would be a, a, a fun...surprise.

Chan puts away her cell phone and starts to follow the group. Aunt Grace looks at him.

AUNT GRAC: Oh, and we spoiled your surprise.

STUDIO BUILDING/ SOUNDSTAGE

Ashleigh walks down a corridor toward a soundstage.

ASHLEIGH: (calling out) Mister Pollard?

필름 스튜디오/건물 복도
스튜디오 안내원이 벽에 기대어 의자에 앉아있고, 몇몇 사람들이 복도에 앉아있고 걸어가고 벽에는 클래식 영화사진들이 일렬로 걸려있다. 애슐리는 들어와 스튜디오 안내원에게 걸어간다.

스튜디오 안내원: 안녕하세요. 어떻게 오셨죠?

애슐리: 롤란 폴라드 감독님을 찾는데요.

스튜디오 안내원: 아, 아까 계셨는데 지금은 모르겠네요.

메트로폴리탄 박물관
개츠비는 무덤앞쪽으로 걸어가고 휴대폰 통화를 한다. 그레이스 고모와 타일러 삼촌은 그를 따라가고 챈은 그녀의 폰에 메시지를 확인하면서 벽 앞에 서있다.

개츠비: (전화기에 대고) 엄마, 가려고 했어요. 애슐리랑 깜짝 등장하려고.

개츠비는 무덤에서 나온다. 그레이스 고모와 타일러 삼촌은 그를 계속 따라간다.

개츠비: (전화기에 대고) 타일러 삼촌과 숙모를 우연히 만났구요. 걱정 마세요. 저녁 때 좋은 시간 갖자구요. 갑자기 나타나도 재밌을 거 같았어요.

챈은 그녀의 폰을 치우고 그들을 따라가기 시작한다. 그레이스 고모는 개츠비를 쳐다본다.

그레이스 고모: 우리가 그 계획을 망쳤네.

스튜디오 빌딩/ 방음스튜디오
애슐리는 방음 스튜디오 쪽의 복도로 걸어간다.

애슐리: (소리를 치며) 폴라드 감독님?

- **look for**
  ~을 찾다
- **spoil**
  망치다
- **corridor**
  복도
- **sound stage**
  사운드스테이지(영화 등의 사운드 필름을 제작하는 방음 스튜디오)

I happened to run into him.
happen to는 '(우연히) ~에게 일어나다' 라는 뜻이고, run into는 우연히 만나다(accidentally meet)는 뜻이다.

I happened to run into him.
그를 우연히 마주쳤다.

A Rainy
Day in
New York

A Rainy
Day in
New York

A Rainy
Day in
New York

ASHLEIGH: (calling out) Rollie?

Francisco Vega, a handsome latin movie star, walks away from a backdrop of an ocean. Vega is wearing a zorro-style ourfit with a mask , which makes him unrecognizable. He looks at Ashleigh.

VEGA: Hello. Can I help you?

Ashleigh looks at Vega.

ASHLEIGH: Have you seen Mister Pollard?
VEGA: Ah, Rollie's gone. He left an hour ago.
ASHLEIGH: Oh. Well, did he seem okay?

Vega, standing and working to take off the mask, gestures at Ashleigh.

VEGA: Well, to (exhales) ...to be honest, he...he, he seemed a little drunk to me.

He pulls off the mask, revealing his face.

VEGA: Are you two friends?

Ashleigh, now recognizing him, looks at Vega with shock.

ASHLEIGH: Oh, my God. You're Francisco Vega.
VEGA: Is that good or bad?
ASHLEIGH: If my roommate was here, (amazed breath) ...she'd hemorrhage.
(exhales and inhales nervously) I mea–, I...I mean, she thinks you're the greatest thing to come along since the morning-after pill.

애슐리: (소리를 치며) **롤리?**

잘 생긴 라틴계 영화스타가 바다 배경의 무대에서 걸어오고 있다. 베가는 조로스타일의 의상을 입고 마스크를 쓰고 있었고, 그것이 그인지 알아 볼 수 없게한다. 그는 애슐리를 쳐다본다.

베가: 누구 찾으세요?

애슐리는 베가를 쳐다본다.

애슐리: 폴라드 감독님 보셨어요?
베가: 롤리는 갔어요. 1시간 전쯤.
애슐리: 괜찮아 보이던가요?

베가는 서서 마스크를 벗으려고 하며 애슐리를 본다.

베가: 음, (숨을 내쉬며) 솔직히… 좀 취한 거 같던데
          요.

그는 마스크를 벗고 거의 얼굴이 드러난다.

베가: 친구분인가요?

애슐리는 이제 그를 알아보고 충격으로 그를 쳐다본다.

애슐리: 세상에…프란시스코 베가네요.
베가: 좋은 거예요, 나쁜 거예요?
애슐리: 제 룸메이트가 있었다면…(놀람의 숨소리를 내며)
          기절했을 거예요.
          (숨을 들이 내쉬며 긴장하며) 당신이 사후 피임약
          다음으로 위대한 존재라고 믿거든요.

- **backdrop**
  (무대의) 배경(막)

- **unrecognizable**
  알아볼 수 없는

- **take off**
  벗다

- **to be honest**
  솔직히 말해서

- **hemorrhage**
  출혈(bleeding)하다

- **morning-after pill**
  피임약

If my roommate was here, she'd hemorrhage.
현재 사실의 반대 의미를 나타내는 가정법 과거시제로, '룸메이트가 여기 있다면 그녀는 충격 받았을 것이다 (hyperbolically meaning she would react with great shock)' 라는 의미이다.

Zoom In

If my roommate was here, she'd hemorrhage.

룸메이트가 있었다면, 기절했을 것이다.

ASHLEIGH: Um...me, too. I– Oh, I– Oh, I can't believe I'm talking to Francisco Vega.

(sighing) Oh! I mean, look at me. I'm...I'm a journalist and I'm reduced to total adolescence. It's, uh, just you're...you're Francisco Vega! (exhales and inhales excitedly)

VEGA: I know that. I guess the key question here is, who are you?

ASHLEIGH: Who, who am I? Is what, that what you're asking, who I am? I'm, uh, my identity?

VEGA: Yeah.

Is it coming to you?

ASHLEIGH: Oh, I, um– Oh, uh– (embarrassed chuckle) I can't believe I'm blank–, I can't believe I'm blanking on it.

VEGA: Check your driver's license.

ASHLEIGH: Right. Yeah, okay. Right.

She opens her purse and takes out her driver's license.

ASHLEIGH: Okay, um, oh, mm...

Ashleigh holds up the driver's license and gestures at Vega.

ASHLEIGH: ...I'm Ash–, I'm Ashleigh Enright.

Vega walks. Ashleigh is standing and putting her driver's license black in the purse.

VEGA: I knew it would be on there.

ASHLEIGH: Yeah. I, um...well, I'm, I work for the Yardley Argus. I write for them.

애슐리: 저도 그렇구요. 내가 프란시스코 베가와 얘
          기하고 있다니. 어떡해…
          (한숨을 쉬며) 전 기자고 고작 대학생인데… 당
          신은 프란시스코 베가잖아요! (숨을 들이 내쉬며
          흥분을 한다)

베가: 그건 나도 아는데 지금 중요한 건 당신은 누
          구죠?

애슐리: 전 누구냐구요? 그걸 물으신 거죠, 난 누군
          가… 제 정체요?

베가: 그래요. 안 떠올라요?

애슐리: 어, 음… (당황해서 웃으며) 어떻게 그게 안 떠오
          르죠?

베가: 면허증 꺼내봐요.

애슐리: 아, 맞다, 네.

애슐리는 가방을 열고 운전면허증을 꺼낸다.

애슐리: 음…

애슐리는 운전면허증을 들고 베가에게 손짓을 한다.

애슐리: 애슐리 엔라잇이에요.

베가는 걸어가고 애슐리는 서서 운전면허증을 가방에 넣고 있다.

베가: 거기 있을 줄 알았어요.

애슐리: 저, 음… 저는… 야들리 아거스 기자예요.

■ me, too.
  나도 그래
  i.e., 'I feel the same way.'

■ adolescence
  청춘기

■ I'm blanking on it.
  그게 기억이 안나
  i.e., 'I cannot recall it'

Is it coming to you?
come to는 '(생각이)나다(들다)' 라는
의미로 'Is your name occurring to
you?' 와 같은 의미로 사용된다.

Is it coming to you?
(생각이) 떠올라요?

VEGA: (nodding) Mm.

ASHLEIGH: And I'm here in New York because I'm interviewing Mister Pollard.

Wow. You look exactly the same, but better.

Ashleigh walk down the corridor. Some studio employees are walking in the corridor.

VEGA: Uh, let me tell you something. You look more beautiful than any journalist I've ever met.

A black door of the studio building is and Vega's trailer is on the street. Some paparazzi are gathered around the front gates of the studio.
Vega enters as he opens the door and walks onto the sidewalk. Male paparazzi #1, standing with the paparazzi, turns and gestures at him.

MALE PAPARAZZI #1: Francisco!

VEGA: You would make a very sexy anchorwoman.

Ashleigh enters through the doorway and follows Vega toward the trailer. A large group of paparazzi runs, shouting questions and snapping photographs.

MALE PAPARAZZI #2: Here! Hey, Francisco! Hey!

ASHLEIGH: How can you say that when you're in the papers every week with those to−die models and actresses?

Vega and Ashleigh stop on the trailer steps, then Vega opens the trailer door. The paparazzi stop on the sidewalk, snapping photographs of them.

VEGA: Get in. Get in, get in.

ASHLEIGH: Where are we going?

MALE: No, wait!

베가: (고개를 끄덕이며) 음…

애슐리: 폴라드 감독 인터뷰로 뉴욕에 왔구요.
우와, 화면과 똑같은데 더 멋지네요.

애슐리는 복도로 걸어간다. 몇몇 스튜디오 직원들은 복도로 걸어간다.

베가: 저도 한마디 하죠. 내가 본 기자 중 최고로
아름다워요.

스튜디오 건물의 뒷문이 있고 베가의 트레일러가 거리에 있다. 몇몇의 파파라치가 스튜디오의 앞문 주변에 모여있다.
베가가 문을 열고 보도로 걸어나간다. 남자 파파라치들이 서있고 그에게 돌아서서 손짓을 한다.

파파라치 1:   프란시스코!

베가: 아주 섹시한 아나운서도 되겠어요.

애슐리는 베가를 따라 트레일러로 간다. 많은 파파라치들이 달려와서 질문을 하고 사진을 찍는다.

파파라치 2:   프란시스코!

애슐리: 항상 엄청난 미녀 모델 배우들만 만나면서
설마요.

베가와 애슐리는 트레일어 계단 앞에 멈추고, 베가는 트레일러문을 연다. 파파라치들이 보도에 멈춰서 사진을 찍는다.

베가: 들어가요.

애슐리: 어디 가요?

파파라치: 기다려요.

- **snap**
  사진을 찍다

- **to-die**
  (대화체 표현)누군가가 엄청나게 아름답다
  (someone is extraordinarily beautiful)

> You look more beautiful than (on)
> any journalist I've ever met.
> 비교급 than (that) 주어 have p.p는 최
> 상급(가장 ~한)의 의미를 가진다.

You look more beautiful than (on) any journalist I've ever met.

당신은 제가 본 기자 중에 최고로 아름다워요.

Ashleigh exits into the trailer as Vega waves his arm at the paparazzi.

VEGA: Not now, guys.

MALE PAPARAZZI #2: Wait. What's goin' on? Francisco!

VEGA: Not now, come on! Give us a break!

MALE PAPARAZZI #1: Hey! Mister Vega! Look this way!

Vega exits into the trailer and closes the door.

Inside the trailer
Ashleigh enters in, then looks around nervously.

ASHLEIGH: Should I be in here?

Vega enters and walks, tossing his mask onto a sofa.

VEGA: Make yourself at home.

Would you like to sit down?

ASHLEIGH: Oh, no, no, no.

VEGA: Would you like a drink?

ASHLEIGH: Oh, no, thanks.

VEGA: Would you like to have dinner with me?

ASHLEIGH: Would I like to have what with you?

VEGA: Yeah. I have no plans but to...get an early bite
and then...

Vega stops and opens the refrigerator.

VEGA: ...you and I can go to a party together.

ASHLEIGH: Oh, a party. Oh, (hiccupping) dinner. Um.

Vega takes two soda cans out of the refrigerator, then looks at Ashleigh.

애슐리는 트레이러 안으로 들어가고 제가는 파파라치들에게 손을
흔든다

베가:　　　찍지 마요! 가만 좀 놔둬요!

파파라치:　　기다려요, 무슨일이에요. 프란시스코

베가:　　　가만 좀 놔둬요!

파파라치:　　베가! 여기 좀 보세요!

베가는 서둘러 트레일러 안으로 들어가고 문을 닫는다.

트레일러안
애슐리는 들어가서 불안하게 주변을 본다.

애슐리:　　　여기 있을까요?

베가는 들어가서 쇼파쪽으로 마스크를 던진다.

베가:　　　편하게 있어요
　　　　　　앉아있을래요?

애슐리:　　　아뇨.

베가:　　　뭐 마실래요?

애슐리:　　　아뇨, 됐어요.

베가:　　　나하고 저녁 먹을래요?

애슐리:　　　당신과 뭘 어째요?

베가:　　　네. 일찌감치 뭐 좀 먹고.

베가는 멈춰서 냉장고 문을 연다.

베가:　　　같이 파티에 가죠.

애슐리:　　　아, 파티요, (딸꾹질을 하며) 저녁…

베가는 소다 두 개를 꺼내 애슐리를 본다.

- **Give us a break .**
  그만 좀 하세요 (Leave us alone의 대화
  체)

- **nervously**
  불안하게, 초조하게

- **toss**
  던지다

- **get an early bite**
  일찍 뭐 좀 먹다

Make yourself at home.
'자신 집에서 처럼 편하게 지내세요'
라는 의미로 '편안히 계세요'(i.e.,
'Behave as freely as if you were at
your own home')'라는 뜻으로 사용된
다.

Make yourself at home.
편하게 있어요.

ASHLEIGH: Well, um, w–what about Tiffany Griffin? I…I mean, I thought you…

VEGA: Ah, don't worry, don't worry.

ASHLEIGH: …you two were a twosome.

VEGA: No, we just broke up.

ASHLEIGH: (hiccups, then breathes tensely)

VEGA: I'm gonna change into my street clothes…while you think about it, okay?

ASHLEIGH: All right. (hiccup) Uh–huh.

Vega opens the bedroom door, then exits into the bedroom and closes the door.

ASHLEIGH: (tense breaths, followed by hiccup) Oh, gosh.

She hold her breath, trying to stop the hiccupping.

애슐리:	티파니 그리핀은요?
베가:	걱정마요.
애슐리:	사귀는 거 아니었어요?
베가:	아니, 헤어졌어요.
애슐리:	(딸꾹질을 하고 긴장하며 숨을 쉰다)
베가:	나 옷 갈아입을 동안 생각해봐요.
애슐리:	좋아요. (딸꾹질을 한다)

베가는 화장실문을 열고 들어가고 문을 닫는다.

애슐리:	(긴장된 숨소리를 내며 딸꾹질을 하며) 세상에.

애슐리는 숨을 참고 딸꾹질을 멈추려고 애쓴다.

■ **twosome**
　두 연인, 커플(romantic couple)

■ **break up**
　헤어지다

■ **hiccup**
　딸꾹질을 하다

She hold her breath, trying to stop the hiccupping.
hold one's breath는 '숨을 죽이다'는 의미이고, try to +동사원형은 '~하려고 애쓰다'는 의미로 사용된다.

om In

She hold her breath, trying to stop the hiccupping.
그녀는 숨을 참고, 딸꾹질을 멈추려고 애쓴다.

A Rainy Day in New York

Asperger syndrome
(아스퍼거 증후군)

TED:	Nah, I'm okay. What's...Gatsby do?
ASHLEIGH:	He goes to Yardley, too. Which he refers to as Forest Lawn University.
TED:	Is he a journalist, too?
ASHLEIGH:	No. He's not really focused professionally. I think, uh, in his wildest dreams he'd like to be Sky Masterson. He's a little eccentric.
TED:	In what way...eccentric?
ASHLEIGH:	Well...I think it has to do with the fact that he and his mom never really hit it off, you know? Uh, she was always forcing him to read everything and learn piano and...I mean, he is really smart. Yeah, he's one of those students who he doesn't have to study for a test and then he just, you know, aces it.
TED:	Sounds like me.
ASHLEIGH:	To tell you the truth, I'm Don't tell anybody, but... ...I think he has a touch of Asperger's.

애슐리는 영화 대본작가인 테드와의 대화에서 남자친구는 어떤 사람이냐는 물음에 "좀 별나다. 엄마와 사이가 안 좋아서 그런 것 같 지만, 정말 똑똑하긴 하다. 공부 안 하고도 시험 잘 본다. '아스퍼거 증후군'이 살짝 있는 거 같다" 라고 한다.

애슐리가 말하는 개츠비의 아스퍼거 증후군은 무엇일까?

아스퍼거 증후군은 발달장애의 일종으로, 사회 관계와 관련된 상호작용에 어려움을 겪고 관심사와 활동이 반복적으로 나타나는 증상을 가진 사람들을 일컫는 말이다. 아스퍼거 증후군의 가장 큰 특징은 사회성 및 커뮤니케이션 능력의 결여이다. 공감능력이 현저히 부족하고 다른 사람의 입장을 고려하고 배려하는 능력이 부족하다. 그러나 지적 능력이 부족한 것은 아니고 오히려 특정한 주제나 사물에 깊이 강하게 관심이 있어 특정분야에 성공한 사람들이 많다. 그 대표적인 인물로 스티븐 잡스, 빌 게이츠, 아인슈타인등이 꼽힌다. 스티븐 잡스가 항상 같은 검은색 옷을 입는 것도 같은 활동의 반복적인 패턴을 보이는 아스퍼거 증후군의 한 부분이라고 한다. 아스퍼거 증후군을 지닌 사람들은 또한 달리기, 암벽 등반과 같은 다른 사람들과의 상호작용이 많이 필요 없는 운동에 뛰어나며, 영화작품으로 '포레스트 검프'를 예로 든다. 그들이 특별히 사회적 성취도가 떨어지는 것

이 아니라 오히려 그 누구보다도 뛰어난 능력을 가지고 있다는 것이다. 그들과 같이 영화 속 개츠비는 '별나고, 공부 안 하고도 시험을 잘 보는 똑똑한 아이'로 묘사되어 있다. 또한, 개츠비와 애슐리가 영화의 첫 부분에서 주고받는 대사를 보면 계속해서 본인들의 관심사만 이야기 하는 것을 볼 수 있다. 이 부분도 자신만의 세계에 갇혀서 본인의 이야기만 하는 아스퍼거 증후군의 커뮤니케이션 능력의 부족을 보여주는 부분이 아닌가 싶다. 그렇다면 이러한 아스퍼거 증후군이 생겨나는 원인은 무엇일까?

　　증후군의 원인은 잘 알 수 없는 상황이지만, 연구된 결과를 보면 유전성을 띤 요인이 처한 어떤 환경에서 드러난다고 한다. 애슐리는 개츠비가 '엄마와의 관계가 안 좋아서 좀 별나다 (He's a little eccentric. I think it has to do with the fact that he and his mom never really hit it off)' 라고 한다. 야스퍼거 증후군은 가정에서 부모와의 관계가 안 좋을 경우 드러난다고 한다. 말을 원래 아주 잘하는 야스퍼거 증후군을 가진 아이가 평소 안 하는 이유는 자신이 원하는 방식대로 계획되고 순차적인 진행이 되어야 만족하는데, 그런 부분이 이루어지지 않을 때 좌절감을 느끼면 아예 말문을 닫는다는 것이다. 아이의 입장에서는 화난 부분을 부모님에게 아주 자세히 이야기를 하는데 부모님이 이해를 못해 답답해 하고, 부모님의 입장에서는 아이가 부모로 존중하지 않고 공격적으로 비난하는 것으로 생각되어 대화단절이 된다는 것이다. 아마도 영화 속의 개츠비도 강압적인 엄마에 의해 관계가 안 좋아진 것으로 보여진다.

취미로 포커 도박을 즐기면서 "인생을 망칠 멋진 방법을 찾아봐야지(Find some brilliant way to ruin my life.)" 라는 말을 하고, 피아노로 재즈를 연주하며 자유롭게 살고 싶어하는 장면이 나오는데, 어머니의 과거비밀을 알게 된 후 앞으로는 본인도 자유롭게 살수 있다는 희망을 가지고, 엄마가 좋아하는 여자친구인 애슐리와의 이별을 해서 현실과 타협하지 않고 본인이 원하는 대로 살겠다는 자유 의지가 마지막 장면에서 보인다.

Chapter 7

애슐리와 베가

Ashleigh & Vega

METROPOLITAN MUSEUM OF ART

Gatsby and Chan walk down the steps in front of the museum. Some people are walking up and down the steps, and it has stopped raining.

GATSBY:	Great, now I gotta take Ashleigh to my mom's...goddamn party.
CHAN:	Well, why is that so bad?
GATSBY:	Why is that so bad, Chan? Because I wanted to spend the night with Ashleigh alone in New York, not with a farrago of WASP plutocrats.
CHAN:	"A farrago of WASP plutocrats"? Sounds like something on the menu at a fusion restaurant.
GATSBY:	I'm not interested in the euro or how many Basquiats somebody owns or whether they prefer a Falcon to a Gulfstream. I mean, these things have no meaning to me.
CHAN:	I notice you haven't renounced your family's money.
GATSBY:	What does that mean?

매트로 폴리탄 박물관
개츠비와 챈은 박물관 계단아래로 내려가고 있다. 몇몇 사람들이 계단을 오르고 내리고 있으며 비는 멈추었다.

개츠비: 젠장, 애슐리와 망할 엄마 파티에 가게 됐네.

챈: 왜 그렇게 싫은데?

개츠비: 왜긴, 애슐리와 오붓하게 뉴욕을 즐기고 싶었는데. 잡탕 와스프 부호들과 말고.

챈: '잡탕 와스프 부호' 무슨 퓨전 레스토랑 메뉴 같네.

개츠비: '유로화가 어쩌네 누가 바스키아 그림이 몇 개네. 전세기는 걸프스트림보다 팔콘이 낫네'. 그런 게 뭐가 그렇게 중요해.

챈: 집안 재산은 포기 못 한 거 같은데.

개츠비: 무슨 뜻이야?

- **farrago**
  잡동사니

- **WASP**
  White Anglo-Saxon Protestant의 약어로 돈이나 사회적 지위가 있는 중상층 백인을 조롱하며 쓰는 대화체 표현

- **plutocrat**
  부호(재벌)
  wealthy people

- **renounce**
  포기하다

CHAN:	That means you could move out…get a job, put yourself through college.
GATSBY:	Oh, yeah? As a what?
CHAN:	Piano player in a dive. Or…maybe a poker player? Dice hustler?
GATSBY:	You're bad, Chan. You're goin' straight to hell.
CHAN:	There's something romantic about gamblers and…old songs…meeting under a clock.
GATSBY:	Yeah…maybe in movies, but this is real life.
CHAN:	Real life is fine for people who can't do any better.
GATSBY:	It was fun killing time with you. Have fun with the blue nevus tonight.
CHAN:	Who?
GATSBY:	Your skin doctor.
CHAN:	Well, at least he knows enough not to wind up in an Egyptian tomb.

KAUFMAN ASTORIA STUDIOS

Paparazzi and fans are gathered around the trailer. The door starts to open.

MALE PAPARAZZI #1:	There he is.
MALE PAPARAZZI #2:	Vega!

Photographers spin around and snap pictures as Vega and Ashleigh come out of the trailer, then walk down the steps.

VEGA:	(to Ashleigh) Okay…here we go.
	(to fans) Thank you for being here.
ASHLEIGH:	(to Vega) Is it always like this?

Vega signs a book for female fan #1.

챈:	그렇게 싫으면 독립해서… 돈 벌어서 학교 다닐 수도 있잖아.
개츠비:	그래? 뭘로 벌까?
챈:	라운지 바의 피아니스트. 아니면… 포커 플레이어나 주사위 도박꾼?
개츠비:	나쁜 여자네. 지옥행 예약이야.
챈:	로맨틱하잖아. 도박사, 옛날 노래들… 시계 밑에서 만나는 약속.
개츠비:	영화에서나 그렇지. 현실에선 아니잖아.
챈:	뾰족한 수 없으면. 그 현실도 괜찮아.
개츠비:	덕분에 즐거웠어. 청색 모반과도 잘되길.
챈:	누구?
개츠비:	그 피부과 의사.
챈:	적어도 미라 관에 숨진않겠지.

쿠프만 아스토리아 스튜디오
파파라치와 팬들은 트레일러 주변에 모여있다. 문이 열리기 시작한다.

남자 파파라치 #1:	저기다.
남자 리포터#2:	베가!

베가와 애슐리가 트레일러에서 내릴 때, 사진사들이 주변에 모여 사진을 찍고 거리로 걸어나간다.

베가:	(애슐리에게) 자, 가죠.
	(팬에게) 와줘서 고마워요.
애슐리:	(베가에게)늘 이런 식이에요?

베가는 여성 팬에게 책에 사인을 해준다.

- **dive**
  (비격식)(어두운 지저분한)술집, 바 (sleazy bar)

- **killing time**
  시간 보내기

- **nevus**
  모반(birthmark), 반점

- **wind up**
  (어떤 장소, 상황에)처하게 되다
  end up in – i.e. 'get trapped inside'

You could move out get a job, put yourself through college.
put somebody through는 '(학비를 내거나 해서)교육을 받게 하다'로 put yourself through college 는 일을 하거나 대출이나 장학금을 받아서 대학 학비를 자신의 돈으로 지불하다('pay for your own college education')는 의미이다.

You could move out get a job, put yourself through college.

너는 돈 벌어서 학교에 다닐 수 있다.

VEGA: (to Ashleigh) This is nothing.

MALE REPORTER #1: (taking book back) Thank you. I love you!

VEGA: (to fans) Okay, I–I'm just signing one, thank you.

MALE REPORTER #1: Francisco!

MALE REPORTER #2: Vega!

VEGA: Sorry, we gotta go. Sorry.

MALE REPORTER #1: Francisco, who's the young lady?

ASHLEIGH: Oh, I'm no one.

MALE REPORTER #1: Yeah, what do you do?

Vega and Ashleigh walk to Vega's limousine, which is parked behind the trailer. Vega opens the door for Ashleigh.

ASHLEIGH: Oh, I'm no one really.

Ashleigh stops in the doorway, then looks back at male reporter #1, standing as he holds a recorder toward her.

ASHLEIGH: I mean…I was Miss Amiability in Scottsdale, but, you know…not really a big deal.

MALE REPORTER #1: And where'd you guys meet?

VEGA: (to Ashleigh) Let's go. Let's go, come on.

Ashleigh waves at the reporters and sits down in the limousine, then Vega closes the door.

MALE REPORTER #2: Who's the girl? Come on!

VEGA: (to Reporters) There's no story here.

Vega walks around the back of the limousine. More reporters and paparazzi cluster around him

VEGA: Okay. Thank you. Thank you for being here.

베가: (애슐리에게) 이건 아무것도 아녜요.

여성팬 #1 : (책을 다시 돌려주며) 고마워요, 사랑해요!

베가: (팬에게) 나중에 해드릴게요. 감사합니다.

남자 리포터 1: 프란시스코!

남자 리포터 2: 베가!

베가: 가봐야 해요.

여자 리포터 1: 프란시스코 여자분은 누군가요?

애슐리: 아무도 아녜요.

여자 리포터 1: 직업은요?

베가와 애슐리는 트레일러 뒤에 주차되어 있는 베가의 리무진으로 걸어간다. 베가는 애슐리를 위해 문을 연다.

애슐리: 정말 아무도 아녜요…

애슐리는 차 문 앞에서 멈추고, 뒤돌아 남자리포터를 본다. 그는 그녀 쪽으로 녹음기를 내밀고 있다.

애슐리: 스카치데일 미인대회 출신이긴 한데 뭐 별 건가요.

남자리포터 1: 두 분 어디서 만나셨죠?

베가: (애슐리에게) 어서 타요.

애슐리는 기자에게 손을 흔들고 리무진에 앉고, 베가는 문을 닫는다.

남자 기자 2: 누군가요? 네?

베가: (리포터에게) 기삿거리 없어요.

베가는 리무진 뒷자리로 간다. 더 많은 기자와 파파라치들이 그 주변에 모여든다.

베가: 와줘서 고마워요.

It's not really a big deal.
big deal은 '대단한 것, 큰 일(not anything of any real importance)'이라는 뜻으로, 여기서는 '그녀가 유명인은 아니다(she is not really a celebrity)'는 의미로 사용되었다.

Zoom In

It's not really a big deal.
별거 아니야.

VEGA: That's it, that's it!

All right. Thank you for coming. Thank you.

Vega exits into the car. Vega closes the door.

Vega and Ashleigh, sit at a table in the expensive uptown restaurant.

ASHLEIGH: There's so much the public wants to know about you.

Ashleigh, who has her notebook open on the table in front of her, sits and gestures across the table at Vega. Several candles burn on the table between them.

ASHLEIGH: Is it true that you were born on the Orient Express right outside of Budapest?

VEGA: Are your two sisters as beautiful as you are? And, uh...please be, be honest. Don't be modest.

ASHLEIGH: Well, um...uh...they are. Yeah.

VEGA: Yeah?

ASHLEIGH: Um, yeah, they, uh, they're actually even prettier.

ASHLEIGH: Yeah. Taylor, especially. She looks a little bit like your girlfriend, Tiffany Griffin.

VEGA: Hm. Could do worse.

ASHLEIGH: Um...so, umm...tsk, are you...are you seriously considering, uh, making a remake of "White Heat"?

VEGA: Do you have a boyfriend?

베가:	그만, 그만.
	와줘서 감사합니다.

베가는 차에 타고 차 문을 닫는다.

베가와 애슐리는 비싼 업타운 레스토랑에 테이블에 앉아 있다.

애슐리:	대중이 궁금해하는 게 정말 많아요.

애슐리는 노트를 펼치고 앉아있고 베가 쪽으로 손짓을 한다. 캔들 몇 개가 그들 사이에 테이블에서 빛나고 있다.

애슐리:	오리엔트 특급열차에서 태어나신 게 사실인 가요?
베가:	두 언니도 당신만큼 예뻐요? 겸손하게 말고 솔직하게요.
애슐리:	네.
베가:	네?
애슐리:	예뻐요. 아니, 저보다 더 예뻐요. 특히 테일 러 당신 여친 티파니와 닮았어요.
베가:	상당한데요.
애슐리:	그리고… '화이트 히트'를 리메이크하실 건 가요?
베가:	남자친구 있어요?

■ **modest**
겸손한

■ **consider**
고려하다

She looks a little bit like your girlfriend.
look like는 '~처럼 보이다, ~와 닮다
(resemble, take after)' 라는 의미이다.

She looks a little bit like your girlfriend.
그녀는 당시의 여자친구와 닮았어요.

Ashleigh, gesturing toward herself, put down the notebook.

ASHLEIGH: Me?

VEGA: Uh… yeah.

ASHLEIGH: Oh.

Ashleigh drinks from her glass of wine.

VEGA: I mean, no, sorry. I should, I sh−, I shouldn't ask that. Um, sorry, I've been drinking and…

…it's just that the, the…the candle lights are coloring your face in…quite an amazing way. I'm, I'm sorry, you have a…a very effective smile. You know? I, I, I couldn't help but ask if you have a boyfriend…or not.

ASHLEIGH: Do I have a boyfriend? Is that what you're asking?

VEGA: Yeah.

Ashleigh taps her fingers together, then gestures nervously at Vega.

ASHLEIGH: (inhales deeply) Well, um…yes and…technically, no. I mean, (inhales) there…there is this boy at Yardley…who's, um, (inhales) I mean…but he's just a boy… you know? He's a mere youth. Um, we've, uh, we've dated a few times.

Ashleigh drinks from her glass of wine.

VEGA: Well…you must be crazy about him. Is he…captain of the football team?

애슐리는 자신을 가리키며, 그녀의 노트를 내려놓는다.

애슐리: 저요?

베가: 네.

애슐리: 오.

배슐리는 와인을 마신다.

베가: 미안해요. 실례를 했네요. 취했나 봐요 게다가… 촛불 빛이 당신 얼굴을… 너무 아름답게 물들여서… 미안한데 당신… 미소가 너무 치명적이라…남친이 있는지 안 물을 수 없었네요.

애슐리: 남친이 있냐구요? 그거 물으신 거죠?

베가: 네.

애슐리는 손가락을 부딪히며 긴장하며 베가에게 손짓을 한다.

애슐리: (깊이 숨을 쉬며) 그게, 음… 네, 그런데… 엄밀히는 아니에요. (숨을 들이마시며) 야들리에 다니는 애인데… 걔는… 그러니까… (숨을 들이마시며) 그냥 남자애예요. 아직 애죠 뭐. 데이트 몇 번 한 게 다예요.

애슐리는 와인을 마신다.

베가: 푹 빠져있겠네요. 풋볼 팀 주장이에요?

- tap
  부딪히다

- technically
  엄밀히 말하면

- mere
  겨우~의, ~에 불과한

I couldn't help but ask if you have a boyfriend.
can't help but + 동사원형은 '~하지 않을 수 없다 (can't help ~ing)라는 의미이고, ask if는 '~인지 아닌지 묻다'라는 뜻이다.

I couldn't help but ask if you have a boyfriend.
당신이 남자친구가 있는지 안 물을 수 없었네요.

ASHLEIGH:	Football? Gatsby? (chuckling) No! No. He doesn't play football. Yeah. He likes to figure out the point spread.
VEGA:	Mm, so a mathematician.
ASHLEIGH:	Mmm...uh, not ex–, not exactly. No, Gatsby's, um...Gatsby's very dear. He's, uh, he's very...amusing. (chuckles and inhales) He's unusual, um...quaint, you know?

Ashleigh drinks from her glass of wine, then waves her hand at Vega.

ASHLEIGH:	(sips wine and swallows) That's the word I would use to describe Gatsby. Quaint. He's, uh, he's exotic, eh, searching, shall, shall we say, for, um... this romantic dream from a vanished age. (chuckles, then inhales deeply)

Ashleigh holds up the glass of wine.

ASHLEIGH:	Um...what is this wine?
VEGA:	It's Chateau Meyney.
ASHLEIGH:	(nodding and exhaling) Oh. I shouldn't imbibe so copiously. Alcohol plays havoc on my cerebral neurons.
VEGA:	(brief chuckle, intrigued) And how?
ASHLEIGH:	Oh, I...I lose my censor. Yeah, I become...loose, uninhibited, passionate, aggressive, um, wicked ...absurd! I just–

애슐리:	풋볼이요? 개츠비가요? (웃으며) 아뇨! (웃으며) 할 줄도 몰라요. 풋볼 몇 점 차로 이길까 예상하는 건 좋아해요.
베가:	수학자 타입인가 봐요.
애슐리:	딱히 그것도 아니고… 개츠비는…아주 귀여워요. 또… 정말 재미있고…(웃고 숨을 들이쉬며) 특이해요. 별나 달까요?

애슐리는 와인을 마시고 베가에게 손짓을 한다.

애슐리:	(와인을 한모금 마시며) 그 말이 딱 이네요, 별나다. 걔는…색달라요. 그래서 추구하는 것도…사라진 시대의 로맨틱한 꿈이죠. (웃으며 깊은 숨을 쉰다)

애슐리는 와인잔을 든다.

애슐리:	이 와인 뭐예요?
베가:	샤또 메네요.
애슐리:	(고개를 끄덕이며 숨을 내쉰다) 오. 이렇게 달리면 안 되는데. 알코올은 제 뇌신경을 박살 내거든요.
베가:	(짧게 웃으며 호기심을 가지며) 어떻게?
애슐리:	필터링이 안 돼요. 그래서…긴장이 풀리고… 거침없고… 열정적이고 공격적이고… 짓궂어지고…이상해져요! 그냥…

- **quaint**
  괴짜

- **imbibe**
  (특히 술을) 마시다: drink

- **copiously**
  풍부[풍성]하게

- **havoc**
  대파괴, 큰 혼란(피해)

- **uninhibited**
  거리낌이 없는

He likes to figure out the point spread.
point spread는 '포인트스프레드(강한 상대가 약한 상대를 패배시키기 위해 기대되는 점수) '이고, figure out은 '계산해 내다, 생각해 내다' 는 의미이다.

Zoom In

He likes to figure out the point spread.
몇점차로 이길까 예측하는 것 좋아해요.

HOTEL ROOM
The hallway door is closed.
ED, a poker player, opens the door. Gatsby is standing in the hall.

ED:	Hello.
GATSBY:	Is this where the poker game is?
ED:	And who are you?
GATSBY:	My name's Gatsby Welles.
ED:	Who?
SID:	Hey, he's okay. That's Hunter's brother.
GATSBY:	I was gonna…take Hunter's chair, if that's all right.
ED:	(remembering) Oh, yeah! Hunter called and said you might…sit in.

Gatsby steps into the room and closes the door.

ED:	You sure you want to play in this game?
SID:	(chuckling) Ha–ha, he's all right. Hunter says he's…a shark, right?

A group of poker players, who are in their 30's and 40's, are sitting around the table. Sid, another of the poker players, stands in front of the table. Jordan, sitting at the table. Gatsby walks toward the table.

SID:	Better watch out for him.
JORDAN:	More like a guppy.
GATSBY:	Yes. (chuckles politely) But if you guys are worried, uh…I got a little somethin'.
SID:	Oh, this kid's loaded!
JORDAN:	Have a seat then, my friend.

호텔 룸

복도 문이 닫힌다.

포커 플레이어인 에드는 문을 연다. 게츠비는 홀에 서 있다.

에드:	안녕하세요.
개츠비:	포커 하는 곳 맞죠?
에드:	누구시죠?
개츠비:	개츠비 웰스요.
에드:	누구요?
시드:	괜찮아, 헌터 동생이야.
개츠비:	형 대신 하기로 했는데.
에드:	(기억을 하며) 아, 헌터가 전화했었지.

게츠비는 방으로 들어오고 문을 닫는다.

에드:	이 판에 정말 끼려고?
시드:	(웃으며) 하하, 헌터 말이 타짜래. 조심하는 게 좋을걸.

한 그룹의 포커 플레이어들이 테이블 주변에 앉아있다. 또 다른 포커 플레이어인 시드는 테이블 앞에 서 있다. 조르단은 테이블 옆에 앉아있다.

시드:	조심하는 게 좋을걸.
조르단:	아마추어 같아보이는데.
개츠비:	(정중하게 웃으며) 못 미더우면 보여드리죠.
에드:	이 친구 두둑하네.
조르단:	어서 앉게, 친구.

■ shark

(속어) 무자비한 도박꾼, 사기꾼

■ Better watch out for him.

You'd better watch out for him으로 You'd 가 생략된 대화체 표현.

■ watch out for

~을 경계하다, 조심하다(be alert)

■ guppy

구피(수족관에서 흔히 기르는 작은 담수어), 아마추어

I was gonna take Hunter's chair.

take one's chair는 '~의 자리를 차지하다, 대신하다' 의미로, take Hunter's chair는 '헌터를 대신한다(i.e., 'take Hunter's place in the game')' 의 의미이다.

Zoom In

I was gonna take Hunter's chair.

헌터를 대신하기로 했어.

A short time later, Gatsby sits amidst the poker players at the table. Ed, Jordan, Sid, Sam and Al sit in a semi-circle around the table.

ED: All right, call.

GATSBY: (very low sigh) This is crazy. Maybe something's happened to her. Maybe she's in some kinda trouble.

JORDAN: Raise, two thousand

GATSBY: Maybe the story led her into danger. Maybe she was kidnapped or murdered. Should I call the police? Of course, then it would be so embarrassing if she turned up alive.

JORDAN: (to Gatsby) Hey, kid. You gonna call or not? The bet's two thousand dollars.

GATSBY: Um... (inhales softly) Tsk. I'll raise you.

He starts to put chips onto the table.

JORDAN: And I re-raise you. All in.

Jordan pushed all his chips into the center of the table.

PIERRE/ GATSBY & ASHLEIGH'S SUITE
Gatsby opens the hallway door and turns on the lights in the suite. He closes the door and walks. He tosses his keycard on a liquor cart. A pack of cigarettes and a roll of money onto the cart. Gatsby then starts to search through his pockets, pulling out more and more rolls of money, until a massive pile of money is piled up on the cart. He opens a television cabinet, picking up the remote control and walking with it. He points the remote control at the television and turns it on.

잠시 후에 개츠비는 테이블에 포커 플레이어들 가운데에 앉아있다.
에드. 조르단. 세드, 샘 그리고 알이 테이블의 반원으로 앉아있다.

에드: 나는 콜.

개츠비: (낮은 한숨을 쉬며) 미치겠네. 애슐리한테 안 좋
은 일이 생겼을지도 모르잖아.

조르단: 이천불 올렸어.

개츠비: 취재하다 위험에 빠졌을지도 납치되거나 살
해당했을지도. 경찰에 신고해야 될까? 근데
그랬다 멀쩡하면 너무 창피하잖아.

조르단: (게츠비에게) 이봐, 동생 콜할 거야? 말 거야?
이천불이야.

게츠비: 음··· (부드럽게 숨을 들이쉬며) 나도 콜.

게츠비는 테이블 위로 칩을 둔다.

조르단: 받고, 올인.

조르단은 그의 모든 칩을 테이블 위에 둔다.

피에르/개츠비와 애슐리의 호텔방
개츠비는 문을 열고 방으로 들어간다. 문을 닫고 걸어 들어간다.
그는 그의 카드키를 술카트에 둔다. 담배 한갑과 돌돌 말은 지폐돈
도 카트로 올려놓는다. 개츠비는 카트가 쌓일 때까지 그의 주머니
에서 더 많은 돌돌 말이 지폐를 찾는다. 그는 티비 캐비닛을 열고,
리모콘을 집어들고 걸어간다. 그는 티비에 리모콘을 가리키며 켠
다.

- **amidst**
  가운데에

- **kidnap**
  납치하다

- **All in**
  포커게임에 쓰이는 용어로, '누군가의 칩에
  모두 베팅을 한다(one is betting all one'
  s chips)' 는 의미

**It would be so embarrassing if
she turned up alive.**
turn up은 '나타나다' 라는 의미이고, 가
정법 과거로 쓰인 문장이다.

**It would be so embarrassing if she
turned up alive.**

만일 그녀가 살아나 나타나면 창피할거야.

ANCHORMAN: (over television) with temperatures in the sixties. Rain is predicted this evening. It will be heavy at times and more of it tomorrow. Mostly cloudy with a chance of showers in the late afternoon.

The television shows a recorded image of Vega walking out of his trailer with Ashleigh.

ANCHORMAN: (over television) On a brighter note, Francisco Vega is in town with his new main squeeze on his arm.

ANCHORMAN: (over television) All our spies could find out is that she's Ashleigh Enright, a beauty queen from Tucson Arizona.

He walks, looking at the television with disbelief.

ANCHORMAN: (over television) Uh, though they were spotted later having drinks ITAL over candlelight and…apparently exchanging sweet nothings.

The television shows an image of Ashleigh, who stops in front of the limousine with Vega and gestures at the reporters around her.

ASHLEIGH: (on television) I was Miss Amiability in Scottsdale, but, you know…not really a big deal.

MALE REPORTER #1: (over television) And where'd you guys meet

MALE REPORTER #2: (over television) Who's the girl? Come on!

ANCHORMAN: (over television) So…good luck, Francisco. We're all rooting for you.

ANCHORWOMAN: (over television) A gorgeous couple. As if they need our help.

앵커맨: (티비에서 나오는 소리) 현재 기온은 약 16도. 저녁엔 비 소식 있는데요. 내일은 더 많이 온답니다. 흐리다 오후 늦게 소나기 예보 있습니다.

티비는 애슐리와 함께 트레일러에서 걸어 나오는 베가의 녹음된 모습을 보여준다.

앵커맨: (티비에서 나오는 소리) 이번엔 좀 밝은 소식으로 프란시스코 베가가 새로운 연인과 나타났군요.

앵커맨: 현재 알려진 바로는 애슐리 엔라잇, 투손 출신의 미인대회 수상자라는군요.

개츠비는 걸어와서 믿지 못하며 티비를 보고 있다.

앵커맨: (티비에서 나오는 소리) 촛불 아래에서 와인을 마시며 사랑을 속삭이는 모습이 포착됐죠.

애슐리의 모습이 티비에 보이고 그녀는 베가와 리무진 앞에 멈춰서 그녀 주변의 기자들에게 손짓을 한다.

애슐리: (티비에서 나오는 소리) 스카치데일 미인대회 출신이긴 한데 뭐 별건가요.

남자기자 1: (티비에서 나오는 소리) 두 분 어디서 만나셨죠?

남자기자 2: (티비에서 나오는 소리) 여자분은 누군가요?

앵커맨: (티비에서 나오는 소리) 잘해봐요, 프란시스코. 우리가 응원할게요.

앵커우먼: (티비에서 나오는 소리) 응원 안 해줘도 잘될 거 같은걸요.

- **chance**
  가능성

- **squeeze**
  애인

- **spot**
  발견하다, 찾다

- **candlelight**
  촛불

- **gorgeous**
  아주 멋진

We're all rooting for you.
root for는 응원하다('hoping for a favorable outcome)라는 의미로, 여기에서는 '애슐리와의 관계를 응원한다'는 의미이다.

We're all rooting for you.
우리가 응원할게요.

MANHATTAN STREETS

Gatsby walks glumly down the sidewalk on fifth avenue.

GATSBY: (voice over) Jesus, I need a drink. I need a drink, I need a cigarette. What I really need is a Berlin ballad.

THE CARLYLE/ BEMELMAN'S BAR

Gatsby sits at a table amidst the patrons in the busy upscale bar. The waiter steps toward Gatsby and looks at his empty glass.

WAITER: May I get you another?

GATSBY: Yeah, why don't you make it a double.

WAITER: (concerned) You want a double?

GATSBY: It's okay, I won't be operating any farm machinery.

The waiter nods at Gatsby, then walks out. Gatsby's cell phone rings, then he picks it up off the table and talks into it.

GATSBY: (into cell phone) Hello? Mom, you gotta give me a chance – I said I was gonna be there tonight. Ashleigh's fine.

GATSBY: (into cell phone) (pauses, then inhales irritably) Yes, I'll wear a tie and I will be there on time, okay? I can't really talk right now.

Gatsby hangs up the cell phone and puts it down on the table. He looks down despondently.

맨하탄 거리
개츠비는 침울하게 5번가 거리를 걸어간다.

개츠비:　(해설)젠장, 한잔해야겠다. 술도 필요하고, 담배도 필요해. 정말 필요한 건 어빙 벌린의 발라드 곡.

칼라일 벨망의 바
개츠비는 번잡한 고급 바에 손님들 사이에 테이블에 앉아있다. 위이터가 개츠비 쪽으로 다가가서 그의 빈 잔을 본다.

웨이터:　한 잔 더 드려요?

개츠비:　네, 더블로요.

웨이터:　(걱정하며) 더블이요?

개츠비:　걱정 마요. 농기계 다룰 일 없으니까.

웨이터는 개츠비에게 고개를 끄덕이며 걸어간다. 개츠비의 휴대폰이 울리고, 그는 테이블에서 그것을 집어 들고 말한다.

개츠비:　(휴대폰에) 여보세요? 엄마, 좀 기다려주세요. 저녁 때 간다니까요. 애슐리는 잘 있어요.

개츠비:　(휴대폰에) (잠시 멈추고 짜증나서) 네, 넥타이도 매고 제 시간에 갈게요, 끊어요

개츠비는 전화를 끊고 테이블 위에 내려둔다. 그는 실의에 빠져 아래를 쳐다본다

- **glumly**
  무뚝뚝하게, 침울하게

- **upscale**
  고급[고가]의

- **hangs up**
  (전화를) 끊다

- **despondently**
  실의에 빠져

May I get you another?
another은 여기서 another glass를 의미해서 '한잔 더 하시겠어요?'라는 의미로 쓰였다.

May I get you another?
한잔 더 드려요?

GATSBY: (voice over) Francisco Vega. A bullshit actor. This guy is incapable of a real moment. All those mannered gestures and all that phony self–promoting liberal politics.

Terry Ford, a beautiful, sophisticated blonde, is sitting in an evening dress at a nearby table.

GATSBY: (voice over) When he offered to set himself on fire to protest climate change, they shoulda let him. If that's Ashleigh's taste...

Gatsby looks up at Terry.

GATSBY: ...the world is full of beautiful women.
TERRY: Sorry, are you talking to me?
GATSBY: Sorry, I was actually talkin'to myself.
TERRY: I know the feeling.

Terry picks up her glass of champagne, then leans back in her chair and smiles.

GATSBY: You ever see the movie "Out of the Past"?
TERRY: (swallows champagne, smacking lips) Excuse me?
GATSBY: Jane Greer and Robert Mitchum.
TERRY: No.
GATSBY: She was bad news.
TERRY: Well, it's the luck of the draw.

Gatsby looks back at her.

개츠비:　(해설)프란시스코 베가, 엉터리 배우. 진심
　　　　이 뭔지도 모르는 엉터리. 매너 있는 척하면
　　　　서.

아름다운 급발의 테리 포드는 이브닝 드레스를 입고 개츠비 근처에
앉아있다.

개츠비:　(해설)진보인 양 지구온난화 반대 분신한다고
　　　　할 때 놔뒀어야 하는데. 애슐리 취향이 그렇
　　　　다면.

개츠비는 테리를 본다.

개츠비:　뭐… 세상은 넓고 미인은 많으니까.
테리:　　저한테 말한 거예요?
개츠비:　아뇨, 저한테 말한 거예요.
테리:　　(웃으며 숨을 들이쉬며) 그 기분 알아요.
개츠비:　영화 '과거로부터' 봤어요?
테리:　　뭐요?
개츠비:　제인 그리어, 로버트 미첨 주연.
테리:　　아니요.
개츠비:　여자가 화근이었어.
테리:　　복불복이죠.

개츠비는 그녀를 처다본다.

- ■ phony
  가짜의

- ■ liberal
  자유의

- ■ set on fire
  ~에 불을 지르다

- ■ draw
  추첨

They shoulda let him.
shoulda는 should have p.p의 대화체
표현으로, should have p.p는 '~했어
야 했는데 (하지 못했다)' 라는 의미로, 과
거의 후회를 나타낸다.

They shoulda let him.
그들은 그를 놔뒀어야 했는데.

GATSBY:	You alone?
TERRY:	I am. Unless you want some company.
GATSBY:	Sure.

Terry picks up her glass and her purse and walks toward him.

TERRY:	Hi.
TERRY:	I'm Terry Ford.
GATSBY:	My name's Gatsby Welles.

Terry stops and shakes hands with Gatsby.

TERRY:	What's the matter, Gatsby? You seem blue.
GATSBY:	My girlfriend dumped me for a movie star.
TERRY:	Oh, are you staying here?
GATSBY:	No, I've been coming here since they used to only serve me ginger ales by law. I love the piano players. And now I'm old enough to order gin and vermouth.
TERRY:	Tsk, time flies.
GATSBY:	Unfortunately, flies coach.
TERRY:	What's that supposed to mean?
GATSBY:	It's not always a comfortable trip.
TERRY:	Tell me about it.
GATSBY:	So, what are you doin' here all alone?
TERRY:	Working.
GATSBY:	What do you do?
TERRY:	I make dreams come true.
GATSBY:	How do you do that?
TERRY:	Use your imagination.

개츠비:	혼자예요?
테리:	네, 그쪽이 불러주지 않는다면.
개츠비:	오세요.

테리는 잔과 가방을 집어들고, 그 쪽으로 걸어간다.

테리:	안녕하세요. 테리 포드예요.
개츠비:	전 개츠비 웰스예요.

테리는 멈춰서 개츠비와 악수를 한다.

테리:	우울해 보이네요?
개츠비:	여친이 절 차고 배우한테 갔어요.
테리:	이 호텔에 묵어요?
개츠비:	아뇨, 술 못 마시던 나이부터 여기 단골이에요. 피아노 연주가 좋아서. 근데 이젠 칵테일을 마실 나이가 됐네요.
테리:	시간이 날아가죠
개츠비:	네, 슬프게도. 이코노미석으로.
테리:	무슨 뜻이에요?
개츠비:	늘 편안한 여정만은 아니라구요.
테리:	그러게요.
개츠비:	여기서 혼자 뭐 해요?
테리:	일해요.
개츠비:	무슨 일 하는데요?
테리:	꿈을 이뤄줘요.
개츠비:	그게 어떻게 가능해요?
테리:	상상력을 발휘해봐요.

- **shake hands with**
  ~와 악수를 하다

- **dump**
  (애인을)차다

- **Time flies.**
  시간은 날아간다. 시간이 빨리간다

- **coach**
  (항공기의) 2등석(economic class
  accommodations in an aircraft)

You seem blue.
blue는 비격식적인 표현으로 '우울한
(depressed)' 이라는 의미를 가진다.

You seem blue.
우울해 보여.

GATSBY:	Tsk…ooh, wow.
TERRY:	Shall we go someplace where we can be more alone?
GATSBY:	Yeah. Sure. Yeah, why not?
TERRY:	Okay. I get five hundred, sweetie.
GATSBY:	Five hundred.
GATSBY:	Right.
TERRY:	I know what you're thinking. Five hundred seems pretty steep, but it's New York.
GATSBY:	How'd you like to make five thousand?
TERRY:	Five thousand?
GATSBY:	Mm–hm.
TERRY:	(suspiciously) To do what?
GATSBY:	Just to be my date for a few hours at a party. Clothes stay on, no fondling, no exchange of fluids. Just a little role playing.
TERRY:	What kinda party?
GATSBY:	Just my mom's big fall…bullshit blowout. I won fifteen G's in a poker game and I need a date with me. Classy item who answers to the name of Ashleigh Enright.

개츠비:	오, 와우.
테리:	좀 더 오붓한 데로 갈까요?
개츠비:	네, 그래요. 그러죠 뭐.
테리:	좋아요. 500 불이야, 자기야.
개츠비:	500불.
테리:	그렇구나.
개츠비:	비싸단 생각이 들겠지만 뉴욕이잖아요.
테리:	오천불은 어때요?
개츠비:	오천불?
테리:	응.
개츠비:	(의심스럽게) 뭐 하는 데요?
테리:	파티에 몇 시간 파트너로 가줘요. 옷 벗을 일도 없고 애무도 섹스도 없어요. 역할 놀이인 셈이죠.
개츠비:	어떤 파티인데요?
테리:	그냥 엄마가 가을에 여는…큰 허세 파티요. 포커에서 만오천불을 땄고 파트너가 필요해요. 애슐리인 척해줄 세련된 아가씨요.

- steep
  비싼(expensive)

- fondling
  애무

- exchange of fluids:
  섹스(exchange of bodily fluids –
  referring to sex)

- G's
  (속어) 'grand'의 줄임말로 수천달러
  (thousand dollars)를 의미함

- Classy
  세련된

Shall we go someplace where we can be more alone?
Shall we go ~?는 '~로 갈까요?'라는
의미로 제안의 뜻을 나타낸다.

Zom In

Shall we go someplace where we can be more alone?

좀 더 오붓한 데로 갈까요?

Chapter 8

파티에서

At the Party

시간 01:04:36 ~ 01:12:24

CLUB
The club is filled with snow business people, wearing business suits and cocktail dresses at the industry party. People stand talking in small groups and other people are sitting at tables.
Ashleigh and Vega walk down a staircase.

ASHLEIGH: I hope I'm dressed okay.

VEGA: You look beautiful.

ASHLEIGH: It looks real fancy.

VEGA: (chuckling) Don't worry, you're perfect.

VEGA: Now, these things can be a little boring... Thank you, thank you for coming.

An older fellow, standing and talking to a woman named Harriet, turns and looks at Vega.

OLDER FELLOW: Vega. How are ya? Nice to see you.

Vega stops and shakes hands with the older fellow.

VEGA: Very good. Good to see you.

OLDER FELLOW: You know Harry.

클럽

클럽은 기업파티에 비지니즈 정장과 칵테일 드레스를 입고 있는 사업하는 사람들로 가득 차 있다. 사람들은 작은 그룹으로 서서 이야기 하고 다른 사람들은 테이블에 앉아 있다.
애슐리와 베가는 계단 아래로 내려간다.

애슐리:　　옷차림이 걱정이네요.

베가:　　　멋있어 보여요.

애슐리:　　다들 화려해 보이는데.

베가:　　　(웃으며) 걱정 마요, 완벽하니까.

베가:　　　좀 지루할 수도 있어요. 같이 와줘서 고마워요.

나이든 동료가 서서 해리어트라는 여성과 이야기를 나누고 있다가 돌아 베가를 본다.

나이든 동료: 베가, 잘 있었나?

베가는 멈춰서 그와 악수를 한다.

베가:　　　그럼요, 반가워요.

나이든 동료: 해리 알지?

- dress
  옷을 입다

- shake hands with
  ~와 악수하다

HARRIET: Hi. Mm.

Vega, stopping with Ashleigh, shakes hands with Harriet, standing beside the older fellow.

VEGA: Hey, yeah, how are you? This guy is the best cook.

(to older fellow) You, you have to do one of those paellas again.

Miller, a glamorously dressed woman, enters and walks toward Vega.

MILLER: Hi, doll.

VEGA: Yeah, hey. (kisses her cheek)

MILLER: I wonder if I can steal you away for two minutes to talk about your fall schedule. I've got a project with your name on it. Yes, now.

VEGA: Oh, okay. Okay.

Vega looks at Ashleigh

VEGA: Do you mind?

ASHLEIGH: No.

VEGA: Just two minutes. Are you gonna be okay?

ASHLEIGH: Yeah.

VEGA: Yeah? Sure? I'll be fast.

Miller and Vega walk past the tall man. Ashleigh, who reaches and takes a glass of wine off the tray of a party waiter.

ASHLEIGH: (to waiter) Oh. Uh, thank you.

해리어트: 안녕.

베가는 애슐리와 멈춰서 해리어트와 악수를 하고 나이든 동료 옆에 서있다.

베가: 네, 잘 지냈어요?이분 최고의 셰프셔.

(나이든 동료에게) 그 **빠**에야 한 번 더 해 줘요.

매력적으로 옷을 입은 여성인 밀러는 베가 쪽으로 걸어온다.

밀러: 안녕, 훈남.

베가: 안녕 (그녀에게 키스를 한다)

밀러: 잠깐 가을 스케줄 의논 좀 하고 싶은데. 자기한테 딱인 작품이 있어.

베가: 알았어.

베가는 애슐리를 쳐다본다.

베가: 괜찮겠어요?

애슐리: 네.

베가: 2 분만 다녀올게요.

애슐리: 그래요.

베가: 괜찮죠? 금방 올게요.

밀러와 베가는 키 큰 남자쪽으로 걸어간다. 애슐리는 파티웨이터의 쟁반위의 와인잔에 손을 뻗어 잡는다.

애슐리: 고마워요.

- paella
  파엘라(쌀, 닭고기, 생선, 채소를 넣은 스페인 요리)

- doll
  (속어) 인형같은여자(요즘에는 모욕적으로 여겨짐)

Do you mind?
상대방에게 정중하게 쓰는 표현으로 '제가 ~해도 괜찮겠어요?' 라는 의미이다. mind는 '신경에 거슬리다, 꺼리다' 라는 뜻을 가지고 있어 대답에 유의해야 하는 표현으로 No는 꺼리지 않는다 즉, 아니다, 괜찮다' 는 긍정적 답이고, Yes는 '꺼린다, 안된다' 라는 부정의 의미를 가진다.

Zoom In

A: Do you mind? B: No.

A: 괜찮겠어요? B: 네. 괜찮아요.

Ashleigh looks at Gabriella. Gabriella summers, a middle-aged celebrity, stands. Ashleigh stops and gestures excitedly at her.

ASHLEIGH: Oh. You're Gabriella Summers.

GABRIELLA: Yes.

ASHLEIGH: Oh, I have so many questions for you!

GABRIELLA: Oh, well.

ASHLEIGH: You know…for my article, um…

GABRIELLA: Okay.

MANHATTAN STREETS

Gatsby and Terry walk down the sidewalk.

GATSBY: It's not that much further. It's just at the corner here.

TERRY: Great. I love to walk.

GATSBY: It's actually the same house I grew up in.

TERRY: Tsk. Oh, so I bet you went to one of those fancy schools, huh?

GATSBY: Yeah, I did.

TERRY: Is it true that all the kids there have charge accounts at Bergdorf's or Prada? They spend lots of money, and do lots of drugs and…blah- dee- blah.

GATSBY: I wouldn't know, I didn't hang out with most of the kids. I just liked to watch old movies and play my vinyl.

TERRY: That's kinda weird. So, I bet you were a bookworm.

애슐리는 가브리엘을 본다. 중년의 유명인 가브리엘 써머스는 서있
다. 애슐리는 멈춰서 그녀에게 손짓을 한다.

애슐리: 가브리엘라 써머스 씨죠?

가브리엘라 써머스: 네.

애슐리: 여쭤볼 게 아주 많아요.

가브리엘라 써머스: 그래요?

애슐리: 기사 때문에요.

가브리엘라 써머스: 네.

맨하탄거리
개츠비와 테리는 보도 아래를 걸어간다.

개츠비: 거의 다 왔어요. 바로 저 코너예요.

테리: 괜찮아요. 걷는 거 좋아요.

개츠비: 이 집에서 자랐어요.

테리: 그럼 좋은 학교 다녔겠네요?

개츠비: 네.

테리: 거기 애들은 백화점이나 명품 매장에 외상
계정이 있다면서요? 돈도 엄청 쓰고 약도 엄
청 해대고?

개츠비: 애들과 안 어울려서 몰라요. 난 옛날 영화
보고 연주나 들어서.

테리: 특이했네. 그럼 책벌레였겠네요.

- charge accounts
  외상거래계정

- hang out
  (…에서) 많은 시간을 보내다
  socialize – spend time

- vinyl
  (속어) 레코드판(음반)(record albums)

- bookworm
  책벌래

That's kinda weird.
kinda는 kind of를 발음대로 철자한 대
화체 표현으로 '약간 좀, 어느 정도' 라는
의미로 쓰인다.

That's kinda weird.
약간 좀 특이하네. 이상하네.

GATSBY: Not really. My mother is this...culture vulture. According to her, I must visit this museum, or I must attend this piano recital, or see this opera. I must read my Henry James, even if Henry James, it puts me to sleep, you know I like Charlie Parker.

TERRY: Who's that?

GATSBY: Forget it, that's all right.

Terry grabs his arm and tugs playfully on it.

TERRY: God, you really are in a bad mood.

CLUB – NIGHT
Ashleigh, holds her notebook open and looks at Gabriella.
Roland stops beside Ashleigh.

ROLAND: There you are.

Ashleigh and Gabriella turn to Roland. He looks apologetically at Gabriella.

ROLAND: Excuse me for the interruption.

ASHLEIGH: You're here.

ROLAND: Yes, I am.

ASHLEIGH: We've been looking everywhere for you

ROLAND: I...had to get my thoughts in order.

ASHLEIGH: Well, I mean, you vanished off the planet...Mister

ROLAND: Mm. Can I speak to you alone for a minute?

ASHLEIGH: I mean, I've actually been dying to talk to you. Your movie was so much better than you led me to believe.

개츠비: 뭐 딱히 그것도… 엄마가 문화 포식자라서. '이 미술관엔 꼭 가라. 이 피아노 연주회엔 꼭 나가라. 이 오페라는 꼭 봐라. 헨리 제임스는 꼭 읽어라. 잠만 쏟아지더구만. 난 찰리 파커가 좋아요.

테리: 누구죠?

개츠비: 됐어요.

테리는 그의 팔을 잡고 장난스럽게 팔짱을 낀다.

테리: 자기 기분이 진짜 안 좋구나.

클럽

애슐리는 노트를 연채로 가브리엘라를 쳐다본다. 로랜드는 애슐리옆에 멈춘다.

로랜드: 여기 있었네요.

애슐리와 가브리엘라는 로랜드에게 몸을 돌린다. 그는 미안하게 가브리엘라를 쳐다본다.

로랜드: 방해해서 죄송해요.

애슐리: 오셨네요.

로랜드: 그래요.

애슐리: 우리가 얼마나 찾아다녔는데요.

로랜드: 생각할 시간이 필요했어요.

애슐리: 연기처럼 사라졌잖아요. 고뇌하는 예술가님.

로랜드: 둘이 얘기 좀 할까요?

애슐리: 저도 너무 얘기하고 싶었어요. 영화는 말씀보다 훨씬 좋았어요.

- **tugs**
  당기다[잡아당기다]

- **playfully**
  장난스럽게

- **apologetically**
  미안하게

- **get ~ in order**
  정리하다

- **vanish off**
  사라지다

- **dying**
  몹시 ~하고 싶어하는
  desperate – very eager

You really are in a bad mood.
be in a good(bad) mood는 '기분이 좋다(나쁘다)'는 의미로 쓰인다.

You really are in a bad mood.
너 기분이 진짜 안 좋구나.

ROLAND: Yes?

ASHLEIGH: (nodding) Mm–hm. Yeah, the climax was, it was so moving. It was very vintage Roland Pollard.

Roland gestures at a chair. Ashleigh sits down in the chair and Roland sits down in a chair.

ROLAND: I was afraid I, um, wasn't going to see you again. Forgive me, I'm, uh...I'm a little drunk.

ASHLEIGH: We were very worried about you.

ROLAND: I spent the day...thinking, re–reflecting about my work, my life. Uh...uhh, I want for us to get to know each other, Ashleigh.

ASHLEIGH: (surprised) You do?

ROLAND: Would you consider coming with me to the South of France?

ASHLEIGH: The where of what?!

ROLAND: Your voice is, is the only voice that's, that's, that's had any clarity for me in ages. The only voice that encouraged me where...where I actually...believed it. Like a muse.

ASHLEIGH: I...mean, I– (inhales and pauses) I–I think you've had too much to drink today. I know I have!

ROLAND: Come with me. You can wake up every morning and smell the orange trees. (pause) I'll talk to you about my new movie and, and I can learn from your unspoiled honesty...and, and y–, and you, you can...smell the orange trees.

로랜드:	그래요?
애슐리:	(고개를 끄덕이며) 클라이맥스도 감동이었고 당신의 최고작이에요.

로렌드는 의자에 손짓을 한다. 애슐리는 의자에 앉고 로랜드도 의자에 앉는다.

로랜드:	다시 못 만날까 봐 걱정됐어요. 미안해요, 나… 좀 취했어요.
애슐리:	우리 걱정 많이 했어요.
로랜드:	하루 종일…내 작업과 인생에 대해 고민했어요. 우리 서로 좀 더 알았으면 해요.
애슐리:	(놀라며) 그래요?
로랜드:	나와 함께 프랑스 남부에 갈래요?
애슐리:	어디의 어디요?
로랜드:	당신 음성은 정말 오랜만에 명확하게 내 영혼을 울린 유일한 소리예요. 그 음성의 힘을 다시금 믿게 됐어요. 마치 뮤즈처럼.
애슐리:	(숨을 들이쉬며 잠시 멈춰서) 너무 취하신 거 같아요. 저도 그렇구요.
로랜드:	같이 가요. 매일 아침 오렌지 나무 향기에 일어나고. (잠시 멈추고)난 내 새 영화 얘길 들려주고 당신의 온전한 솔직함에서 뭔가 배우고. 당신은… 오렌지 향기를 즐기고.

- moving
  감동적인(emotionally effecting)

- vintage
  (특정 인물의 작품들 중) 최고의

- forgive
  용서하다

- reflect
  깊이(곰곰히) 생각하다

- in ages
  오랫동안
  a very long time

- muse
  (작가, 화가등에게 영감을 주는)뮤즈
  (inspiration)

- unspoiled
  훼손되지 않은

I spent the day thinking about my work.
spend + 시간(돈)+ -ing는 '~하는데 시간(돈)을 보내다(쓰다)' 라는 의미이다.

 Zoom In

I spent the day thinking about my work.
나는 하루 종일 내 작업과 인생에 대해 고민했어.

ASHLEIGH: I, I think you're c–confusing me with this, like, total other Ashley. The L–E–Y spelling.

She picks up her glass of wine and drinks from it.
A short time later, Ashleigh walks through the crowd. She looks excitedly at him.

ASHLEIGH: (laughing) Hey, I thought that was you!

TED: You're here!

Ashleigh, who has a glass of whiskey in her hand, clinks her glass against Ted's glass.

ASHLEIGH: I'm here! Everybody's here. Roland's here!

TED: Oh, yeah. I, I, I, I came with him.

ASHLEIGH: (sipping drink) Mm!

TED: I was try–, I was trying to figure out a way to contact you. I have–I apologize for today.

ASHLEIGH: Oh, that's okay.

TED: You were very, very understanding.

ASHLEIGH: I felt really bad for you.

TED: No, no, no. No, no, no, no, no, no, no, no, I'm fine. I'm fine. Uh, I–I'm, I'm as, I'm about as well as could be expected.

ASHLEIGH: Yeah.

Ted picks up his glass of liquor and drinks from it.

ASHLEIGH: Well, I mean, yeah. Yeah, I mean, for a guy that, you know, just discovered that, mmm...his wife was with his best friend, you know. I mean, you are at a party!

애슐리: 감독님의 애슐리와 절 헷갈리시나 봐요.
L-E-Y 로 끝나는 애슐리.

그녀는 와인잔을 들고 마신다.
잠시 후에, 애슐리는 군중 속으로 걸어간다. 그녀는 그를 흥분해서
쳐다본다.

애슐리: (웃으며) 작가님인 줄 알았어요!

테드: 여기 있었네요!

애슐리는 손에 술잔을 들고 테드의 잔에 소리를 내며 부딪힌다.

애슐리: 네! 다들 여기 있어요, 롤리도.

테드: 네, 같이 왔어요.

에슐리: (술을 조금 마시며) 음!

테드: 당신 연락처를 찾고 있었어요. 아깐 미안했
어요.

애슐리: 괜찮아요.

테드: 당신의 이해심 고마워요.

애슐리: 많이 속상하시죠?

테드: 아니, 괜찮아요. 예상했던 만큼이에요.

애슐리: 네.

테드는 술잔을 들고 마신다.

애슐리: 네, 그게 참…부인이 절친과 바람난 걸 알았
으니…그래도 파티에 왔네요!

- confusing
  혼란스러운

- crowd
  사람들, 군중

- clink
  쨍그랑하는 소리를 내다

- understanding
  이해심 있는

I'm about as well as could be expected.
as ~as 는 '만큼 ~한' 이라는 의미로 동
등비교를 나타낸다.

I'm about as well as could be expected.

예상했던 만큼이에요.

TED:	I'm at a party. I got home, I got to my apartment, and I was wondering why Connie's infidelity, it w-, i–it w-, it didn't wound me as deeply as it should...you know? A–a–all I could keep, I–I kept thinking about, I remembered what you said about my movies. And I thought, my God, why is Ashleigh's...approbation so meaningful to me? It, it really, it was. And I, i–it struck me. It struck me. You and I were thrown together. We, we, we were tryin' to f–, w–, find a wandering rogue Roland Pollard, we had an adventure together, and in the movie version, in my movie version the guy...looks up and he realizes he, he's, he's fallen in love with the girl.

Ashleigh, wobbling drunkenly, reacts with surprise.
A short time later, Vega stands at another section of the bar as miller, sitting shakes her head at him.

VEGA:	I've played that role so many times.
MILLER:	Writing like this does not come along every day.

Ashleigh walks. She waves her hand drunkenly at Vega.

ASHLEIGH:	Hi!
VEGA:	(turning to Miller) Hey, y–
MILLER:	I'm gonna call Sammy if I don't hear from you by Friday.
VEGA:	Yes, you call Sammy. All right. Ciao.

테드:	그러게요. 집에 가서 곰곰이 생각했죠. 아내의 외도가 왜 이 정도밖에 안 속상할까. 그러다 당신이 내영화에 대해 말한 게 생각났죠. 당신의 인정은 왜 이렇게 감동적일까? 그때 알았어요. 우린 갑자기 하나가 된 거예요. 방황하는 롤리를 같이 찾으면서 함께 모험하다, 내 영화 버전으로 하자면, 그 남자는…올려다보며 그녀와 사랑에 **빠진** 걸 깨닫죠.

애슐리는 취해서 비틀거리며 놀라서 반응한다.
잠시 후에 제가는 다른 곳에 서있고 밀러는 서서 그에게 고개를 젓는다.

베가:	그런 역은 많이 했잖아.
밀러:	이런 대본은 흔치 않아.

애슐리는 걷는다. 그녀는 베가에게 취해서 손을 흔든다.

애슐리:	저 왔어요.
베가:	(밀러에게 몸을 돌리며) 왔군요.
밀러:	금요일까지 연락이 없으면 샘한테 전화할게.
베가:	알았어, 안녕.

- **infidelity**
  (배우자나 애인에 대한)부정

- **wound**
  상처를 입히다

- **approbation**
  승인, 찬성

- **wander**
  방황하다

- **wobbling**
  흔들거리는

- **drunkenly**
  취해서

He's fallen in love with the girl.
fall in love with는 '-와 사랑에 빠지다'라는 의미로, 현재완료(have fallen)시제로 사용되어 '(과거에서 현재까지도) 사랑에 빠져있다'는 의미이다.

He's fallen in love with the girl.
그는 그녀와 사랑에 빠져 있다.

Vega and miller kiss on the cheeks as Ashleigh sips from her glass of whiskey.
Vega turns back to Ashleigh as Miller walks away from the bar.

VEGA: (turning to Ashleigh, chuckling) I'm sorry it took me so long.

ASHLEIGH: ...it's so funny. 'Cause my father would always
say, you know, when drinking you should never
mix grain and grape together, but...nah, I think
they go really good!

VEGA: Yeah. Hey, you know what? I think we should
split.

ASHLEIGH: We should split?

WELLES TOWNHOUSE/ FOYER
Gatsby's mother stands at the bottom of the steps of a grand staircase, shaking
hands with a female guest. Gatsby's father stands on the steps in the lavish
townhouse, shaking hands with a make guest.

MOTHER: Gatsby

Terry and Gatsby stop in the foyer. Gatsby looks at mother as Terry hands her
coat to a servant.

MOTHER: If you always intended to come, you should have
told us. You know I am not fond of surprises.

Terry and Gatsby look at mother and father.

GATSBY: Mother...Dad...this is my girlfriend, Ashleigh
Enright.

TERRY: Hi, how are you?

MOTHER: How lovely to meet you, Ashleigh.

TERRY: You...too.

FATHER: Hello, it's a pleasure.

베가와 밀러는 볼에 키스를 하고 애슐리는 위스키를 마신다. 베가
는 애슐리쪽으로 몸을 돌리고 밀러는 바에서 멀리 걸어나간다.

베가: (애슐리 쪽으로 몸을 돌리고 웃으며) 너무 오래 걸려
서 미안해요.

애슐리: 재밌네요. 아빠가 늘 위스키와 와인은 섞어
마시지 말라셨는데 섞어도 아주 좋은걸요.

베가: 네, 우리 이제 나가죠.

애슐리: 나가요?

웰즈 타운 하우스/현관

개츠비의 엄마는 여성 손님과 악수를 하며 웅장한 계단아래에 서 있
다. 개츠비의 아빠는 호화스러운 타운하우스에 서서 남자 손님들과
악수를 하고 있다. 엄마는 개츠비를 쳐다본다.

엄마: 개츠비!

테리와 개츠비는 현관에 서 있다, 개츠비는 엄마를 보고있고 테리
는 도우미에게 코트를 건네준다.

엄마: 올 거였으면 미리 말해주지. 엄마 놀라는 거
안 좋아하잖니.

테리와 개츠비는 엄마와 아빠를 쳐다본다.

개츠비: 엄마, 아빠… 여자친구 애슐리 엔라잇이에
요.

테리: 안녕하세요.

엄마: 반가워요, 애슐리.

테리: 저두요.

아빠: 어서 와요.

- **sip**
  홀짝거리다, 조금씩 마시다.

- **split**
  (속어)떠나다(leave)

- **lavish**
  호화로운

- **servant**
  고용인, 도우미

- **be fond of**
  ~을 좋아하다

I'm sorry it took me so long.
'It takes + 사람 + 시간' 은 '시간이 ~
걸리다' 는 의미로 쓰인다.

I'm sorry it took me so long.
너무 오래 걸려서 미안해요.

Terry steps toward father and shakes his hand.

TERRY:	Hi, how are you?
FATHER:	Hi. I'm well, thanks.
TERRY:	Nice to meet you.
FATHER:	I've done business with your father.

Father turns and walks up the stairs. Mother, Gatsby and Terry follow him up the steps.

TERRY:	Yes, he speaks very highly of you.
FATHER:	Aha! Actually, I've never met him. It's his bank.
TERRY:	Yeah, he's got so many banks.

WELLES TOWNHOUSE/ LIVING ROOM
The townhouse is filled with party guest, and Terry is sitting on a sofa, chatting with an older man named Leonard. Eli, a middle-aged man, enters with two glasses of champagne.

ELI: So, how are things at Yardley?

Eli stops beside Gatsby and hands him both glasses of champagne.

GATSBY: Aah, it's very quiet, you know. We get a lotta snow in the winter, that sorta thing. Very rural, but...I chose it because they have a great Kurdish Studies program, yes, yes...

LEONARD: Have you thought more about a career? Your father was bemoaning the fact that you were still undecided.

Gatsby hands a glass of champagne to Terry, then sits down beside her on the sofa. Two women named Wand and Dana stand beside the sofa and Hunter and Lily are standing behind the sofa. Gatsby looks at Leonard.

테리는 아빠쪽으로 걸어가 악수를 한다.

테리:	잘 지내시죠?
아빠:	네, 고마워요.
테리:	반갑습니다.
아빠:	난 아버지하고 거래해요.

아빠는 몸을 돌려 계단으로 올라가고 개츠비와 테리는 그를 따라 계단으로 올라간다.

테리:	아버지가 칭찬 많이 하셨어요.
아빠:	직접 뵌 적은 없어요. 그분 은행과 거래하는 거지.
테리:	네, 아버지 은행이 좀 많죠.

웰스 타운 하우스/거실
타운 하우스는 파티 손님들고 가든차 있고 테리는 레오나드라는 나이든 남자와 이야기 하며 소파에 앉아있다. 중년인 엘리는 두 잔의 샴페인을 가지고 들어온다.

엘리:	학교 생활은 어떠니?

엘리는 개츠비 옆에 멈춰서 그에게 삼페인 두병을 건넨다.

개츠비:	조용해요. 겨울엔 눈이 많이 오고 시골답죠. 전 쿠르드어 강의가 좋아서 거기로 간 거예요.
레오나드:	진로는 아직 못 정했니? 네 아빠가 걱정하던데.

개츠비는 테리에게 샴페인 잔을 건네고 소파에 그녀 옆에 앉는다. 완다와 다나라고 불리는 두 여자는 소파 옆에 서 있고 헌터와 릴리는 소파 뒤에 서 있다. 개츠비는 레오나드를 쳐다본다.

- **do business**
  거래하다

- **rural**
  시골의, 지방의

- **bemoan**
  한탄하다, 슬퍼하다

- **hand**
  건네주다

He speaks very highly of you.
speak highly(well) of는 '~을 칭찬하다, 좋게 말하다' 이고 speak ill of는 '~을 욕하다, 험담하다' 라는 의미를 가진다.

He speaks very highly of you.
그가 당신에 대해 칭찬 많이 했어요.

283

GATSBY:	Well, you know, I have, Leonard and, um…I want to go into nuclear physics…uh, maybe open a little store, sell dark matter.
HUNTER:	He's kidding you. No, um, he likes to sit at the piano and sing. And play blackjack.
WANDA:	And when you were a boy, your mother wanted you to be a concert pianist.
GATSBY:	(grinning and nodding) Mmmm, ah, yes, well, she always had big plans for me.
HUNTER:	Yeah…she did.
LEONARD:	How 'bout you, Ashleigh? What are your plans?
GATSBY:	Well, eh, she wants to be a journalist, actually.
DANA:	T.V. or print?
GATSBY:	Yeah, political stuff.
TERRY:	I'd like to do the weather.
GATSBY:	She'll report from all the…trouble spots.
TERRY:	On the weather.
HUNTER:	Great.

WELLES TOWNHOUSE/ DINING ROOM
Father steps toward mother, who is standing at the buffet table getting some food. Terry walks to the table, then mother looks up at her. Terry picks up a snack and smiles at mother, then walks toward the living room door.

FATHER:	You've been…staring at Ashleigh all night.
MOTHER:	There is something about that girl.
FATHER:	She's quite pretty. Mm, sophisticated for a young girl.

개츠비:	네, 생각해 봤는데… 핵물리학을 공부해서 암흑 물질을 팔아 볼까 해요.
헌터:	얘 장난치는 거예요. 피아노 치며 노래하는 거 또 블랙잭을 좋아해요.
완다:	너 어렸을 때 네 엄마가 피아니스트 만들려고 했잖니.
개츠비:	(웃으며 고개를 끄덕이며) 늘 절 위한 큰 포부를 가지셨었죠.
헌터:	그랬어.
레오나드:	애슐리는 계획이 뭔가?
개츠비:	기자가 되고 싶어해요.
다나:	TV 아님 지면?
개츠비:	정치쪽.
테리:	TV 기상 캐스터요.
개츠비:	분쟁 지역 소식.
테리:	그 지역 날씨요.
헌터:	좋네.

웰스 타운하우스/다이닝 룸
아빠는 음식을 가지러 뷔페 테이블에 서 있는 엄마쪽으로 걸어간다. 테리는 테이블 쪽으로 걸어가고 엄마는 그녀를 쳐다본다. 테리는 스낵을 집고 엄마를 보고 웃고 그 때 거실 문으로 걸어간다.

아빠:	애슐리 얼굴 뚫어지겠어. 뭐 문제 있어요?
엄마:	뭔가 좀 이상해요.
아빠:	예쁘기만 한데. 나이에 비해 세련됐고.

■ blackjack
블랙잭(카드게임)

You've been staring at Ashleigh all night.
stare at은 '~을 응시하다, 빤히 쳐다보다' 라는 뜻이고, 현재완료진행(have been staring)으로 쓰여 '저녁 내내 계속 빤히 쳐다보다' 는 강조의 의미로 쓰였다.

You've been staring at Ashleigh all night.
애슐리를 저녁 내내 쳐다 보내.(애슐리 얼굴 뚫어지겠어).

VEGA'S LOFT BUILDING

Ashleigh and Vega get out of Vega's limousine, which has stopped in front of his building. As the limousine moves down the street, they hurry toward the building. Rain has started falling again.

INT. VEGA'S LOFT

VEGA: Come on in.

Vega and Ashleigh enter, then Vega turns on the lights and illuminates the loft.

ASHLEIGH: Wow. Look at this place.
VEGA: Nice, isn't it?

Vega walks to toward the living room area.

VEGA: What was that all about with...Ted Davidoff and, and Rollie Pollard?
ASHLEIGH: We were just talking.
VEGA: Yeah?
VEGA: All right. Well, don't worry. I'm sure they were very interested in that story you're writing.
ASHLEIGH: Mm, yeah, today's been quite a story.
VEGA: And...that's just the beginning. Please...sit down. Relax.

Ashleigh sits down on the sofa and looks around.

ASHLEIGH: This is really amazing.

WELLES TOWNHOUSE/ LIVING ROOM

Gatsby sits glumly at the bar as hunter, standing beside him, pours himself a glass of scotch.

베가의 로프트 건물
애슐리와 베가는 베가의 리무진에서 내려서 그의 건물 앞에 멈춘다. 리무진이 거리로 이동할 때, 그들은 빌딩으로 서둘러 간다. 비는 다시 오기 시작했다.

베가의 로프트 건물 실내.

베가:　　　들어와요.

베가와 애슐리는 들어가서 베가는 불을 켜고 복층 방을 밝힌다.

애슐리:　　우와, 대단하네요.
베가:　　　괜찮죠?

베가는 거실로 걸어간다.

베가:　　　테드랑 롤리하고는 무슨 얘길 그렇게 했어요?
애슐리:　　그냥 얘기요.
베가:　　　그래요?
베가:　　　그랬구나. 걱정 마요. 당신 기사에 관심 많았을 테니까.
애슐리:　　오늘 정말 대박이었어요.
베가:　　　그리고… 그건 시작에 불과해요. 앉아요. 편안하게.

애슐리는 소파에 앉아서 주변을 둘러본다.

애슐리:　　집이 정말 좋네요.

웰즈 하우스 거실
개츠비는 바에 앉아 있고 헌터는 그옆에 서서 잔에 술을 따른다.

- turn on
  ~을 켜다.

- illuminate
  (~에 불을)비추다

- be interested in
  ~에 관심을 가지다

- quite a story
  대단한 이야기

- glumly
  무뚝뚝하게, 침울하게.

Today's been quite a story.
quite a story는 '대단한 이야기(대박 스토리)' 라는 의미로 쓰여, '정말 대박이었어' 라는 의미를 가진다.

Today's been quite a story.
오늘 정말 대박(대단한 스토리)이었어요.

HUNTER: She's very charming. And hot! You didn't say Ashleigh was hot.

GATSBY: I told you she was sexy.

HUNTER: She older than you?

GATSBY: Huh?

HUNTER: She looks older.

GATSBY: That's what you want, a little experience.

HUNTER: (pause) You'd better grow up and get a profession. You think a girl like that wants to live hand to mouth?

GATSBY: Funny you should put it that way.

Gatsby looks down.

헌터:	아주 매력 있네. 야하고! 그런 말은 안 했잖아.
개츠비:	섹시하다고 했잖아.
헌터:	너보다 연상이니?
개츠비:	뭐?
헌터:	연상 같아 보여.
개츠비:	그런 거 원했구나. 경험이 좀 있는…
헌터:	(잠시 멈추여) 그럼 직장부터 구해야지. 저런 여자가 입에 풀칠하며 살길 바라겠냐?
개츠비:	뭔가 알고 하는 소리 같네.

개츠비는 아래를 내려다 본다.

■ live hand to mouth
하루살이 생활하다, 간신히 지내다

You'd better grow up and get a profession.
You'd는 You had의 줄임말로, had better+ 동사원형은 '~하는게 좋겠다'는 충고의 의미로 사용된다.

You'd better grow up and get a profession.
너는 성숙하고 직장을 구해야지.

A Rainy
Day in
New York

Culture Vulture

GATSBY: (voice over) That's my girlfriend, Ashleigh Enright. My dad knew one of her father's banks in Arizona, and naturally, with those family credentials, my mother wants us to get married, sight unseen.

영화의 첫 부분에서, 개츠비는 엄마가 얼굴도 보지 않고 배경만으로 어머니의 이상형이라고 하는 여자친구 애슐리를 소개하는 부분이 나온다. 이렇게 개츠비의 엄마가 상류층을 추구하는 분이라는 것을 첫 장면부터 소개한 것은 상류층의 배경이 이 영화의 중요한 한 부분이라는 것을 알 수 있다.

GATSBY: Not really. My mother is this…culture vulture.

위 대사에 개츠비는 자신의 가족들을 'culture vulture' 라고 표현한다. 그렇다면, Culture Vulture란 무엇일까?
Culture Vulture는 culture(문화) 와 vulture(독수리)가 합쳐져서 '문화의 포식자 독수리라는 의미' 로, '문화광' 즉, 정통문화영역인 클래식, 미술, 그리고 문학 등에 지대한 관심이 있는 사람을 말한다.

TERRY: I bet you went to one of those fancy schools, huh?
GATSBY: Yeah, I did.
TERRY: Is it true that all the kids there have charge accounts at Bergdorf's or Prada? They spend lots of money, and do lots of drugs and…blah-dee-blah.

테리는 개츠비에게 "화려한 학교" 즉 유서있는 학교들을 다녔을 것이라고 말하고, '거기 애들은 백화점이나 명품 매장에 외상 계정이 있다면서요? 돈도 엄청 쓰고 약도 엄청 하고?' 라도 말을 한다. 이 대사에서 암시하듯이, 개츠비의 집안은 꽤 권위 있는 부자 집안으로, 문화 광이신 개츠비의 어머니는 교양 있어 보이기 위해, 남들의 시선을 의식하며 개츠비에게 미술관과 피아노 연주회, 오페라 등 상류층 사람들이 즐겨보는 것들을 보라고 요구하는 것을 아래의 대사를 보면 알 수 있다.

GATSBY: According to her, I must visit this museum, or I must attend this piano recital, or see this opera. I must read my Henry James, even if Henry James, it puts me to sleep, you know?

다음에 나오는 "A farrago of WASP plutocrats"는 개츠비 가족들을 지칭하는 말이다. farrago는 '뒤죽박죽' 이라는 뜻으로, 대화에서는 잘 쓰이지 않는 단어를 사용함으로써 시적인 느낌을 주고, WASP는 'White Anglo-Saxon Protestant' 의 줄임말로, 전형적인 미국의 백인 중상층들을 말하며, 특히 돈이 많거나 사회적 지위가 높은 사람들을 비꼬아 표현한 말이다. plutocrats는 부유한 사람들이 돈을 이용해서 정치적으로 영향력을 행사하는 금권 정치가들을 말한다.

GATSBY: Why is that so bad, Chan? Because I
            wanted to spend the night with Ashleigh
            alone in New York, not with a farrago of
            WASP plutocrats.

CHAN: "A farrago of WASP plutocrats"? Sounds
            like something on the menu at a fusion
            restaurant.

또한, 아래 대사에서도 우리에게 다소 생소한 'Basquiats'와
'Falcon to a Gulfstream'이 나온다

GATSBY: I'm not interested in the euro or how many
            Basquiats somebody owns or whether they
            prefer a Falcon to a Gulfstream. I mean,
            these things have no meaning to me.

　장 미셸 바스키아 (Jean-Michel Basquiat)는 흑인 미술 작가로 주로 백인우월주의를 비판하는 작품들을 남겼다. 그는 작은 골목의 그래피티 작가로 활동하다가 미국에서 하위문화에 대한 관심이 높아짐에 따라 그 후에는 그의 작품성을 인정받아 '검은 피카소' 라고 불렸다. 그의 그림 가격은 그의 사망 이후 더 증가하였고, 2017년, 바스키아(Basquiats)의 그림 '무제' 는 1억 달러를 넘긴 가격에 낙찰되었을 정도로 고가의 작품이다.

　그러나 개츠비는 culture vulture 를 자신의 어머니를 비하하는 발언으로 사용한다. 자신의 가족들과 다르게 자유로운 성향인 개츠비는 가족들과 다른 자신에 괴리감을 느낀다. 개츠비는 작가 바스키아(Basquiats)를 언급하여 바스키아(Basquiats)의 백인우월주의를 비판하는 작품을 수집하는 자신의 어머니와 어울리는 부유한 백인들을 비꼬아 표현한다. 또한, 팰콘(Falcon)과 걸프스트림(Gulfstream)은 전세기의 모델 이름으로 같은 맥락에서 자신의 어머니의 자선 행사에 참석하는 부유한 사람들과 어울리기 싫다는 설명을 하고 있다.

하지만, 게츠비가 부유층에 대해 비아냥 거리며 부정적으로 이야기를 하지만 아래의 대화에서 보듯이 로맨택 보다는 현실세계에서는 본인도 어쩔수 없는 부모의 돈 때문에 독립하지 못한다는 것을 보여주는 개츠비의 이중적인 측면이 보인다.

CHAN:	I notice you haven't renounced your family's money.
GATSBY:	What does that mean?
CHAN:	That means you could move out...get a job, put yourself through college.
GATSBY:	Oh, yeah? As a what?
CHAN:	Piano player in a dive. Or...maybe a poker player? Dice hustler?
GATSBY:	You're bad, Chan. You're goin' straight to hell.
CHAN:	There's something romantic about gamblers and...old songs...meeting under a clock.
GATSBY:	Yeah...maybe in movies, but this is real life.

또한, 개츠비는 culture vulture인 어머니를 싫어하지만, 애슐리가 부유한 은행장 딸이며 이쁘고 귀여운 여자친구라고 챈에게 자랑을 한다.

CHAN: Who's Ashleigh? The rodeo queen you're
             dating?
GATSBY: She's not a cowgirl.
GATSBY: She comes from one of the biggest banking
             families in Tucson. She, she was a
             debutante, actually.

다음의 대사에서도 개츠비가 본인의 문화적 지식을 자랑하듯 Charlie Parker가 좋다고 하는데 테리가 누구인지 모른다며 누구냐고 묻자 고개를 저으며 'Forget it(됐어요)' 이라 하며 본인이 속한 상류층에 대해 테리는 모를 것 이니 그만 두자는 무시하는 듯한 모습을 볼 수 있다.

GATSBY:　　　I like Charlie Parker.
TERRY:　　　Who's that?

Gatsby looks down and shakes his head.

GATSBY:　　　Forget it, that's all right.

이렇듯 문화 광 (culture vulture)의 모습은 미국 상류층에 속하기 위해 문화에 대한 지속적인 관심을 가지려고 노력하는 개츠비의 엄마와 또한 아들 개츠비도 그에 따르도록 하게 하는 모습에서 볼 수 있다. 그렇지만 그들이 인위적으로 노력하는 것은 결국 개츠비와 애슐리의 사랑에서는 곧 끝이 나게 된다. 아마 그들이 이틀 동안 오는 비를 맞으면서 각자 혼란과 혼동의 시간을 보내면서 그들이 갖고 있던 위선과 편견을 씻어 내린 것 아닌가 한다. 비가 오는 날 개츠비와 개츠비의 엄마 모두가 솔직해지고 비밀을 감추지 않고 털어내는 모습들이 이 영화의 제목과 인물들이 돋보이는 영화인 것 같다.

Chapter 9

혼돈의 시간

Chaos

시간 01:12:25 ~ 01:21:30

VEGA'S LOFT/ LIVING ROOM
Ashleigh sits by herself on the sofa and holds a cigarette in her hand. She is talking to herself as vega is getting drinks.

ASHLEIGH: Keep your hand on the wheel, Ashleigh. I mean...God, he obviously wants to go to bed with you. I mean, how do you feel about this? (finishing blowing smoke, then inhales and sighs) You have a boyfriend. (licks lips pensively) Yes, but...I mean, this is Francisco Vega! I mean apart from him being so sexy, it's, I mean, he's...an international icon? À la Mahatma Gandhi. How can you say no? This is a story you can tell your grandchildren.

VEGA: May I show you upstairs?

ASHLEIGH: Oh, um...sure.

VEGA: If you like it here, you're gonna love it over there.

Ashleigh walks. Vega is standing with two glasses of whiskey.

VEGA: I got us some whiskey.

베가의 로프트/거실

애슐리는 소파에 혼자 앉아있고 손에 담배를 잡고 있다. 그녀는 혼잣말을 하고, 베가는 술을 가지러 간다.

애슐리:	정신 바짝 차려, 애슐리. 너와 자고 싶어하는 게 뻔하잖아. 어쩌면 좋겠어?
	(담배연기를 내뿜고, 숨을 들이쉬며 한숨을 쉰다) 넌 남친이 있어. (깊은 생각에 빠져 입술을 핥으며) 그래, 하지만…프란시스코 베가잖아! 엄청 섹시한데다가 세계적인 아이콘이잖아. 말하자면 마하트마 간디 같은. 어떻게 거부할 수 있겠어? 손주들한테 들려줄 얘깃거리가 될 텐데
베가:	위층 구경해볼래요?
애슐리:	좋아요.
베가:	여기가 맘에 들었다면 위층도 좋을 거예요.

애슐리는 걷는다. 베가는 두 잔의 위스키를 가지고 서있다.

베가:	위스키요.

- Keep your hand on the wheel
  정신 바짝 차려(Maintain your self-control)

- pensively
  깊은 생각에 잠겨 , 수심에 잠겨

- À la
  ~와 같은 식으로(in the manner of)

He hands one of the glasses to Ashleigh. They walk up the stairs.

ASHLEIGH: Is this where you sleep?

VEGA: Yeah. When I sleep.

VEGA'S LOFT/ BEDROOM
Ashleigh and Vega walk up the steps to the bedroom.

VEGA: Look. You, you can see the whole apartment from here. special.

ASHLEIGH: (with glass to lips) It's nice.

The bedroom is open—walled, like a balcony, and looks out over the entire apartment.

VEGA: Yeah, I know. I know.

Vega puts down his glass on a table, then kisses Ashleigh passionately.

ASHLEIGH: (surprised grunt) Vega (overlapping) (intense moaning while kissing)

Ashleigh puts down her glass, then starts to pull off her sweater and blouse. Vega kneels down in front of Ashleigh, pulling on her skirt.

VEGA: Let me help you.

Ashleigh pulls off her sweater and blouse, then Vega looks excitedly at her.

VEGA: Ho—ho! Look at you!

Vega pulls off Ashleigh's skirt. The intercom buzzes.

VEGA: Oh, who the hell is that?

그는 애슐리에게 한잔을 건네준다. 그들은 계단위로 올라간다.

애슐리:　위에서 주무세요?

베가:　네 잘 때는요.

베가의 위층/침실
애슐리와 베가는 침실로 계단을 올라간다.

베가:　아래층이 다 내려다보여요. 그게 좀 특별하
　　　　죠.

애슐리:　(입에 잔을 가져가며) 멋지네요.

침실은 개방형 벽을 가지고 있고 발코니처럼 아파트 전체가 보인
다.

베가:　그쵸. 그렇다니까요.

베가는 테이블에 잔을 내려놓고 열정적으로 애슐리에게 키스를 한
다.

애슐리:　(놀라서 끙끙거리며) 베가. (긴장하고 신음소리를 내며
　　　　키스를 한다)

애슐리는 그녀의 잔을 내려 놓고, 그녀의 스웨터와 블라우스를 벗
기 시작한다.
베가는 애슐리 앞에서 무릎을 꿇고 그녀의 스커트를 잡아 당긴다.

베가:　도와줄게요.

에슐리는 그녀의 스웨터와 블라우스를 벗고, 베가는 그녀를 흥분해
서 쳐다본다.

베가:　기가 막히네!

베가가 에슐리의 스커트를 벗긴다. 인터콤이 울린다.

베가:　젠장, 누구야.

- **open-walled**
  개방형 벽면

- **passionately**
  열정적으로

- **kneel down**
  (무릎을) 꿇어 앉다

- **the hell**
  도대체(강조 의미)

Let me help you.
Let me + 동사원형은 '내가 ~해 줄게
(요)' 라는 의미이다.

Let me help you.
내가 도와 줄게요.

Vega drops the skirt on the floor. He stands up and gestures at Ashleigh, who is now in her bra and panties.

VEGA: Gi–, give me a sec.

He talks into the intercom.

VEGA: (into intercom) Yes?

TIFFANY: (over intercom) It's Tiffany. I'm home!

Vega turns off the intercom, then reacts with panic.

ASHLEIGH: But I thought you two weren't together anymore.

VEGA: (panicked breath) Wait a sec. (frantic panting) It's gonna be fine.

ASHLEIGH: ...you think it's okay? I mean, you said that you weren't together anymore.

Vega gestures at a door.

VEGA: You have to hide there.

Camera dollies a narrow balcony walkway, which leads toward a second stairwell at the back of the loft.

VEGA: Go, go behind that door.
Go, go, go. She can't see you. Go! Go, go, go!

Ashleigh walks hesitantly down the walkway. The sound of Vega running down the stairs to the living room is heard. The doorbell buzzes again. Vega rushes into the foyer and opens the front door.

TIFFANY: Surprise!

Tiffany Griffin, Vega's beautiful actress girlfriend, enters from the foyer with her luggage.

베가는 스커트를 마루에 떨어뜨린다. 그는 일어서서 브라와 팬티를
입고 있는 애슐리에게 손짓을 한다.

베가:　　　잠깐만요.

베가는 인터콤에 이야기한다.

베가:　　　(인터콤에 대고) 네?

티파니:　　(인터폰에서 들리는 소리) 나야, 티파니!

베가는 인터콤을 끄고, 기겁한다.

애슐리:　　헤어졌다고 했잖아요.

베가:　　　(허둥지둥하는 숨소리로) 잠깐만요. (정신 없이 헐떡거
　　　　　　리며) 괜찮을 거예요.

애슐리:　　괜찮아요? 끝난 거 맞죠?

베가는 문을 가리킨다.

베가:　　　저기, 문 뒤에 숨어요.

카메라는 위층의 뒤에 계단 쪽으로 향하는 좁은 발코니를 비춘다.

베가:　　　가요, 보면 안 돼요! 어서 어서!

애슐리는 서둘러서 통로 아래로 간다. 계단 아래로 달려가는 베가
의 소리가 들린다. 도어벨이 다시 울린다. 베가는 현관으로 서둘러
가고 현관문을 연다.

티파니:　　써프라이즈!

베가의 아름다운 여배우 여자친구인 티파니 그리핀은 짐을 가지고
현관으로 들어간다.

■ **panicked**
　 허둥지둥하는

■ **frantic**
　 정신없이(미친 듯이) 서두는

■ **panting**
　 헐떡거리는, 가슴이 두근거리는

■ **stairwell**
　 계단

■ **foyer**
　 로비, 현관

> **You said that you weren't
> together anymore.**
> not ~ anymore는 '더 이상 ~ 않다(not
> ~ any longer, no more, no longer)
> '라는 의미이다.

You said that you weren't together anymore.
당신들 헤어졌다고 했잖아요.

VEGA: What are you doing here?

TIFFANY: We wrapped two days early. I'm so glad you're home... it's starting to pour!

Tiffany takes off her wet jacket.

TIFFANY: I just got off the plane. I bet you weren't expecting me.

VEGA: I, I, I, I, I'm loving this, yeah, but...

Vega dashed, then Tiffany gestures at him with confusion.

TIFFANY: (calling after him) Francisco, why are you— What are you doing running around?

Tiffany rolls her suitcase.

VEGA: Just, uh, (frantic breaths) getting ready for you!

Vega dashed into the bedroom area, snatching Ashleigh's skirt off the floor and her glass of whiskey off the table. The sound of Tiffany walking up the stairs is heard.

VEGA: (frantic breaths) Welcome back.

TIFFANY: I just got off the plane. We wrapped two days early!

VEGA: Wow!

TIFFANY: I came right from Teterboro. I know you find being surprised arousing.

VEGA: Yeah, yeah. Did?

Tiffany starts to kiss Vega passionately.

베가: 어떻게 된 거야?

티파니: 촬영이 이틀 일찍 끝났어. 집에 있어 다행이네, 비 오는데.

티파니는 젖은 자켓을 벗는다.

티파니: 막 공항에서 왔어. 깜짝 놀랐지?

베가: 이런 거 좋아, 근데…

베가는 달려가고 티파니는 당황해서 그에게 손짓을 한다.

티파니: (그를 부르며) 왜 그렇게 뛰고 야단이야?

티파니는 가방을 끌고간다.

베가: 그냥… (정신없이 숨을 쉬며) 자기 맞을 준비!

베가는 침실로 달려가서 애슐리의 스커트를 바닥에서 주워 치우고 위스키잔을 테이블에서 치운다. 티파니가 계단을 올라오는 소리가 들린다.

베가: (정신없이 숨을 쉬며) 어서 와.

티파니: 비행기에서 막 내렸어. 이틀이나 일찍 끝나다니.

베가: 와우!

티파니: 공항에서 바로 왔어. 자기 이런 거에 흥분하잖아.

베가: 그럼 그럼.

티파니는 베가에게 키스를 한다.

- **wrap**
  (영화) 촬영 종료

- **pour**
  마구 쏟아지다(rain very heavily)

- **takes off**
  벗다

- **get off**
  내리다

- **dash**
  (급히) 서둘러 가다

- **snatch**
  움켜쥐다

- **arousing**
  자극적인

I'm loving this.
여기서 '이런 거 좋아' 라는 의미는 '너가 도착한 것이 좋다' 라는 의미이다.('I am excited about your arrival').

I'm loving this.
이런 거 좋아.

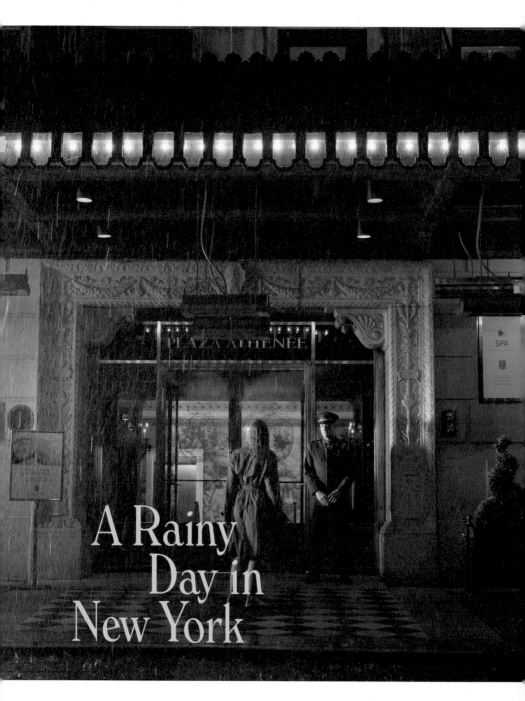

A Rainy
Day in
New York

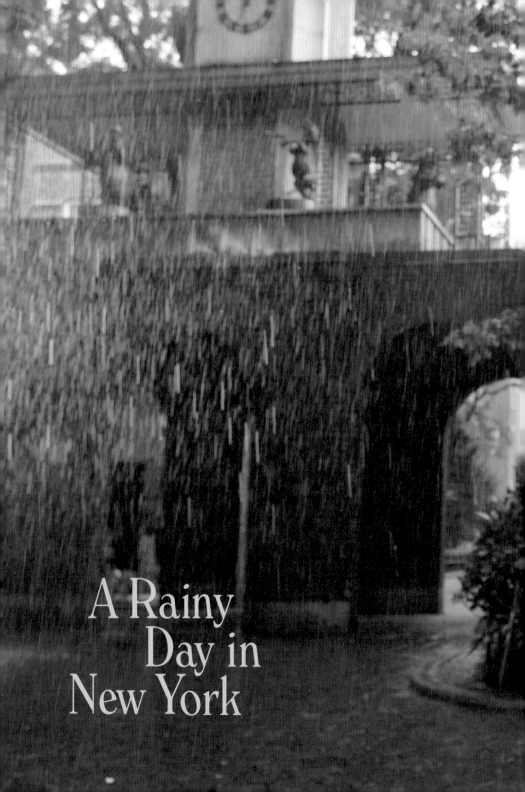

A Rainy
Day in
New York

TIFFANY: (kissing him) Mm, baby. Mm, I've missed you.

Ashleigh steps off the walkway and sneaks down the stairs toward a small back room. A glass door leading out to a fire escape is and a raincoat is on a hook on the wall.

VEGA: (slightly muffled) Yeah, me too.

As Ashleigh walks down the steps, she trips and knocks against a bookcase. A book falls to the floor. Tiffany, who has heard the book fall, leans back and looks at Vega.

TIFFANY: What was that?

Ashleigh hurries across the room to the back door. She unlocks the door.

VEGA: I didn't hear anything.

Tiffany stands up.

TIFFANY: No, I'm sure I heard something.

Ashleigh opens the back door to the fire escape. Rain is pouring down outside the loft.

TIFFANY: One sec.

Ashleigh, putting on the raincoat, walks to the back door. She opens the door and starts to step onto the fire escape.

VEGA: (calling after Tiffany) Hey— (worried breaths) Come back, that was nothing!

Tiffany walks down the stairs. She picks the book up off the floor, then looks around. She puts the book back on the shelf, then locks the back door. She walks up the stairs.

티파니: (키스를 하며) 우리 자기. 보고 싶었어.

애슐리는 복도에서 작은 뒷 방쪽의 계단으로 내려간다. 비상계단으로 연결되는 유리문이 있고 우비가 벽에 걸려있다.

베가: (소리를 죽이며) 나도 보고 싶었어.

애슐리가 계단 아래로 내려갈 때 북케이스에 걸려 소리를 낸다. 책이 바닥에 떨어진다. 책이 떨어지는 소리를 들은 티파니는 뒤로 기대서 베가를 쳐다본다.

티파니: 무슨 소리지?

애슐리는 서둘러서 방을 지나 뒷문으로 간다. 그녀는 문을 연다.

베가: 아무 소리 안 났는데.

티파니는 일어선다.

티파니: 아냐, 분명히 났어.

애슐리는 화재비상구 뒷문을 연다. 비가 쏟아 붓는다.

티파니: 잠깐만.

애슐리는 우비를 입고 뒷문으로 간다. 문을 열고 화재 비상구로 나간다.

베가: (티파니를 부르며) 이리 와, (걱정스러운 숨소리를 내며) 아무 소리 안 났어.

티파니는 계단 쪽으로 간다. 바닥에서 책을 줍고 주변을 둘러본다. 그녀는 책을 책꽂이에 올리고 뒤문을 보고 잠근다. 그녀는 계단으로 올라간다.

- **walkway**
  통로(보도)
- **sneak**
  살금살금(몰래) 가다
- **unlock**
  열다
- **fire escape**
  (화재 대피용) 비상계단(사다리)

She unlocks the door.
unlock은 '열다' 는 의미이다.

She unlocks the door.
그녀는 문을 연다.

Ashleigh hurries back through the rain to the door. She tries to open the door, but it is locked.

Ashleigh climbs down the fire escape ladder to the ground, she turns and runs down an alley to the street. Ashleigh stops on the sidewalk, then gestures frantically at a couple.

ASHLEIGH: Uh, do you know which way the Waldorf Hotel is?

WELLES TOWNHOUSE/ STUDY
Gatsby and mother walks into the study.

GATSBY: What's on your mind, Mother?

MOTHER: I want to have a word with you.

Gatsby sits down on a sofa.

GATSBY: Oh, no. No, please don't do this to me tonight, Mom. I'm not, I'm not really in the mood for one of your tête-à-têtes where I come out on the short end as always. I, I really couldn't take it tonight...

MOTHER: (sighs)

GATSBY: ...okay? Where's Ashleigh?

MOTHER: I asked her to leave.

Gatsby looks at mother with surprise, then gestures at her.

GATSBY: What?! Why?!

MOTHER: Don't give me that Ashleigh bullshit. I smelled hooker the second she walked through the door.

GATSBY: Mother, do you hear yourself?

MOTHER: Damn right I hear myself.

GATSBY: I'm shocked. I, uh...

애슐리는 서둘러 다시 빗속의 문으로 간다. 그녀는 문을 열려고 하지만 문이 잠겨있다.
애슐리는 다시 비상계단 아래로 내려간다. 그녀는 거리 복도로 달려간다. 애슐리는 보도에 멈춰서 커플에게 몹시 흥분해서 손짓을 한다.

애슐리: 월도프 호텔이 어느 쪽인지 아세요?

웰스 타운하우스/서재
개츠비와 엄마는 서재로 걸어 들어온다.

개츠비: 왜 그래요, 엄마?
엄마: 둘이 얘기 좀 하게.

개츠비는 소파에 앉는다.

개츠비: 엄마, 오늘은 안 돼요. 좀 봐줘요. 지금은 정말 엄마랑 독대할 기분 아니라구요. 보나마나 내가 질 텐데. 말싸움하기 싫어요.
엄마: (한숨을 쉰다)
개츠비: 애슐리는 어딨어요?
엄마: 내가 내보냈다.

개츠비는 놀라서 엄마를 보고, 그녀에게 손짓을 한다.

개츠비: 네? 왜요?
엄마: 애슐리 같은 소리 그만해. 보자마자 창녀인 거 알았다.
개츠비: 엄마 제정신이세요?
엄마: 제정신이고말고.
개츠비: 충격이네요, 참…

- **frantically**
  미친 듯이, 극도로 흥분하여

- **I'm not really in the mood.**
  나는 정말 그럴 기분이 아니야.

- **tête-à-têtes**
  (불어에서) 둘만의 사담
  private discussions between two people

- **take**
  참다(bear, endure)

- **hooker**
  (속어) 창녀(prostitute)

- **hear oneself**
  '자신의 말이 들리다' 라는 의미.
  '너 그거 지금 말이라고 하는 거야? 제정신이야?'

A: What's on your mind?
B: I want to have a word with you.
have a word with는 '~와 잠깐 이야기를 나누다' 라는 의미이다.

A: What's on your mind?
B: I want to have a word with you.
A: 무슨 일이에요?
B: 잠깐 이야기 좀 나눴으면 하는데.

Gatsby puts his glass of liquor down on the floor.

GATSBY: (pauses, then sighs) Okay, I apologize. Um...tsk, I met her in the bar at the Carlyle and I gave her five thousand bucks to pretend she was Ashleigh... who has dumped me.

MOTHER: Five thousand?

It was worth that much for you to make a fool of your father and me?

GATSBY: I was in a bad mood. It was my idea of a joke. So it was a bad joke, okay? I won a lot in a card game, so, uh, it was an act of rebellion.

MOTHER: It was an act of hostility.

GATSBY: Hostility and rebellion.

MOTHER: Rebellion against what? Private schools, a nice home, summers in Europe?

GATSBY: Against a life of pretentious appropriateness. Appropriate friends, appropriate schools, appropriate women that you may or may not approve of.

MOTHER: Tsk, you resent me because I set a high bar.

GATSBY: Mother, I don't resent you because you set a high bar. I just want you to see me. I'm never gonna be like Hunter. I'm not gonna roll off the assembly line and make you proud.

MOTHER: You lied to me when you said that you were too busy to come to my party, that you were too busy at work, snowed under at Yardley.

개츠비는 그의 술잔을 바닥에 내려놓는다.

개츠비: (멈추고 한숨을 쉰다) 맞아요, 죄송해요.
칼라일 바에서 만났는데 오천불 주고 애슐
리인 척해달랬어요. 갠 절 찼거든요.

엄마: 오천불?
그 큰 돈을 들여 부모 망신을 시킨 거야?

개츠비: 너무 우울해서 친 장난인데 영 아니었네요.
마침 포커로 돈도 땄겠다…반항 한번 해봤
어요.

엄마: 적대감을 보인 거지.

개츠비: 적대감과 반항심이요.

엄마: 뭐에 대한 반항? 사립학교, 좋은 집.유럽 여
름 휴가?

개츠비: 허세 가득한 버젓함이요. 버젓한 친구들,
버젓한 학교. 엄마가 인정해줘야 하는 여자
들.

엄마: 내 기준이 높다고 원망하는 거니?

개츠비: 그런 게 아니라 절 있는 그대로 봐주길 바라
요. 전 형과는 달라요. 집안의 자랑이 못 될
거라구요.

엄마: 엄마 파티에 오기 싫어서. 학교 과제가 많다
고 거짓말까지 하고.

- **bucks**
  (비격식)달러(dollars)

- **dump**
  (비격식)(애인을)차다

- **make a fool of**
  조롱하다, 놀리다

- **rebellion**
  반항심

- **hostility**
  적대감

- **appropriateness**
  타당한, 어울림

- **approve of**
  인정하다

- **set a high bar**
  기준이 높다

- **assembly line**
  (대량 생산의) 일관 작업(열), 조립 라인

- **roll off the assembly line**
  개인적인 특이성 없이, 가족이나 사회에서
  이전에 배출된 사람과 같은 사람을 만들어
  낸다는 조롱하는 말투의 표현

I am in a bad mood.
기분 안좋아.

I am in a bad mood.

기분이 안좋아.

GATSBY:	You know what, Mom? I did lie to you. Because I didn't want to come to your party, all right? I wanted to spend the day with Ashleigh in the city... and have a great time.
MOTHER:	Where is Ashleigh?
GATSBY:	I told you. She dumped me. We became separated. This city has its own agenda.
MOTHER:	And your rage with me is so great that you express it by bringing home a whore?
GATSBY:	An escort, Mother.
MOTHER:	Oh, let's not split pubic hairs.
GATSBY:	Anything to shake up that collection of appropriate snobs.
MOTHER:	So you, you bring her to my gala as your girlfriend...to make a fool of me?
GATSBY:	You know what, Mom? I'm sorry. I don't know why I'm like this. I don't know where I get this perverse streak in my system from. I don't know.
MOTHER:	You get it from me.
GATSBY:	Oh, yeah, I get it from you? Oh, yeah, the queen of good taste.
MOTHER:	All right. You're a big enough boy to hear the whole inappropriate story. I met your father...in the exact same line of work...an escort service...or more to the point, hooking...as that working girl you tried to slip past us as Ashleigh Enright.

개츠비:	네, 거짓말했어요. 파티에 오기 싫었고 애슐리와 멋진 주말을 보내고 싶었거든요.
엄마:	걘 어디 있니?
개츠비:	제가 말했잖아요. 절 차고 사라졌어요. 이 도시가 방해를 했는지.
엄마:	그렇다고 내가 미워서 창녀를 집에 들여?
개츠비:	파트너 대행이요.
엄마:	그게 그거지 뭘.
개츠비:	속물들 파티 분위기 좀 깨려구요.
엄마:	그래서 그런 앨 여자친구라고 데려와 엄마를 바보 만들어?
개츠비:	알겠어요. 죄송해요. 저도 제가 왜 이런지 모르겠어요. 누굴 닮아 이렇게 삐딱한지 모르겠어요.
엄마:	날 닮아서 그래.
개츠비:	엄마를 닮아요? 행여나요. 고상한 취향의 여왕님.
엄마:	그래. 이제 너도 부적절한 얘기를 소화할 나이가 됐으니까. 내가 아빠를 만난 것도 그런 일을 하면서였어. 파트너 대행. 좀 더 정확히는 창녀. 네가 애슐리라고 속이려고 한 그 아가씨처럼.

- **whore**
  매춘부

- **shake up**
  흔들어 놓다. 방해하다(disturb)

- **snobs**
  속물

- **gala**
  파티

- **perverse**
  (사고방식 · 태도가) 비뚤어진[삐딱한]

- **streak**
  사람의 성격에서 특히 좋지 못한 구석(데), 행태

- **line of work**
  업무

- **to the point**
  간단 명료한(간결한) (=pertinent)

- **hooking**
  working as a prostitute

- **slip past**
  ~을 슬쩍 통과하다(=get by unnoticed)

Let's not split pubic hairs.
split hairs는 '머리카락 한가닥 한가닥 나누다. 즉 '사소한일에 지나치게 신경쓰다' 라는 뜻으로, Let's not spirit hairs는 '시시콜콜 나누지 마라. 그게 그거다' 라는 뜻으로 사용된다.

Zoom In

Let's not split pubic hairs.
그게 그거지.

GATSBY: What?

MOTHER: Lower your eyebrows.

(very soft breaths) I knocked on your father's hotel room door because that's how I made my living. Fresh from Gary, Indiana. Providing the...lonely male of the species with a little casual recreation. For a fee. Except in your father's case, we fell in love. And not did we marry, Winston used my hard-earned nest egg to start the company that has enabled us to live a, a pretty privileged life. You following?

Gatsby looks at mother with astonishment.

MOTHER: Am I goin' too fast?

And I put myself through school so my brilliant young son can laugh at my pretentions. What I'm, what I'm saying is that...if I have bent over too far in my pursuit of the finer things and of cultivating an image, and... if I have caused you some discomfort... it's only an overzealous ex-professional hustler from the Midwest trying to eradicate...unsavory remnants of many hotel rooms I still wake up screaming over. And if you can't understand where you get your mysterious urge to consort with the demimonde...you have my genes. And I'm sorry to lay this X- rated tale on my sweet college boy, but something tells me that the time is right.

개츠비: 뭐요?

엄마: 인상 쓰지 말구.

(숨을 들이쉬며 멈추고) 네 아빠호텔 방을 노크했어 그렇게 먹고 살았으니까 인디애나주 개리에서 갓 올라와서 외로운 남자들에게 가벼운 오락거리를 제공했다고나 할까. 유료로. 아빠와는 달랐던 게 서로 사랑에 빠진 거지. 우린 결혼도 했고. 내가 모아뒀던 돈으로 아빠 회사를 차렸는데 잘돼서 특권층의 삶까지 누리게 됐어. 알아듣고 있지?

개츠비는 놀라서 엄마를 쳐다본다.

엄마: 너무 빨라?

열심히 일해 학교도 나왔더니 잘난 어린 아들이 내가 허세라고 비웃는구나. 그러니까 내 말은… 혹시 내가 좋은 것들을 좇고 좋은 이미지를 만드는 데 있어 지나 쳤다면… 또 그래서 널 불편하게 했다면 그건 중서부 출신 전직 매춘부가 어떻게든 과거를 지우려던 거야. 호텔방의 안 좋은 기억 때문에 지금도 악몽에 시달려. 왜 그런지 이해는 안 가지만 왠지 모르게 화류계와 어울리고 싶다면 엄마 유전자를 받은 거야. 사랑스런 대학생 아들한테 이런 불미스런 얘기가 미안하지만 이제 때가 된 거 같았어.

- **Lower your eyebrows.**
  인상 쓰지 말구

- **bent over too far**
  ~에 너무 많이 기울이다(쏟다)
  i.e., 'been too excessive'

- **cultivate**
  (말·행동 방식 등을) 기르다(함양하다)

- **overzealous**
  지나치게 열성적인

- **hustler**
  (속어) 매춘부, 창녀

- **eradicate**
  근절하다, 뿌리뽑다

- **unsavory**
  불미스러운, 비도덕적인

- **remnant**
  남은 부분

- **consort**
  (남들이 좋지 않게 생각하는 사람들과) 어울리다

- **demimonde**
  화류계, 매춘부

You following?
여기에 follow는 '이해하다, (내용을)따라 잡다' 라는 의미로, 대화체에서 '내 말 알아듣고 있지(Are you understanding the implications of this?)' 라는 의미로 사용된다.

You following?
알아듣고 있지?

Chapter 10

새로운 시작

A New Day

시간 01:21:31 ~ 01:32:30

HOTEL PLAZA ATHENEE
The rain pours down in front of the hotel.
Ashleigh enters on the sidewalk and walks to the door, then realizes she is at the wrong hotel. She stands under the awning, looking around.

THE CARLYLE/ BEMELMANS BAR
The bar is now closed and a waiter is cleaning up around the tables. Gatsby enters through a door, walking slowly across the room toward a piano. Maitre D'enters, then gestures at the waiter.

MAITRE D:	Uh, just put up the chairs and then...you're done. All right?

The Maitre d walks and smiles at Gatsby, who is sitting down at the piano.

MAITRE D:	Oh, hey, Gatsby.
GATSBY:	Hey, Johnny. (heavy sigh)

Gatsby starts to play Irving Berlin's "They say it's wonderful" on the piano. Ashleigh, wearing the raincoat and soaking wet, enters through the doorway, then stops and looks at Gatsby. Ashleigh walks barefoot across the room to him. Ashleigh stops beside the piano, then Gatsby looks up at her. Gatsby stops playing the piano.

플라자 호텔
비가 호텔 앞에 쏟아 붓는다.
에슐리가 보도 위로 가고 문쪽으로 걸어고 그 때 그녀는 잘못된 호텔에 있다는 것을 깨닫는다. 그녀는 차양천막에 서서 주변을 둘러본다.

칼라일 호텔/베멜만스의 바
바는 문을 닫고, 웨이터는 테이블 주변을 청소하고 있다. 개츠비는 문으로 들어가고 피아노 쪽으로 방으로 천천히 걸어간다. 매이트레드는 웨이터에게 손짓을 한다.

매이트레드: 의자 정리만 하고 가.

매이트레드는 게츠비에게 걸어가서 웃고, 개츠비는 피아노에 앉는다.

매이트레드: 개츠비 왔구나.
개츠비: 안녕, 자니 (무거운 한숨을 쉰다)

개츠비는 Irving Berlin 의 They say it's wonderful 을 연주하기 시작한다. 우비를 입고 다 젖은 채로 애슐리는 문으로 들어가서 개츠비를 보고 멈춘다. 애슐리는 맨발로 그에게 걸어간다. 애슐리는 피아노 옆에 멈춰서고 개츠비는 그녀를 올려다본다. 개츠비는 피아노 연주하던 것을 멈춘다.

■ barefoot
　맨발의

323

GATSBY:	I saw you on television.
ASHLEIGH:	Well...nothing happened. I'm really exhausted. I've been walking forever. And then I got lost on the train.
GATSBY:	Ashleigh, you were with a famous movie star.
ASHLEIGH:	Well, but nothing happened.
GATSBY:	I'd love to believe you.
ASHLEIGH:	Just...too many drinks. Too much weed. I'm, I'm just a little too tired to explain. I...Tomorrow, I promise. But really, Gatsby, nothing happened.
GATSBY:	Well, then take off your raincoat, okay? And I'll get you some black coffee.
ASHLEIGH:	Oh. Oh, I can't. I have no clothes underneath.

PIERRE/ GATSBY & ASHLEIGH'S SUITE
It has stopped raining. Gatsby walks across the room. Ashleigh, wearing a sweater and pants, walks across the room.

ASHLEIGH:	So, to Roland Pollard, it was...like a...a spiritual thing. You know, I was a muse. Some inspiration, 'cause he's really going through a rough creative period. And also, my name's totally the same as his first wife's...who also went to Yardley! Who he's never really gotten over. And then Ted Davidoff...I mean, he was just... absolutely traumatized by this affair that his wife was having with his best friend. And there I was, you know, just a person there to talk to, to...to hold his hand during a crisis, you know?
GATSBY:	What about Francisco...Vega?

개츠비:	너 TV 에서 봤어.
애슐리:	아무 일 없었어. 피곤해 죽겠어, 얼마나 걸 었는지 전철도 잘못 타고.
개츠비:	너 스타 배우랑 있었잖아.
애슐리:	근데 아무 일 없었어.
개츠비:	나도 믿고 싶다.
애슐리:	너무 많이 마시고 너무 많이 피웠어. 그래서 말할 기운도 없어 내일 다 설명해줄게. 근데 정말 아무 일 없었어.
개츠비:	일단 코트 좀 벗어. 내가 커피 갖다줄게.
애슐리:	안 돼, 안에 옷 안 입었어.

피에르 호텔 개츠비와 애슐리의 호텔방

비는 멈추었다. 개츠비는 방으로 걸어간다. 애슐리는 스웨터와 바
지를 입고 방으로 걸어온다.

애슐리:	롤란 폴라드가 원했던 건 정신적인 거였어. 내가 자기 뮤즈라며. 영감을 주… 심한 슬 럼프를 겪고 있거든. 그리고 첫 번째 부인과 이름도 같았는데 학교도 야들리를 나왔대. 아직도 못잊고 있더라구. 그리고 테드 다비 도프는 완전 트라우마에 빠져있었어. 부인 이 자기 절친과 바람을 피웠거든. 근데 그 위기의 순간 옆에서 위로해줄 사람이 나밖 에 없었던 거지.
개츠비:	프란시스코 베가는?

- **nothing happened.**
  아무 일 없었어

- **weed**
  마리화나(marijuana)

- **take off**
  벗다

- **underneath**
  ~의 밑(아래/안)에

- **spiritual**
  정신적인

- **inspiration**
  영감

- **go through**
  겪다 경험하다

- **traumatize**
  정신적 외상을 초래하다, 엄청난 충격을 주
  다

- **affair**
  불륜 (관계)

I'd love to believe you.
I'd 는 I would 의 줄임말이고, would
love to + 동사원형은 '~하고 싶다
(would like to + 동사원형)는 의미이다.

I'd love to believe you.
나는 널 믿고 싶다.

Ashleigh puts the clothes in her suitcase. Gatsby gestures at her.

GATSBY: Uh, James Dean, minus the acting chops.

ASHLEIGH: Aah, Francisco Vega was just after my body. But I was onto him. And I got terrific material for a hot story "I Dated a Hunk". So what about you?

Gatsby has started smoking a cigarette in the cigarette holder.

ASHLEIGH: How was going to your mom's soiree?

GATSBY: (puffs silently on cigarette)

Gatsby glances at Ashleigh, then puts the cigarette holder down in an ashtray.

GATSBY: It was pretty nice, actually. Yeah, we got into sort of a crazy conversation...and ...for the first time in my life, she surprised me in a good way. And now I feel closer to her.

ASHLEIGH: Mmm, must've been a big talk. What'd you discuss?

GATSBY: The oldest profession.

ASHLEIGH: Journalism?

GATSBY: (shaking his head) Mm–mn.

ASHLEIGH: Ah. No, that's the second oldest.

GATSBY: Tsk, let's put it this way, she's a lot more than I gave her credit for. I've sold her short.

ASHLEIGH: What a shame we never got to take that carriage ride.

Gatsby glances at Ashleigh, then looks at his wristwatch.

애슐리는 가방에 옷을 넣는다. 개츠비는 그녀를 쳐다본다.

개츠비: 연기 재능은 **뺀** 제임스 딘.

애슐리: 프란시스코 베가는 내 몸만 원했어. 하지만 안 넘어갔지. 대신 재밌는 기삿거린 얻었어 '섹시남과의 데이트'. 넌 어땠어?

개츠비는 시가렛홀더로 담배를 피기 시작했다.

애슐리: 엄마의 파티는?

개츠비: (담배를 조용히 훅 내뱉으며)

개츠비는 애슐리를 쳐다보며, 시가렛 홀더를 잿털이에 둔다.

개츠비: 아주 좋았어. 엄마와 황당한 대화를 나누게 됐는데…좋은 의미로 엄마에게 놀랐어. 평생 처음 많이 가까워진 느낌이야.

애슐리: 뭔가 거창한 대화였나 보네. 무슨 얘기였어?

개츠비: 역사상 가장 오래된 직업.

애슐리: 기자?

개츠비: (고개를 저으며) 음…

애슐리: 아니다. 그건 두 번째지.

개츠비: 내 생각보다 훨씬 내실 있는 분이었다고 할까? 내가 엄마를 과소평가했어.

애슐리: 마차를 못 탄 게 너무 아쉽다.

개츠비는 애슐리를 보고 그의 손목시계를 본다

- **chop**
  재능

- **soiree**
  파티
  party or reception held in the evening, typically in a private home

- **put**
  설명하다(express)

- **I've sold her short**
  내가 그녀를 과소평가했어
  'I've underestimated her'

- **carriage**
  마차
  a horse-drawn carriage

I was onto him.
be onto somebody는 '~의 잘못에 대해 알다'라는 의미로, '그의 의도를 알았다(I was aware of his intentions)'는 의미로 쓰였다.

I was onto him.
나는 그를 알아챘다.

GATSBY: We can still do it. Yeah, we have plenty of time we can get it in. Said the john to my mom.

ASHLEIGH: (confused) What?

Gatsby puts down the cigarette holder and shakes his head.

GATSBY: Nothing.

GATSBY: Look, we should probably leave our luggage downstairs. As you know, I'd hate to miss our bus back to Yardley.

CENTRAL PARK

It is Grey and overcast, but not raining.
Ashleigh and Gatsby sit in the back of a carriage. A carriage driver drives the carriage down a path in the park.

GATSBY: New York on a misty day.
Can't tell why it means somethin' to me, but it means everything.

Ashleigh looks up at the sky, then looks him.

ASHLEIGH: (frowning) Hm. It's my one carriage ride and the weather's gloomy.

ASHLEIGH: I couldn't really sleep last night. You hear all those fire engines?.

GATSBY: I did.
"The roaring traffic's boom…the silence of my lonely room…"

ASHLEIGH: (grinning excitedly) I know that! That's from Shakespeare, right?

개츠비: 지금이라도 타면 돼. 얼마든지 끼워 넣을 수 있어. '엄마의 고객들이 말했겠지'.

애슐리: (당황해하며) 뭐?

게츠비는 시가렛 홀더를 내려놓고, 고개를 젓는다.

개츠비: 아냐.

개츠비: 짐은 아래층에 두고 가자. 학교 가는 버스 놓치면 큰일이잖아.

센트럴 파크
회색 구름이 덮혀 있으나 비는 안 온다.
애슐리와 개츠비는 마차 뒤에 앉아있다. 마차 운전사는 공원길 아래로 마차를 운전한다.

개츠비: 안개 낀 뉴욕.
왜 그런지 모르겠지만 나한텐 정말 소중해.

애슐리는 하늘을 올려다보고 그를 쳐다본다.

애슐리: (인상을 찌푸리며) 단 한 번 마차를 타는데 날씨가 이렇게 꿀꿀하다니.

애슐리: 어젯밤에 통 못 잤어 소방차 소리 들었지?

개츠비: 응.
찻길의 으르렁대는 굉음. 내 외로운 방의 적막…

애슐리: (흥분해서 웃으며) 나 알아! 셰익스피어 맞지?

- **john**
  (속어) 창녀의 고객(client of a prostitute)

- **overcast**
  구름이 뒤덮인, 흐린

- **gloomy**
  우울한, 침울한

We can get it in.
get something in은 '스케줄에 그것을 억지로 넣다(squeeze it into our schedule)'라는 의미이다.

We can get it in.
그것을 넣을 수 있어.

Gatsby looks away from her.

GATSBY: (inhales as if to speak, but shuts his mouth)

Gatsby looks down and shakes his head.

GATSBY: (to driver) Sir, could you stop for a second?
ASHLEIGH: Why are we stopping?

The carriage stops. Gatsby turns and looks at Ashleigh.

GATSBY: Ashleigh, you go back to Yardley. Okay? I'm gonna stay in New York.
ASHLEIGH: What? (confused chuckle)

Gatsby shakes his head at her.

GATSBY: I need the carbon monoxide to survive.

Ashleigh reacts with confusion.

ASHLEIGH: Well...what are you talking about?
GATSBY: I don't, I don't know. We're two different creatures, right?
ASHLEIGH: What, uh...?
GATSBY: Yeah, you like the sound of crickets and I like the rattle of the taxis. You blossom in the sun and me, eh, I come into my own under grey skies.
And look, you were a big hit here. You, you were a crackerjack reporter.
You were loved spiritually, emotionally and physically by three gifted men, right?

개츠비는 그녀에게서 먼 곳을 쳐다본다.

개츠비: (말하려고 숨을 들이 쉬다가 다시 입을 닫는다)

개츠비는 아래를 내려다 보고 고개를 젓는다.

개츠비: (운전사에게) 저, 잠깐만 세워주시겠어요?
애슐리: 왜 세워?

마차는 멈춘다. 개츠비는 애슐리를 돌아 본다.

개츠비: 넌 학교로 돌아가. 난 뉴욕에 남아야겠어.
애슐리: 뭐? (황당한 웃음으로)

개츠비는 그녀에게 고개를 젓는다.

개츠비: 난 살려면 일산화탄소가 필요해.

애슐리는 황당하게 반응한다.

애슐리: 그게 무슨 소리야?
개츠비: 글쎄… 너랑 난 너무 딴판이잖아.
애슐리: 뭐? 어?
개츠비: 넌 귀뚜라미 소릴 좋아하고 난 덜컹대는 차
　　　　　소리를 좋아하고, 넌 햇빛 아래 피어나고 난
　　　　　회색 하늘 아래 힘이 나고.
　　　　　또 넌 여기서 스타였잖아. 일류 기자였다
　　　　　구. 멋진 세 남자에게 정신적으로 감정적,
　　　　　육체적으로 사랑받았잖아.

- **looks away from**
  ~로부터 눈길을 돌리다

- **cricket**
  귀뚜라미

- **rattle**
  덜커덕(달그락/덜컹)거리는 소리

- **hit**
  대 성공, 히트(success)

- **crackerjack**
  진짜 멋진(근사한)사람 (exceptional
  ability)

I come into my own.
come into one's own은 '자기의 진가
를 발휘하다(I flourish), 인정을 받게 되
다' 라는 의미이다.

I come into my own.
나는 진가를 발휘한다.

GATSBY: Yeah–yeah, you don't want to be with me. Y–you deserve better than me.

ASHLEIGH: Right, but I, eh...you're dropping out of Yardley?

GATSBY: Mmmmm...if I don't sound too pretentious, I want to review my other options. (quick breath, then to driver) Excuse me, sir, do you think it's possible to take her to the Pierre Hotel?

Gatsby starts to climb out of the carriage.

ASHLEIGH: Wait. Wait, I don't?

Gatsby takes a wad of cash out of his jacket.

GATSBY: Look, you take this, right?

ASHLEIGH: I Gatsby, I don't understand.

He hands the money to Ashleigh.

ASHLEIGH: I don't really understand.

GATSBY: Right? You take this...and you get your luggage, and then just make your way safely back to Yardley, okay?

ASHLEIGH: And so you, so you But. you're not coming back to Yardley?

The carriage starts to move again, carrying Ashleigh down the path. Gatsby walks alongside the carriage.

GATSBY: I, I... I don't know, Ashleigh. I, I gotta figure some stuff out in my life.

ASHLEIGH: Wait.

개츠비: 넌 나한테 아까워. 더 좋은 사람 만나야지.

애슐리: 좋아. 그런데.. 너는 학교 중퇴하려구?

개츠비: 허세 부리려는 건 아니지만 다른 가능성이 있을 거야. (빠르게 숨을 쉬며, 운전사에게) 얘 좀 피에르 호텔에 데려다 주시겠어요?

개츠비는 마차에서 내리기 시작한다.

애슐리: 기다려.

게츠비는 그의 자켓에서 현금 뭉치를 꺼낸다.

개츠비: 자, 받아.

애슐리: 개츠비, 이해가 안되.

그는 애슐리에게 돈을 건낸다.

애슐리: 개츠비, 어쩌려고?

개츠비: 짐 찾아서 학교로 잘 돌아가.

애슐리: 넌 안 돌아갈 거야?

마차는 애슐리를 태우고 다시 이동하기 시작한다. 개츠비는 마차 옆을 걸어간다.

개츠비: 모르겠어. 내 인생에 대해 고민 좀 해보고

애슐리: 기다려봐.

- drop out of
  중퇴하다

- pretentious
  허세 부리는, 가식적인

- wad
  뭉치

- alongside
  옆에, 나란히

You deserve better than me.
deserve는 '~을 받을 만하다(누릴 자격이 있다)' 는 의미이다.

 Zoom In

You deserve better than me.
나보다 더 좋은 사람 만나야지.

GATSBY: But look, have a great trip, and you tell everybody at, uh, Yardley, I said goodbye, all right?

Ashleigh looks back at Gatsby, who is obscured as the carriage moves away from him.

ASHLEIGH: But...wait. So you're not coming back to Yardley? Wait, I Gatsby? Um...wait, sir, I'm... (shouting) Gatsby, I don't understand! I...Um, I But we're... Oh...

It starts to drizzle. Ashleigh glances up at the sky, then looks at the carriage driver.

ASHLEIGH: Oh, eh...God, um, could you hurry? I think it's starting to rain.

CENTRAL PARK

A heavier rain has started to fall. Gatsby walks through the archway under the clock. He strolls, then he around and looks up at the clock. The clock starts to sound its musical chimes, signaling it is now 6 o'clock. Gatsby turns and walks backwards, looking up at the clock. Hands on the clock point to 6:00 and the carousel of animal statues on it has started moving around the clock.

Gatsby checks the time on his wristwatch, then looks under the underpass.

Chan, wearing a white T-shirt and a purple skirt, walks out from under the underpass. Chan stops, then Gatsby stops in front of her.

GATSBY: How did I know you'd be here?

CHAN: You didn't think I was gonna blow this moment, did you?

GATSBY: What about the skin doctor?

개츠비: 조심히 가고 친구들한테 인사 전해줘.

애슐리는 개츠비를 다시 돌아보고, 마차가 이동하면서 개츠비가 안 보인다.

애슐리: 넌 야들리로 안 간다는 거야? 개츠비! 저, 잠깐만요… 개츠비, 이해가 안 가!

비가 보슬보슬 내리기 시작한다. 애슐리는 하늘을 쳐다보고 마차 운전사를 쳐다본다.

애슐리: 오, 이런… 서둘러주실래요? 비가 오는 거 같은데.

센트럴 파크
비가 더 심하게 오기 시작한다. 개츠비는 시계아래에 아치웨이 아래를 통과한다. 그는 걷고 방향을 돌려 시계를 올려다본다. 시계는 6시를 알리는 음악소리를 내기 시작한다. 개츠비는 뒤로 다시 걸어가서 시계를 위로 쳐다본다. 시계바늘은 6시를 가리키고, 시계에 동물 조각상의 회전목마가 시계주변을 이동하기 시작한다.

개츠비는 손목시계를 확인하고 지하도를 쳐다본다.

하안셔츠와 보라색 스커트를 입은 챈이 지하도 아래에서 걸어 나온다. 챈은 멈추고 개츠비는 그녀 앞에 멈춘다.

개츠비: 네가 올 줄 내가 어떻게 알았을까?
챈: 내가 이런 기회를 놓치겠어?
개츠비: 피부과 의사는 어쩌고?

- **obscure**
  모호하게 하다

- **drizzle**
  (비가) 보슬보슬 내리다

- **archway**
  아치 (지붕이 덮인) 길, 아치형 입구

- **chime**
  (차임벨) 소리

- **hand**
  (시계) 바늘

- **underpass**
  아래쪽 도로(철도)

You didn't think I was gonna blow this moment, did you?
blow는 '놓치다 (wreck , miss)' 라는 의미이다.

om In

You didn't think I was gonna blow this moment, did you?
내가 이런 기회(순간)을 놓치겠어?

CHAN: Very handsome. Very rich and very clever, but I'm here.

GATSBY: For a kisser who's a maximum of an eight?

Chan smiles, then caresses his hair.

CHAN: It's fall. By spring I'll have you up to ten.

They kiss as the rain falls on them. They walk and they wrap their arms around one another and smile. They stop and kiss again.

Scene fades to black.

챈: 아주 잘생겼어. 완전 부자에 똑똑하기까지
근데 여기 왔어.

개츠비: 기껏해야 키스 8점짜리 만나러?

챈은 웃으며 그의 머리를 만진다.

챈: 지금 가을이니까 봄까지 10점 만들어줄게.

비가 오고 그들은 키스를 한다. 그들은 서로 팔을 감싸고 걷는다.
그들은 멈추고 다시 키스를 한다.

장면은 어두워 진다.

■ caress
애무하다, 어루만지다

I'll have you up to ten.
up to는 '~까지' 라는 의미이다.

I'll have you up to ten.
10점까지 만들게 해 줄께.

A Rainy
Day in
New York

A Rainy
Day in
New York

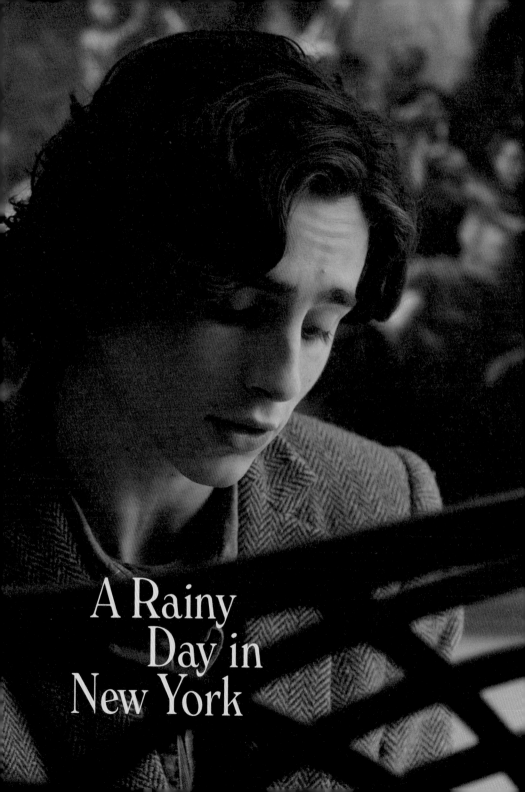

A Rainy
Day in
New York